THE BIBLE'S ANSWERS
TO **100** OF
LIFE'S BIGGEST
QUESTIONS

THE BIBLE'S ANSWERS
TO **100** OF
LIFE'S BIGGEST
QUESTIONS

Norman L. Geisler and Jason Jimenez

BakerBooks

a division of Baker Publishing Group
Grand Rapids, Michigan

© 2015 by Norman L. Geisler and Jason Jimenez

Published by Baker Books
a division of Baker Publishing Group
P.O. Box 6287, Grand Rapids, MI 49516-6287
www.bakerbooks.com

Printed in the United States of America

Library of Congress Cataloging-in-Publication Data

Geisler, Norman L.
    The Bible's answers to 100 of life's biggest questions / Norman L. Geisler and Jason Jimenez.
        pages cm
    Includes bibliographical references.
    ISBN 978-0-8010-1694-3 (pbk.)
    1. Bible—Miscellanea. 2. Christian life—Biblical teaching—Miscellanea. I. Jimenez, Jason, 1979– II. Title.
    BS612.G44 2015
    220—dc23   2014030693

15 16 17 18 19 20 21   7 6 5 4 3 2 1

Contents

Foreword

We (Josh and Sean) have spent much of our lives and ministries trying to help people answer the tough questions of life. Even though culture has changed drastically over the past few decades, one thing remains the same: *people have questions and they want answers*. Being prepared with answers to tough questions is not just *our* job though. The Bible says all believers are to be ready with an answer to everyone who asks (1 Pet. 3:15). And that includes *you*! That's why we are so thrilled that Norm and Jason have written this Q&A book. This book is written for the Christian who needs clear and convincing answers to some of the most challenging questions of the day. If you have questions, this is the book for you.

No longer do you have to worry or be afraid when someone asks you a tough question about your faith. This book will equip you with solid answers to questions most Christians struggle to answer. Not only will it help you build confidence to defend the faith, but it will also be an encouragement as you grow in your faith.

We believe Christians from all walks of life will benefit from Norm and Jason's biblical and practical approach to tackling one hundred of life's biggest questions. Their way of laying out the book not only gives you (the Christian reader) biblical answers but also provides practical application and additional resources that will help you go deeper in your study.

We deeply value resources designed to help Christians grow in their faith—and we have no doubt that this book fits that description. As you read and explore the valuable answers in this book, you will come to better understand what it is that you believe and will come away with a stronger conviction as to why you believe it.

We highly recommend this Q&A book, which covers such a wide range of thought-provoking questions with such insightful responses. The beginner will not feel overwhelmed, and the expert will find some insights to deepen his or her faith. This is truly an outstanding resource that we hope many believers will get, study, and share with their friends.

Josh and Sean McDowell

Preface

Have you ever asked a question of someone you expected would know the answer, and to your surprise, he or she struggled to give a response? That's a bit unsettling, isn't it? But now, let us turn the question on you. How many times have you been asked a question about the Bible or the Christian faith and been unable to give an answer? Not a great feeling, *is it?* Both situations are unpleasant, and it is why most Christians freak out over being asked a question for fear they won't be able to give an answer.

We can relate. In the course of our ministry careers, we have been asked everything from the most elaborate to the most simplistic questions by people of every age and walk of life. That's not to say we've gotten the answers right all the time, but we try our best to answer people's questions with God's honest truth. But it takes a lot of discipline and a considerable amount of time to be able to answer people's questions.

The sad reality is that far too few Christians spend time studying—leaving most Christians helpless to answer even the most basic questions about their faith. Statistics show that a whole new generation is abandoning the church because of a lack of biblical knowledge. This indeed is troubling because questions—particularly spiritual questions—demand answers and shouldn't be sidestepped.

That's why we joined forces to write this Q&A book. We wanted to offer a resource with real and relevant answers in a time of great uncertainty. To provide a resource that not only gives Christians of all ages credible answers but brings comfort and assurance as well.

No longer can we afford to ignore the doubts and questions so many Christians have. We must be about the business of equipping Christians so they can be sure of what they believe, while confidently offering clear and convincing answers as to why they believe it. That's why we feel it is necessary to address the serious concerns and questions Christians have, from the purpose of life to life after death—and everything in between.

But having the right answers is only part of the equation (Prov. 18:13). What is equally important is to extend the same level of care toward the person asking the question as we give to the answer—which is the very approach taken in writing this book. We not only answer each question from a biblical perspective but also provide the reader with practical application and additional resources to go deeper. Thus, the end product is an answer book (with a family focus) to one hundred of life's most challenging questions that Christians, both young and old, can read and understand.

It is our fervent prayer that this answer book will help Christian readers learn more about their faith and be emboldened to go out and offer biblical answers to those searching for truth. You will find that offering solid answers to people's questions will be a blessing not only to them but to you as well (Prov. 15:23).

Acknowledgments

We want to thank our wives, Barbra Geisler and Celia Jimenez, for their support and unending devotion that greatly inspired us to complete this book.

We also want to thank Les Stobbe, our literary agent, for his hard work and representation to get this book published with Baker Books, and for the help of Paula Canington, Jeff Carroll, and Doug Goforth for providing research assistance.

A big thanks goes out to Josh and Sean McDowell for enthusiastically supporting this project and to Bobby Conway and the team at One Minute Apologist for partnering with us to produce short videos to coincide with the answers in the book.

We are also grateful to the wonderful staff at Baker Publishing Group for their outstanding professionalism and friendly interaction during crucial changes in the manuscript.

Finally, we want to thank all the brave souls who raised their hands and tolerated long lines just to ask questions. We are forever grateful to you for trusting us as reliable sources to answer your questions.

PART 1

Questions about God and Truth

1 What Is Truth?

Answer

Who would have thought that a belief in absolute truth would be under attack in our day and age? Today, young people are embracing a "feel-good" truth to satisfy their appetites, and, paradoxically, pastors and churches are shifting toward a one-size-fits-all mentality of truth.

But we've seen this dismissal of truth before. Centuries ago, standing right in front of Pontius Pilate was the embodiment of truth, Jesus Christ. Jesus confronted Pilate by saying, "You say that I am a king. In fact, the reason I was born and came into the world is to testify to the truth. Everyone on the side of truth listens to me" (John 18:37). But despite the overwhelming proof of Christ's innocence, and his indisputable claim to be God, Pilate responded flippantly, "What is truth?" (John 18:38).

Rather than discover the truth, Pilate rejected it to appease the Jews and maintain his status with the emperor. But what Pilate (and most Americans) failed to realize is that truth is of the utmost importance, for without it, we know nothing.

So what is truth?

Simply put, *truth is telling it like it is.* That is, truth corresponds with the way things really are. This acrostic will help you remember what is TRUE about truth:

Transcendent: Truth comes from God, and he has revealed it to his creation. Take gravity, for example. Newton didn't *determine* gravity; he merely *discovered* its existence. In the same way, humans *know* truth because God reveals it in his creation and in his Word, the Bible.

Real: Truth matches (corresponds to) the facts in the real world. Two opposing things can't be true at the same time and in the same sense. That would be a contradiction.

Universal: Truth applies to all people, at all times, and in all locations. For example, $1 + 1 = 2$ is a universal truth that is not challenged or denied.

Exclusive: Truth is absolute. Though opinions about truth change, truth, on the other hand, remains the truth and therefore cannot change. Beliefs change but not truth.

Application

Be careful not to buy into the self-defeating belief that truth is relative, for even the assertion that there is no absolute truth claims to be absolutely true. There are many people today who push their thinking on Christians to be more tolerant and accept the belief that truth is not absolute or exclusive. King David wrote, "Lead me in your truth and teach me, for you are the God of my salvation" (Ps. 25:5 ESV). God is truth, and your life is in far better hands than if you trust the lies spouted out in the world.

Bible References

1 Kings 22:16; Psalms 5:9; 15:2; 86:11; Proverbs 8:7; John 8:32; 15:26

Books

Truth Decay, by Douglas Groothuis
Total Truth, by Nancy Pearcey
The Truth War, by John MacArthur
Truth in Religion, by Mortimer Adler

Website

Matt Slick, "What Is Truth?," Christian Apologetics & Research Ministry, http://www.carm.org/what-is-truth

DVD

Truth Project, Focus on the Family

Online Video

Norman L. Geisler, "What Is Truth?," The One Minute Apologist, http://www.oneminuteapologist.com/searchpage#what-is-truth[1]

2 Whose Truth Is True?

Answer

Several years ago, I (Jason) was talking to a student about Jesus Christ. After I shared the gospel with him, he looked at me and said, "That's all great and stuff, but that's just *your* truth."

After poring over many proofs of Christianity, the student wasn't fazed a bit. He thought all those *truths* about Jesus were cool. Just one problem—they didn't apply to him.

This speaks to the growing movement of *postmodernism*, which not only questions propositional truth and authority but also goes as far as stating that truth is unknowable. (The basic ideas of postmodernism have existed since the early days of humankind. In the Garden of Eden, Adam and Eve rejected God's absolute standard in exchange for their own selfish gain.)

This postmodern view of truth may seem acceptable to some, but it's a contradiction. Think about it: *How do postmodernists know truth is unknowable?* To say truth is unknown is to *know* something about truth. This is complete nonsense. It is undeniable that truth is knowable.

> ### Law of Noncontradiction
>
> Aristotle referred to the Law of Noncontradiction (LNC) as the "first principle of knowledge." The LNC is self-evident and unavoidable. Something can't both exist and not exist at the same time and in the same sense (A is not non-A).

But in the midst of so many different religious beliefs, *whose truth is true?*

Christianity is all about "testing all things" to determine what is right and wrong (1 Thess. 5:21). To do so, however, you must appeal to an absolute position; otherwise, there is nothing on which to base your findings or draw concrete conclusions. Any meaningful statement must be true or false; it must be affirmable or deniable.

This leads to three alternatives to determine whose truth is true:

1. *All religious views are true.* This is known as *religious pluralism*. It is important to point out, however, that most religions don't hold to such a belief. Why? It's absurd. Based on the Law of Noncontradiction (A is not non-A), it's impossible for all religions to be true. It is impossible to

affirm God exists and deny he exists at the same time and in the same sense. Christianity, for example, believes in God, but atheism and religions such as Buddhism deny God exists. Either there is a God or there is not. It can't be both.

2. *All religious views are false.* It's possible that all religious views are false, but to know that, it must be measured by an absolute standard that corresponds to the truth. In this case, there would be a religious view above the rest that is true.

3. *One religious view is exclusively true.* Considering that truth is absolute and exclusive, it's reasonable then to assume that this truth claim is exclusively true. There is one view that is true, and everything opposed to it is false. But how do you figure out which religious view is the right one?

Ravi Zacharias posits three tests that any statement or belief system must pass: (1) logical consistency (*Are there contradictions?*), (2) empirical adequacy (*Is there any proof?*), and (3) experiential relevance (*Does it work in real life?*). For a statement or belief system to be logically consistent it must not contradict itself, but correspond to reality (that which is true). Moreover, the belief system must not only correspond to reality, but also cohere with the facts of reality (empirical adequacy). In other words, there must be evidence to substantiate its truth claims. And finally, a view or belief system must be viable to live by in the real world (experiential relevance). That is, its actions and values must comply with objective morality that we instinctively know is right.

Allow us to demonstrate how these three tests of truth (logical consistency, empirical adequacy, and experiential relevance) come in handy in very practical ways. Take, for instance, directions. It matters a great deal to have the right directions in order to reach your destination. If you program the wrong coordinates into a GPS, it will lead you to the wrong location. Similarly, when you are sick, it matters a great deal that your doctor gives the right diagnosis to determine the right course of treatment. So if following the right directions and receiving the right treatments matter, *how much more so when it comes to spiritual matters?*

Application

Though our views or emotions concerning truth change, truth stays the same. Holding fast to God's truth will bring you the greatest rewards and have the biggest impact on those around you. Don't underestimate the influence of those who disregard absolute truth for something more alluring. Take the advice of John: "Test the spirits to see whether they are from God" (1 John 4:1).

Bible References

Psalm 145:18; Matthew 7:15; John 4:23–24; 8:32; Ephesians 5:15–17; 1 Thessalonians 5:21; 2 Peter 2:1–3; 1 John 1:5–7; 4:1

Books

Relativism: Feet Firmly Planted in Mid-Air, by Francis Beckwith and Greg Koukl

Why Should Anyone Believe Anything at All?, by James Sire

Website

Rick Wade, "Truth: What It Is and Why We Can Know It," PROBE Ministries, http://www .probe.org/site/c.fdKEIMNsEoG/b.5207651/k.F625/Truth_What_It_Is_and_Why_We_ Can_Know_It.htm

DVD

The Truth Project, Focus on the Family

Online Video

Norman L. Geisler, "Truth and Relativism," The One Minute Apologist, http://www.one minuteapologist.com/searchpage#geisler-relativism

3 Is There a God?

Answer

Deep down inside each human being is a God-shaped vacuum waiting to be filled. There are many lost people searching for answers to the purpose and meaning of life, and many of them have no inkling that their questions of identity and eternal destiny are answered only in God. That's why it's critical that Christians understand and can confidently articulate proof of this basic and most fundamental truth: there is a God.

To help show you evidence for God's existence, we put together a simple acrostic—GOD: *goodness*, *origin*, and *design*. Let's take one letter at a time.

Goodness

The apostle Paul stated that all people have "no excuse" because the "law is written on their hearts" (Rom. 2:1, 15 ESV). This is to say that there are objective moral laws about what is good that are binding on all people and by which we must live. Thus, the Moral Law Argument can be summarized as follows:

1. Moral law implies a moral lawgiver.
2. There is an objective moral law.
3. Therefore, there is an objective moral lawgiver.

Moral laws not only *describe* certain behaviors but also *prescribe* what ought to be. We know in our hearts that we should do good and not bad because there is an objective moral law that governs everyone. If there is no God, then there is no ultimate moral standard by which to differentiate right and wrong. But evidence shows that moral laws are *objective* for all humans on the basis that God is the objective moral lawgiver. We all know that we should do to others what we want them to do to us. Thus, we know that stealing, rape, and killing are wrong because we do not want anyone to do those things to us.

Origin

There is overwhelming evidence that the universe had a beginning. In 1915, Albert Einstein developed the general theory of relativity. This theory is now almost universally accepted because of all the scientific evidence for it. Essentially, this theory holds that time, space, and matter all had a beginning point. In the 1920s, Edwin Hubble (after whom the Hubble Space Telescope is named) captured magnificent evidence of the expanding universe (which gave enormous proof that the universe had a beginning).

The argument for the origin of the universe goes like this:

1. Everything that had a beginning has a cause.
2. The universe had a beginning.
3. Therefore, the universe has a cause.

Premise 1 is based on the Law of Causality: every effect must have a cause. Based on science and pure reason, we know that *something cannot come from nothing.*

Premise 2 identifies that the universe must have a cause greater than itself. This is evidenced by a great SURGE:

Second Law of Thermodynamics: The universe is running out of useable energy. It's like the unwinding of a clock.

Universe expansion: The universe is spreading from a beginning point.

Radiation echo: There are traces of *afterglow* from the expansion of the universe from the beginning point.

Galaxy seeding: A great mass of energy has been discovered in outer space just as many scientists predicted.

Einstein's theory: This shows that the universe had a beginning and that time, space, and matter are all needed for everything to exist.

Design

One of the oldest and most popular arguments for the existence of God is the Design Argument. You can better understand it this way:

1. Every complex design has a designer.
2. The universe has a highly complex design.
3. Therefore, the universe has a designer.

All reasonable persons infer a designer when comparing the presidential faces on Mount Rushmore to the grandeur of the Grand Canyon. Common observation shows that it took a designer to produce Mount Rushmore, while the Grand Canyon features came about by gradual succession of wind and erosion.

THE DESIGN OF THE UNIVERSE

Let's take a look at one very finely tuned constant of the universe: *gravity*. If the gravitational force were even slightly altered, the world could not sustain life.

THE DESIGN OF THE WORLD

It's quite amazing to think that the earth is the only known planet in the universe that contains and sustains life. There are many reasons for this, but allow us to list two essential reasons.

The first reason is the *placement of the earth*. The earth is uniquely placed in the Milky Way galaxy (between the Sagittarius and Perseus spiral arms) so as not to be threatened by hazardous conditions of giant molecule clouds or supernova explosions. Another amazing fact of the earth is its proximity to the moon. The size of the earth and the distance to the moon causes the earth's axis to tilt perfectly at 23.5 degrees (allowing for annual seasons to occur).

The second reason is the *condition of the earth*. The earth's atmosphere has the perfect amount of oxygen, carbon dioxide, nitrogen, and hydrogen to be a habitable planet for life to survive and thrive. For example, oxygen comprises 21 percent of the atmosphere. If the amount were any higher, it would create massive fires; if it were any lower, life would suffocate.

THE DESIGN OF HUMAN LIFE

Yet even more incredible than the divine design of the universe and the world is the human body. The amount of genetic information contained in the human brain alone exceeds all the information in all the books in the Library of Congress. Therefore, common sense tells us that just as it takes a sculptor to sculpt a statue, we must assume it takes a Creator to create the amazing detail of human life.

Application

It's important not to take for granted the many blessings given by God. He created you in his image and has formed within you amazing talents and spiritual gifts to bring him glory, honor, and praise. Being created in his image grants every human being special status and makes human life sacred. David shouted, "Great is the LORD, and greatly to be praised, and his greatness is unsearchable. One generation shall commend your works to another, and shall declare your mighty acts" (Ps. 145:3–4).

Bible References

Genesis 1–2; Psalm 19:1–6; Romans 1:19–20

Books

Christian Apologetics, chapter 13, by Norman L. Geisler
20 Compelling Evidences That God Exists, by Kenneth Boa and Robert Bowman Jr.
Mere Christianity, by C. S. Lewis

Website

Marilyn Adamson, "Is There a God?," EveryStudent.com, http://www.everystudent.com/features/isthere.html

DVD

The Reason for God, Timothy Keller

Online Video

Ken Boa, "Does God Exist?," The One Minute Apologist, http://www.oneminuteapologist.com/searchpage#does-god-exist-boa

4 Who Made God?

Answer

This question not only makes Christians feel uneasy when asked by atheists but has also been known to trip up quite a few parents when asked by their four-year-old.

Although it may seem that this question lands a blow to belief in God, the truth is that, if you understand its implications, it's actually quite simple to answer. The short answer: No one made God. He always was (Exod. 3:14); he never had a beginning (Ps. 90). After all, something had to be there forever or there would not be something here now (John 1:3; Col. 1:16–17; Heb. 1:2).

So either God or the universe had a beginning. But the evidence presented in question 3, *Is there a God?*, is that the universe is not eternal. The Second Law of Thermodynamics reveals that the universe must have had a beginning since it is running out of useable energy. Therefore, the God who made the universe must be without a beginning. Why? Because the Law of Causality says that everything that has a beginning had a beginner. It is ridiculous to assert that nothing can make something but is entirely reasonable to assert that someone (i.e., God) can make something out of nothing. Therefore, God is the *uncaused* (eternal), *first* (originator) *cause* (Creator) who created everything that exists.

Application

God, who is timeless, changeless, and immaterial, created time, space, and matter. There is no one like our God! Asaph declares in Psalm 77:13–14, "Your ways, God, are holy. What god is as great as our God? You are the God who performs miracles; you display your power among the peoples."

Bible References

Exodus 3:14; Jeremiah 23:23–24; Malachi 3:6; John 4:24; Acts 17:24–25; James 1:17

Books

Who Made God? And Answers to Over 100 Other Tough Questions of Faith, edited by Norman L. Geisler and Ravi Zacharias

The Case for the Creator, by Lee Strobel

Systematic Theology: In One Volume, by Norman L. Geisler

Website

Peter S. Williams, "Who Made God?," BeThinking, http://www.bethinking.org/god/who-made-god

DVD

12 Points That Show Christianity Is True, Norman L. Geisler

Online Video

Bobby Conway, "Who Made God?," The One Minute Apologist, http://www.oneminute apologist.com/searchpage#who-made-god

5 Who Is God?

Answer

If you ask this question of Muslims, they will say Allah is God. Jews believe God is Yahweh (the God of Israel). Mormons believe God is Elohim (a created being who progressed into godhood).

One year I (Jason) took the liberty of asking the question *Who is God?* to people of all ages at my church. Here are some of the responses Christians in an evangelical church gave me:

God is the higher power.

God is Creator of everything.

God is everything.

God is all-powerful.

God is love.

God is my Father.

There is so much to write about God and yet so much we can't even fathom. Nonetheless, God has revealed enough in his creation (general revelation) and in his Word (special revelation) to help us understand who he is.

The Trinity

The *Trinity* (or *tri-unity* [3-in-1] of the Godhead) is an important doctrine to know concerning the nature of God. Christians are not *tri-theistic* (belief in three gods); they are *monotheistic* (belief in one God). Christianity teaches that God is one in nature (Deut. 6:4; see Isa. 44:6–8) and eternally revealed in three distinctive yet united personhoods: Father, Son, and Holy Spirit. Each member of the Trinity has a distinct role, but they share a unique, yet eternally equal relation within the Godhead. This means there is a plurality in God's unity but not in his nature.

The Sovereignty of God

God is the Most High, who has unlimited control and supreme power over heaven and the inhabitants on earth. He alone is the Creator and Sustainer of everything that has its existence according to his complete purpose and will (Eph. 1:11). Nebuchadnezzar, an unlikely character in the Bible, provides one of the most striking passages on the sovereignty of God:

> At the end of the days I, Nebuchadnezzar, lifted my eyes to heaven, and my reason returned to me, and I blessed the Most High, and praised and honored him who lives forever, for his dominion is an everlasting dominion, and his kingdom endures from generation to generation; all the inhabitants of the earth are accounted as nothing, and he does according to his will among the host of heaven and among the inhabitants of the earth; and none can stay his hand or say to him, "What have you done?"
>
> Daniel 4:34–35 ESV

Trinity
Father—Matthew 6:9; John 5:45; 1 Corinthians 8:6; Hebrews 12:9; 1 Peter 1:2
Son—John 1:1; 8:58; Revelation 2:8
Holy Spirit—Acts 5:3–4; Psalm 139:7–12; 1 Corinthians 2:10–11
Trinity—Matthew 3:15–17; 28:19–20; 1 Corinthians 12:4–6; 2 Corinthians 13:14

As Nebuchadnezzar described, God alone has the absolute and perfect right to reign and exercise his authority over the earth (Ps. 22:28) and to govern the stars of heaven as he sees fit (Pss. 103:19; 135:5–6).

The Self-Existence of God

Saying God is self-existent means he is absolutely independent of anyone or anything. The phrase comes from the word *aseity*, which literally means "of oneself." The self-existence of God is recorded by Moses in Exodus 3:14 when God announced from the burning bush, "I AM WHO I AM." In this one statement, God revealed to Moses his *Is-ness* (self-existence) and opened the door to all the other amazing attributes that describe who he is. God is:

1. *Simple* (absolutely one): God is the only Creator of the heavens and the earth (Gen. 1:1; Deut. 6:4; Isa. 40:28; Ps. 148; Heb. 11:3).
2. *Eternal*: There is no beginning or end to God (Deut. 33:27).
3. *Immutable* (unchanging): God is eternally perfect with no potentiality to change (Mal. 3:6; Heb. 6:17–18).
4. *Infinite* (limitless and boundless): Everything that exists proceeds from God (Ps. 147:5; Isa. 66:1). Thus, God experiences no growth or improvement from his perfectly infinite nature.
5. *Omnipotent* (all-powerful): God is fully capable of holding and sustaining everything by his infinite power (Exod. 6:3). Therefore, everything outside of God is dependent on him for existence because he has existed for all eternity.

The Self-Sufficiency of God

Since God exists eternally and independently of everything (see question 4, *Who made God?*), it is reasonable to deduce that he is also self-sufficient and, therefore, needs nothing to elevate his essence. That is, God is unaffected by the external causes of his creation, and he seeks no greater good to change his being because he himself is absolutely perfect in his unchanging nature. The self-sufficiency of God is supported by various passages in the Bible. In Hebrews 1:2, the writer maintains that "[God] made the universe." The prophet Isaiah writes, "The LORD is the everlasting God, the Creator of the ends of the earth. He will not grow tired or weary, and his understanding no one can fathom" (40:28). Elsewhere, Isaiah records these words of God: "I am the LORD; that is my name! I will not yield my glory to another or my praise to idols. See, the former things have taken place, and new things I declare; before they spring into being I announce them to you" (42:8). Hence, since the beginning of time, it was God who was the *Originating Cause* that caused everything to exist.

The Bible not only establishes God as the *Originator* of created things but also affirms that God is the *Sustainer* of all things created. For instance, not only did God create the *origin* of the universe, but he also remains active in the *operation* of it. The Bible makes frequent mention of God as the Sustaining Cause who holds everything together (Col. 1:17; Rev. 4:11). The writer of Hebrews contends: "God . . . *upholds* the universe by the word of his power" (1:3 ESV). Daniel declares that God is over the "times and the seasons" (2:20–21). Solomon describes God's sustaining power with these words: "By me kings reign and rulers issue decrees that are just; by me princes govern and nobles—all who rule on earth" (Prov. 8:15–16; see 21:1). And finally, Samuel affirms God as Sustainer by mentioning that the provision and destiny of humans lie in the hands of God: "The LORD brings death and makes alive; he brings down to the grave and raises up. The LORD sends poverty and wealth; he humbles and he exalts. He raises the poor from the dust and lifts the needy from the ash heap; he seats them with princes and has them inherit a throne of honor" (1 Sam. 2:6–8).

The Power of God's Sovereign Control

To help you better grasp the self-existence and self-sufficiency of God, allow us to provide four properties that maintain the power of God's sovereign control.

OMNIPRESENCE OF GOD

God, who has no origin, is infinite and presently involved everywhere in his creation all at once. That is, there is nowhere God is not present in his creation. It is important to point out, however, that the omnipresence of God is not a necessary part of his nature but rather a free act of his will regarding his creation. Isaiah records, "The LORD is the everlasting God, the Creator of the ends of the earth" (40:28). David ponders, "Where can I go from your Spirit? Where can I flee from your presence?" (Ps. 139:7; see Jer. 23:23–24). Undoubtedly, Isaiah, David, and Jeremiah all recognized the omnipresence of God over creation. There is absolutely no limitation to the presence of God. He is not *limited* to the *boundaries* of the universe; instead, he is *boundless* to the *limitations* of the universe.

OMNISCIENCE OF GOD

Scripture also states that God "[knows] the end from the beginning" (Isa. 46:10). David adds, "[God's] understanding has no limit" (Ps. 147:5). Job sarcastically asks, "Can anyone teach knowledge to God?" (21:22). God's knowledge is infinitely perfect because it is linked to his absolutely perfect nature.

OMNIPOTENCE OF GOD

God has the absolute power to do all things that he wills to do. Abraham asks this rhetorical question: "Is anything too hard for the LORD?" (Gen. 18:14). David proclaims, "The earth is the LORD's, and everything in it, the world, and all who live in it" (Ps. 24:1). Since God created the universe, it follows that he is the rightful owner of as well as the sovereign ruler over all things. There is nothing in existence that exists without the sovereign rule of God or that is outside his knowledge. It is important to point out, however, that there are certain things God cannot do. God cannot deny himself (2 Tim. 2:13); he cannot do wrong (Hab. 1:13); he cannot be tempted (James 1:13); and he cannot lie (Titus 1:2).

OMNISAPIENCE OF GOD

Finally, the fourth property is the *omnisapience of God*. *Omnisapience* literally means God is "all wise." This is at the root of God's sovereignty because in order for God to be sovereign over all things, he must be able to devise and achieve perfection with complete wisdom—producing no gimmicks or flaws. Thus, God's actions are accomplished perfectly in his infinitely pure wisdom, which exalts his own glory forever. The apostle Paul passionately writes, "God, the blessed and only Ruler, the King of kings and Lord of lords, who alone is immortal and who lives in unapproachable light, whom no one has seen or can see. To him be honor and might forever" (1 Tim. 6:15–16).

Application

The nature of God may blow your mind, but it by no means violates logic or reasoning. Just as God has revealed himself to be perfectly united in the Godhead, so you should remain united in Christ as you worship and obey him.

Bible References

Exodus 34:5–7; Numbers 23:19; Ezra 8:22; Psalms 33; 84:11–12; Isaiah 40:13–14; 1 Corinthians 1:9; 2 Corinthians 9:8; Colossians 1:16–17; 1 John 1:5

Books

Knowing God, by J. I. Packer

Systematic Theology: In One Volume, by Norman L. Geisler

The Knowledge of the Holy, by A. W. Tozer

Website

Josh McDowell, "Attributes of God," Josh.org, http://www.josh.org/?s=Attributes+of+God&cat=-3%2C-4%2C-5%2C-6%2C-7%2C-8

DVD

How Great Is Our God, Louie Giglio

Online Video

Bobby Conway, "Who Is God?," The One Minute Apologist, http://www.oneminuteapologist.com/searchpage#who-is-god-bobby

6 Are Miracles Possible?

Answer

I (Norm) was speaking on a secular campus some time ago when I was challenged about my belief in miracles. A student asked, "How can you possibly believe Jesus turned water into wine?" I replied, "It happens all the time. The rain comes down into the earth, up through the vine into the grape, and the grape turns into wine. All Jesus did was speed up the process." That basically ended the conversation.

C. S. Lewis said, "If we admit God, must we admit miracle? Indeed, indeed, you have no security against it. That is the bargain."[2] But men like Benedict Spinoza (1632–77) and David Hume (1711–76) argued against miracles. Spinoza claimed that the laws of nature can't change—but miracles do just that. Miracles are a violation of natural laws. Hume, on the other hand, denied the credibility of miracles because they are rare and lack eyewitness testimony.

Despite Spinoza's and Hume's attempts to refute miracles, the evidence for miracles is overwhelming. We live in a theistic universe. The fact that the universe was created with intelligent

Differences between Natural Occurrences and Supernatural Occurrences

Natural	Supernatural
Regular	Irregular
Repeatable	Not Repeatable
Predictable	Not Predictable

design and that objective morality is binding on all humankind points to God. Think about it. The known universe appears to have a radius of 14 billion light years. The moon is 240,000 miles away from the earth, and the sun is about 93 million miles away. Neptune is an outstanding 2.7 to 2.9 billion miles away from the earth! And yet each planet, star, and galaxy has been placed and programmed to contribute to the rest of the universe with precision. *Is this all coincidental or supernatural?*

Miracles are not hard to believe when you consider that the greatest miracle took place when God created the universe (Gen. 1:1; Job 26:10; Ps. 33:6; Jer. 10:12). Once the universe is explained by the order of a Creator, then the miracles of parting the Red Sea, turning water into wine, and Jesus rising from the dead are all possible.

Simply put, *a miracle is a special act of God that interrupts the regular or natural course of events.* Often a miracle confirms a *message* of God through a *messenger* of God. Peter rose up and proclaimed these words on the day of Pentecost: "Men of Israel, hear these words: Jesus of Nazareth, a man attested to you by God with *mighty works* and *wonders* and *signs* that God did through him in your midst, as you yourselves know" (Acts 2:22 ESV).

Moreover, another validation for the miracles of God is the reliability of the New Testament. If the New Testament is true, then its claims about Jesus and miracles are true as well. (See question 15, *Is the Bible true?*)

Application

Most people are looking for a miracle in their life. The fact that God created the heavens and the earth and sent his Son to forgive you of your sins are incredible miracles that shouldn't be taken for granted. Doubting that miracles exist is to doubt God's power and ability to perform them. If this has been an area of doubt, put your faith back in God and start believing in him for the unbelievable!

Bible References

Genesis 1–2; Exodus 7:14–25; Numbers 22:21–35; 2 Kings 13:21; Matthew 9:27–31; Mark 7:31–37; John 2:1–11; 11:38–44; 21:1–14

Books

Miracles and the Modern Mind: A Defense of Biblical Miracles, by Norman L. Geisler
Miracles, by C. S. Lewis

Website

Norman L. Geisler, "Miracles and Modern Scientific Thought," Leadership University, http://www.leaderu.com/truth/1truth19.html

DVD

Does God Exist? Building the Scientific Case, TrueU

Online Video

Norman L. Geisler, "Are Miracles Possible?," The One Minute Apologist, http://www.oneminuteapologist.com/searchpage#are-miracles-possible

7 If God, Why Evil?

Answer

Suffering is undeniable. Whether it is the loss of a loved one, a painful experience, or a battle with severe emotional or physical pain, no one is immune to the reality of suffering. It eventually comes knocking on each of our doors.

But how can an all-powerful and all-good God allow evil and suffering? This objection to God's coexistence with evil happens to be one of the strongest arguments for atheism. But a proper examination of the question leans more favorably to the Christian perspective.

Atheists argue that if God is all-powerful and all-good, then he would remove evil completely. Since evil is prevalent in the world, atheists conclude that God does not exist. This sounds convincing at the outset, but with a little thought, the whole argument crumbles.

Let's examine the atheists' argument more carefully:

1. If God is all-powerful, then he can defeat evil.
2. If God is all-good, then he would defeat evil.
3. But evil is not defeated.
4. Hence, there is no all-powerful and all-good God.

There is a serious flaw in the argument, however, which is apparent when it is restated as follows:

1. If God is all-powerful, then he can defeat evil.
2. If God is all-good, then he would defeat evil.
3. But evil is not *yet* defeated.
4. Hence, there is no all-powerful and all-good God.

As any thoughtful person can see, the conclusion does not follow because it assumes that evil will never be defeated. It ignores the fact that God may not be finished yet. In fact, if there is an all-powerful and all-good God, then we know that evil will one day be defeated. Follow the logic below:

1. If God is all-powerful, then he can defeat evil.
2. If God is all-good, then he would defeat evil.
3. But evil is not yet defeated.
4. Hence, evil will one day be defeated.

How do we know that evil will one day be defeated? Because God, who is all-powerful, can do it, and being all-good, he wants to do it. Therefore, it will be done. The very nature of God guarantees it.

Furthermore, there is another serious problem with the atheists' argument. How do they know some things are actually evil unless they know what is truly good (evil is a lack of good)? To put it another way, how can they know there is injustice in the world unless they have some ultimate standard of justice by which they measure it? But if there is an ultimate moral law, then there must be an ultimate moral lawgiver.

Again, the atheists' argument boomerangs on them, for in their attempt to eliminate God, they presuppose there is a God.

Application

Jesus forewarned that in this world we will face various trials and sufferings. But then he said something very comforting: "But take heart! I have overcome the world" (John 16:33). Things may be tough now, but we can rest assured that in the end God will make all things new in his perfect time (Rev. 21–22).

Bible References

Genesis 3; 50:20; Psalm 23; Habakkuk 1:13; Matthew 6:13; Romans 12:21; James 1:13; 1 John 2:13; Revelation 21–22

Books

If God, Why Evil?, by Norman L. Geisler
If God Is Good: Faith in the Midst of Suffering and Evil, by Randy Alcorn
The Problem of Pain, by C. S. Lewis

Website

Randy Alcorn, "How Could a Good God Allow Evil and Suffering?," Eternal Perspective Ministries, http://www.epm.org/resources/2001/Apr/9/how-could-good-god-allow-evil-and-suffering

DVD

God, Evil, and Suffering, vol. 10, Ravi Zacharias International Ministries

Online Video

Norman L. Geisler, "If God Exists, Why Evil?," The One Minute Apologist, http://www.one minuteapologist.com/searchpage#if-god-why-evil

8 Is the God of the Old Testament a Monster?

Answer

The culture today is more interested in painting God as a cosmic bully than a merciful God. Most of the media, elite schools, and staunch atheists claim that the God of the Bible is a cruel and ruthless deity who caused mass genocide in the Old Testament.

Here are some of the hotly debated passages in the Old Testament that supposedly back up this view of God.

Then the LORD rained on Sodom and Gomorrah sulfur and fire from the LORD out of heaven.

Genesis 19:24 ESV

You must devote them [Canaanites] to complete destruction.

Deuteronomy 7:2 ESV

Then they devoted all in the city to destruction, both men and women, young and old, oxen, sheep, and donkeys, with the edge of the sword.

Joshua 6:21 ESV

And the men of Israel turned back against the people of Benjamin and struck them with the edge of the sword, the city, men and beasts and all that they found. And all the towns that they found they set on fire.

Judges 20:48 ESV

Now go and strike Amalek and devote to destruction all that they have. Do not spare them, but kill both man and woman, child and infant, ox and sheep, camel and donkey.

1 Samuel 15:3

By simply isolating these Old Testament passages, it's no wonder people think God is a brutal monster.

Bearing in mind that these horrific incidents did occur, we need proper precautions and examination of the context before drawing any conclusions.

1. The Bible declares that God is a loving, merciful, and perfectly just God. (See question 7, *If God, why evil?*) He would never commit an unjust and brutal act. It's against his very nature as love (1 John 4:16).
2. Each of these passages needs to be interpreted in its proper context, not taken out of context to try to prove a point.

God of the Old Testament

God is merciful—Deuteronomy 4:31; 13:17; 2 Samuel 22:26; 2 Chronicles 30:9; Nehemiah 9:17–19; Jeremiah 3:12; Daniel 9:9 (also read the mercy books: Exodus, Psalms, Jeremiah, Hosea)

God is loving—Exodus 34:6–7; Numbers 14:18–19; Deuteronomy 5:10; 7:9; 1 Chronicles 16:34; 2 Chronicles 1:8; Ezra 3:11; Nehemiah 1:5; Psalm 5:7

God is holy—Exodus 5:11; Leviticus 11:44; Deuteronomy 7:6; Joshua 5:15; 24:19; 1 Samuel 2:2; 1 Chronicles 16:10; Psalm 11:4

God is forgiving—Exodus 34:7; Numbers 14:18–19; Nehemiah 9:17; Psalm 25:18; Jeremiah 31:34

3. These actions were taken because each nation refused to accept God and his laws. God had extended mercy long enough. The Amalekites, for example, had been given over four hundred years to repent of their sins.

4. It was customary according to Israeli rules of engagement to warn of coming invasion, giving women and children the opportunity to flee prior to war. Furthermore, many of these cultures that God permitted to be destroyed were so completely corrupt that there was no hope for the next generation. Therefore, this was an act of mercy on God's part because it may have saved many children before the age of accountability (2 Sam. 12:23; Isa. 7:16).

5. Each incident was limited to a particular group at a particular point in history. These nations were relentless in their attempts to murder the people of Israel, yet you don't hear people complaining about that! God protected Israel from her enemies by providing the very elements to keep his promises and people safe (Matt. 2:4–6; Rom. 3:2). What kind of God would he be if he abandoned his promises to Israel and allowed wicked people to kill them off? Instead, God delivered the people of Israel and used them as a model of his great love and mercy to the other nations.

God's holiness and justice require those who perpetrate evil to be punished. God never changes. Therefore, God demonstrated the same love and mercy in the Old and New Testaments (2 Pet. 3:9).

Application

Rest assured that God is a loving and merciful God who acts justly all of the time (Gen. 18:25). But God is also holy, and he cannot tolerate sin (Hab. 1:13). Therefore, he must judge sin.

Bible References

Exodus 5:11; Numbers 14:18–19; Deuteronomy 4:31; Nehemiah 9:17–19; Daniel 9:9

Books

The Case for Faith, by Lee Strobel

Is God a Moral Monster? Making Sense of the Old Testament God, by Paul Copan

A Popular Survey of the Old Testament, by Norman L. Geisler

Website

Paul Copan, "Is Yahweh a Moral Monster?," Evangelical Philosophical Society, http://www.epsociety.org/library/articles.asp?pid=45

DVD

Promises of God, Deepening Life Together Series

Online Video

Bobby Conway, "How Can a Loving God Kill People in the Old Testament?," The One Minute Apologist, http://www.oneminuteapologist.com/searchpage#how-can-a-loving-god-kill-people

9 Would a Loving God Send People to Hell?

Answer

The idea of being tormented in eternal agony isn't something people like to think about, let alone bring up in casual conversation. That's why most people avoid talking about hell or rule it out altogether.

What Is Hell?

Hell is reserved for sinners who have willfully rejected the gift of salvation through Jesus Christ as Lord and Savior.

Hell, literally, is a place of suffering, punishment, and eternal separation from the presence and glory of God (Matt. 5:22; 10:28; Mark 9:43; 2 Thess. 1:9; 2 Pet. 2:4).

Let's face it. Hell is a controversial subject. But despite the apparent aversion people have to talking about hell, it is a necessary truth that Christians need to grasp and address with others. After all, Christians believe that those who reject the gospel of Jesus Christ will end up in hell forever.

It's important to mention that skeptics view hell as inhumane, cruel, and barbaric. The problem with this assessment is that it is based more on personal feelings than on an objective look at the evidence.

The existence of hell is rooted in the nature of God. His holiness and justice require the existence of a hell. Habakkuk says that God is "of purer eyes than to see evil and cannot look at wrong" (1:13 ESV). The apostle John emphasizes that "God is light; and in him is no darkness at all" (1 John 1:5).

God is perfect (Matt. 5:48) and, therefore, executes his justice perfectly (Gen. 18:25) and with no favoritism (Rom. 2:11).

Of course, God is also love and is "not willing that any should perish" (2 Pet. 3:9 NKJV) but "desires all men to come to the knowledge of the truth" (1 Tim. 2:4). In fact, God so loved the whole world that he gave his only Son to suffer for us so that we need not be separated from him (John 3:16; see 1 John 2:2).

Since God is love (1 John 4:7–8), however, it is against his nature to *coerce* people to love him. That would be a contradiction. It would be like saying he *forces* people to freely choose him. God's love cannot act *coercively* but rather *persuasively*. Those who receive God are rewarded, and those who reject God are condemned. Jesus said, "Jerusalem, Jerusalem, you who kill the prophets and stone those sent to you, how often I have longed to gather your children together, as a hen gathers her chicks under her wings, and *you were not willing*" (Matt. 23:37).

If God is love and humans are free, then there must be a hell. Not only would it be a contradiction for God to force people to love him, but it would also be hell for them to be forced to love the One they hate.

Application

Do you realize that Jesus talked more about hell than about heaven? He doesn't desire that any should go to hell but that all will receive the free gift of salvation and spend eternity in heaven with him (John 1:12; 3:16–21; Rom. 10:9–10). As a Christian, be grateful for your salvation and be emboldened to share the gospel and, hopefully, save many from going to hell.

Bible References

Matthew 5:22–30; 10:28; 13:49–50; 22:13; 23:23; 25:41; Luke 16:19–31; 2 Thessalonians 1:7–9; Hebrews 9:27; 2 Peter 2:4–5; Jude 1:12–13; Revelation 19:20; 20:11–15

Books

"Hell," in *The Big Book of Christian Apologetics*, by Norman L. Geisler

"A Loving God Would Never Torture People in Hell," in *The Case for Faith*, by Lee Strobel

The Great Divorce, by C. S. Lewis

Website

"How Can a God of Love Send Anybody to Hell?," Christian Answers Network, http://www.christiananswers.net/q-grace/hell-and-god.html?zoom_highlight=how+can+a+god+of+love+send+anybody+to+hell

DVD

Hell's Best Kept Secret, Ray Comfort

Online Video

Bobby Conway, "Is Hell Unjust?," The One Minute Apologist, http://www.oneminute
apologist.com/searchpage#is-hell-unjust

PART 2

Questions about Creation, Science, and the Bible

10 How Did the Universe Come to Be?

Answer

The opening line of Genesis puts it succinctly: "In the beginning God created the heavens and the earth" (1:1). The Bible teaches that through an act of God the temporal creation of the universe came from nothing (*ex nihilo*).

Creator	Creation
Uncreated	Created
Necessary	Contingent
Eternal	Temporal
Infinite	Finite
Changeless	Changing

Christianity teaches that God is the *Originating Cause* (Eph. 3:9) who created the space-time universe and is also the *Sustaining Cause* that keeps everything together (Col. 1:17). Moses declared, "For in six days the LORD made the heavens and the earth, the sea, and all that is in them, but he rested on the seventh day" (Exod. 20:11).

According to Gottfried Wilhelm Leibniz (1646–1716), a German philosopher and mathematician, everything that exists has a cause for its existence. We know the universe exists and didn't get here on its own. God is the necessary being who produces external causes that don't exist necessarily because they are contingent on something greater than their own existence.

But there are two other options: (1) *Naturalism* teaches that nothing created the universe—it just came to be with no real explanation. (2) *Pantheism* teaches that God and the universe are one and eternally the same. The problem with naturalism is that it holds to a contradictory claim that *nothing created something* or *something created itself*. But this is fundamentally irrational. Pantheism, on the other hand, is fundamentally flawed because it identifies the universe as eternal, when the Second Law of Thermodynamics proves that wrong.

Second Law of Thermodynamics
In a closed, isolated system, the amount of useable energy decreases. That is, matter and energy deteriorate gradually over time. Also, things tend to move from order to disorder, not the reverse.

Thus, it is reasonable to conclude that God created the universe out of nothing (*ex nihilo*).

Application

To know there is a God who created the universe and controls all things ought to give you great comfort. Evolutionists attempt to rule out a Creator, but thankfully, as a Christian, you know God as a personal Creator, and we are made in his image.

Bible References

Genesis 1–2; Job 26:10; Isaiah 40:22; John 1:3; Colossians 1:17; Hebrews 1:3

Books

God's Design for Heaven and Earth: Our Universe, by Richard and Debbie Lawrence
Why the Universe Is the Way It Is, by Hugh Ross
A New Look at an Old Earth, by Don Stoner

Website

John D. Morris, "Did God Create with the Appearance of Age?," Institute for Creation Research, http://www.icr.org/article/did-god-create-with-appearance-age

DVD

Science and Evidence for Design in the Universe, Ignatius Press

Online Videos

Andrew Murtagh, "Can the Universe Come from Nothing?," The One Minute Apologist, http://www.oneminuteapologist.com/searchpage#can-the-universe-come-from-nothing
William Lane Craig, "What Is the Fine-Tuning Argument for the Existence of God?," The One Minute Apologist, http://www.oneminuteapologist.com/searchpage#what-is-the-fine-tuning-argument-for-the-existence-of-god

11 Is Evolution a Viable Option?

Answer

Although macroevolution is the dominant scientific theory taught in schools and upheld in academia, the majority of the public still holds to a belief in creation.

But how is this possible? How is it that the majority of people still don't buy into the explanation of evolution? We will provide three essential flaws to the theory of evolution, but first, here's evolution in a nutshell:

> **Evolution** (common ancestry) is simply defined as a gradual development of simple life forms into more complex life forms brought about by natural processes.

Thus, for evolution to be a viable option, it must be able to explain (1) the origin of the universe, (2) the origin of first life, and (3) the origin of new life forms.

1. *The origin of the universe*: According to cosmic evolution, the universe just *popped into existence*. Though evolutionists now admit the universe had a beginning, they deny any designed cause or purpose behind the existence of the universe. Thus, evolution offers no real explanation for the existence of an incredibly big and complex universe. (See fig. 1.)

2. *The origin of first life*: Biological evolutionists teach that a *primordial soup* (simple organic chemicals) produced the first life a few billion years ago as the earth was shaped, formed, and cooled down. But the earth had to be incredibly fine-tuned from the start in order for the necessary and specific conditions to be balanced precisely to produce life. Some evolutionists even speculate that life arose on another planet and was transported here. But this is simply speculation; there is no real evidence for it. Further, if life arose elsewhere, the same problem exists, namely, that nonlife does not produce life. (See fig. 2.)

3. *The origin of new life forms*: Evolution teaches that certain genetic mutations occurred among species that eventually caused them to transition into completely new species with all new genetic information. This is known as *macroevolution*. The evolutionist bases this idea on

observing slight changes or modifications in species within their environment (*microevolution*). Yet, macroevolution is a huge leap from the slight modifications that we witness and has absolutely no evidence to support it. What we do observe and can verify is that there is a single common ancestor of humankind (Adam and Eve). Humans beget humans and dogs beget dogs (Gen. 1:21–24). Thus, evolutionists make unwarranted claims that have never been proven that different species emanated from a single cell, or *common ancestry*. (See fig. 3.)

Figure 1. The Origin of the Universe

Figure 2. The Origin of First Life

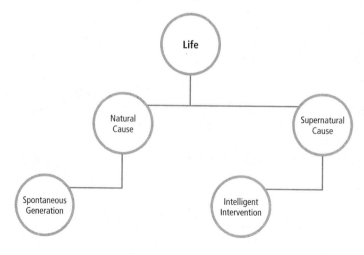

Figure 3. The Origin of New Life Forms

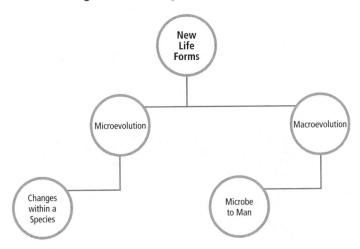

Most revealing is that Darwin himself admitted, in his book *Origin of Species* (written in 1859), to the lack of evidence for "intermediate links" in the fossil record. The fossil evidence (as a whole) is even greater than in Darwin's day, and yet it still does not show evidence of macroevolution.

What the fossil record does show, however, are fully formed and fully functional species. This confirms the obvious: transitional forms cannot survive with missing or evolving parts, especially considering *survival of the fittest*.

Someone may ask, "What about Archaeopteryx?" Isn't this a great example of a transitional species from a feathered dinosaur to modern birds?

The problem with Archaeopteryx is that it's not a transitional life form that evolved from a reptile to a bird. Rather, Archaeopteryx appears in the fossil record as a fully developed bird. Thus, Archaeopteryx is not a missing link between birds and reptiles. It's a bird.

In the end, what the evidence points to is a designer who created a good design and applied it to various other species to gain the best results.

Application

When talking with evolutionists, make sure not to assume what they believe, and don't allow them to make up evidence in support of evolution. Some great questions to ask evolutionists are:

What do you mean by evolution?

If there is no God, why is there something rather than nothing?

45

Where did the first life come from?
Doesn't there have to be preexisting life for life to exist?
What caused nonliving chemicals to produce life?
How did nonintelligent matter produce intelligent life?

Bible References

Genesis 1–2; 5:1–3; Psalms 8; 33; Isaiah 42:5–9; Acts 17:26; Romans 1:20–27; 2 Peter 3:3–6

Books

Darwin's Doubt: The Explosive Origin of Animal Life and the Case for Intelligent Design, by Stephen C. Meyer

Refuting Evolution, vols. 1 and 2, by Jonathan Sarfati

Darwin on Trial, by Phillip Johnson

Website

Evolution News and Views, http://www.evolutionnews.org

DVD

Icons of Evolution, Randolf Productions

Online Video

Norman L. Geisler, "Is Evolution a Viable Option?," The One Minute Apologist, http://www.oneminuteapologist.com/searchpage#is-evolution-a-viable-option

12 Are Science and the Bible Compatible?

Answer

The scientific world has convinced millions to believe that the stories of the Bible and the facts of science are mutually exclusive. To many scientists, the Bible is nothing more than an antiquated religious book filled with fairy tales and make-believe stories.

But this couldn't be further from the truth. Science and the Bible are not mutually exclusive. The Bible and nature have no conflict because what's in nature, the Bible affirms. The conflict arises (oftentimes) between theology and science. This is to be expected. Both scientists and Bible interpreters are fallible and continue to make investigative discoveries about nature and the Bible.

The Bible has much to say about creation. The Creator who created all things also inspired the very words of the Bible. The Bible openly declares, "The heavens declare the glory of God, and the sky above proclaims his handiwork" (Ps. 19:1).

At the turn of the nineteenth century, many

The Bible Is Scientific
The beginning of the universe—Genesis 1:1
The round earth—Proverbs 8:27; Isaiah 40:22
The earth suspended in space—Job 26:7
The Second Law of Thermodynamics—Psalm 102:25–26
The universe made from tiny elements—Colossians 1:16–17; Hebrews 11:3

secular thinkers began to teach naturalism (denial of God) and separate Christianity's role in the scientific community. Until then, most originators and primary developers of key scientific disciplines were God-fearing scientists who believed in the Bible for both personal and scientific work:

Galileo Galilei (1564–1642)—astronomy, mathematics, and physics

Johannes Kepler (1571–1630)—astronomy

Blaise Pascal (1623–62)—mathematics, physics, and theology

Robert Boyle (1627–91)—chemistry

Isaac Newton (1642–1727)–dynamics

Michael Faraday (1791–1867)—electromagnetics

Gregor Mendel (1822–84)—genetics

Contrary to what the modern science world asserts, the history of science demonstrates the significant and influential role Christianity has played in the development of modern science. It's more than fair to say that the Bible and science are compatible.

Application

Christianity is not a blind faith—it is a reasonable faith. It understands the benefits of science. When honest and objective scrutiny has been applied to the claims of the Bible, not one piece of it has been disproved. You can be confident that what the Bible says is true.

Bible References

Job 26:7; 38:4–30; Psalm 19; Isaiah 40:12, 28; John 3:12; Romans 1:20; Colossians 1:16; 2:3; Hebrews 1:3; 2 Peter 3:10–12

Books

A Fine-Tuned Universe: The Quest for God in Science and Theology, by Alister McGrath

The Fingerprint of God, by Hugh Ross

The Biblical Basis for Modern Science, by Henry Morris

Website

"The Bible and Science Agree," Creationism.org, https://www.creationism.org/articles/BibleSci.htm

DVD

Philosophy, Science and the God Debate: Oxford Professors Dispute the Assault on Christianity, John Lennox, Alister McGrath, Keith Ward, Christopher Jervis, and Malcolm Turner

Online Video

Norman L. Geisler, "Is the Bible without Error in Science and History?," The One Minute Apologist, http://www.oneminuteapologist.com/searchpage#is-the-bible-without-error

13 What Happened to the Dinosaurs?

Answer

Dinosaurs have captured the imagination of children and scientists for many years. There are countless tales as to what exactly happened to the dinosaurs. Old Earthers believe dinosaurs became extinct after a massive meteor hit the earth over 65 million years ago.

Young Earthers argue that Genesis 1:21 states that God created "the great creatures of the sea." If this is the case, then dinosaurs were created with every other kind of animal and existed alongside humans. But the alleged footprints of humans with dinosaurs turned out to be a fraud, leaving us with no real fossil evidence that dinosaurs and human beings lived at the same time.

Young Earthers insist (based on fossilized bones) that most dinosaurs appear to have been rapidly submerged in water and embedded in muddy deposits by a catastrophic worldwide flood event. All the millions upon millions of discovered fossil graveyards have verified this time and time again.

As for how Noah got dinosaurs on the ark, Young Earthers point out that the ark was extremely large and designed with perfect dimensions (450 feet long; 75 feet high; 45 feet wide) and over 1.5 million cubic feet of space to house more than enough animals, supplies, and food as well as to store waste. It was practical for Noah to have carried eggs or dinosaurs in their infancy. After the animals came off the ark, many (including dinosaurs) became extinct with the change of climate after the global flood. Many died from disease or an inability to adapt; others were killed by hunters or through competition with other species (Gen. 9:2–3; 10:8–12).

Old Earthers do not have this problem since they believe dinosaurs were extinct long before the time of Noah. Indeed, some believe the flood was geographically local and did not include dinosaurs to begin with. It may have been anthropologically universal in that it wiped out nearly the entire human race (1 Pet. 3:20), which was still cradled in the Mesopotamian area.

Dinosaur

In 1841, Sir Richard coined the term *dinosaur*, which literally means "terrible lizard." That's why the word *dinosaur* doesn't appear in the English translations of the Bible, because they originated from the Geneva and King James versions in the sixteenth and seventeenth centuries.

But many passages of the Bible allude to massive dinosaurs, both land animals and living creatures of the sea.

Dragons—Psalms 74:13; 148:7; Isaiah 13:22 KJV
Behemoth—Job 40:15–19; 41:12
Leviathan—Job 41:1–34; Isaiah 27:1
Great Monster—Ezekiel 29:3; 32:2

Application

So no matter whether the earth is thousands or millions of years old, there is no contradiction between the existence of dinosaurs and the Bible. Each explanation gives what they believe to be a reasonable account for the disappearance of dinosaurs. The resources below provide the alternative views regarding dinosaurs.

Bible References

Job 40:15–19; 41:1–34; Psalms 74:13; 148:7; Isaiah 13:22; 27:1; Ezekiel 29:3; 32:2

Books

The Great Dinosaur Mystery Solved, by Ken Ham

Dinosaurs and Creation: Questions and Answers, by Daniel DeYoung

Websites

Ken Ham, "Dinosaurs and the Bible," Answers in Genesis, http://www.answersingenesis.org/articles/1999/11/05/dinosaurs-and-the-bible

Reasons to Believe, "Dinosaurs," http://www.reasons.org/rtb-101/dino

DVDs

The Bible Explains Dinosaurs, Ken Ham

Mystery of the Dinosaurs: The Biblical Solution, Mike Snavely

Online Video

Jason Jimenez, "What Happened to the Dinosaurs?," The One Minute Apologist, http://www.oneminuteapologist.com/searchpage#what-happened-to-dinosaurs

14 Was There Really a Worldwide Flood?

Answer

There are essentially two camps: local flood versus global flood. Many Old Earthers point to the fact that the Bible often uses universal language to describe local areas (Acts 2:5; Col. 1:23). Some Young Earthers, however, insist there is scientific evidence for a global flood.

The Surface Features of the Earth

All over the world, people have discovered fossilized animals and plants embedded in thick, sedimentary layers that were laid down by water. Many of the rock strata were laid down very quickly, preserving various species and plant life. Based on evidence from the Grand Canyon's Coconino Sandstone (covering over two hundred thousand square miles) to Australia's Hawkesbury Sandstone in Sydney, Young Earthers are convinced that these and countless more features point to a global flood. Old Earthers believe these formations resulted from many local floods that occurred in different places at different times over the centuries.

The Dimensions of Noah's Ark

The dimensions of the ark are like those of a modern cargo ship. It was 450 feet long, 75 feet high, and 45 feet wide (Gen. 6:15). That means the inside of the ark had over 1.5 million cubic feet of space. That's plenty of room to store the thousands of animals needed to repopulate the earth. (The ark was also sturdy enough to survive the harsh weather conditions.) Young Earthers point out that if the flood were only localized, there would have been no need for Noah to build a massive cargo ship. Old Earthers counter, however, that all those animals were needed to repopulate the massive area where the local flood occurred.

Ancient Accounts of Flood Stories

Young Earthers offer as additional proof of a global flood over five hundred flood myths that depict the flood account in the book of Genesis. These myths share similar details that make you wonder how it is that distinct people groups all around the world (Mexico, Romania, India, and Sudan) share a flood account that can be traced back for thousands of years. It is fairly obvious that as Noah and his descendants got off the ark and began to repopulate the earth they took the flood story with them. In time, the flood story simply evolved as people adapted it to their distinct cultures. These stories would have spread as the people were later dispersed around the world from the Tower of Babel (Gen. 11). But Old Earthers point out that the universal flood stories do not necessarily prove a universal flood.

Old Earthers insist that worldwide *stories* do not prove a worldwide *flood*. These stories only show that, however wide the flood was, the human race (and the stories of the flood) moved out from there to the entire world. Actually, both views could be true since the flood could have been worldwide *anthropologically* (as far as human beings are concerned), since they may have all lived in a limited area, but not worldwide *geologically*. That is, the flood might not have literally covered the entire globe.

Application

The main point of the flood is about the wickedness of humankind. Genesis 6:5–7 reads:

The LORD saw how great the wickedness of the human race had become on the earth, and that every inclination of the thoughts of the human heart was only evil all the time. The LORD regretted that he had made human beings on the earth, and his heart was deeply troubled. So the LORD said, "I will wipe from the face of the earth the human race I have created—and with them the animals, the birds and the creatures that move along the ground—for I regret that I have made them."

Yet despite the wickedness of humans, God found favor in Noah and saved him and his family by instructing him to build an ark (Gen. 6; 1 Pet. 3:20; 2 Pet. 2:5). Thus, the flood represents the judgment of sin, the ark represents redemption, and the sign of the rainbow represents God's faithful protection (Gen. 9:11–17).

The resources below provide alternative views of the flood.

Bible References

Genesis 6–9; 10:1, 32; 11:10; Matthew 24:38–39; Luke 17:27; Hebrews 11:7; 1 Peter 3:18–22; 2 Peter 2:5

Books

The Genesis Flood, by Henry Morris

Refuting Compromise, by Jonathan Sarfati

The Genesis Question: Scientific Advances and the Accuracy of Genesis, by Hugh Ross

Websites

"The Flood," Answers in Genesis, answersingenesis.org/the-flood/

Hugh Ross, "Exploring the Extent of the Flood," parts 1–3, Reasons to Believe, http://www.reasons.org/articles/exploring-the-extent-of-the-flood-part-one; http://www.reasons.org/articles/exploring-the-extent-of-the-flood-what-the-bible-says-part-two; http://www.reasons.org/articles/exploring-the-extent-of-the-flood-part-three

DVDs

Noah's Flood: Washing Away Millions of Years, Terry Mortenson

How Well Designed Was Noah's Ark?, Werner Gitt

Online Video

Jason Jimenez, "Was There a Worldwide Flood?," The One Minute Apologist, http://www.oneminuteapologist.com/searchpage#was-there-a-worldwide-flood

15 Is the Bible True?

Answer

Do you know the number one reason why young people leave the Christian faith? They stop believing the Bible is true.

This sweeping problem of doubt among young people touches on something of great importance. Young people aren't leaving the faith primarily because they want to live a life of sin and rebellion. Many of them are leaving the faith over the simple fact that they have lost faith in the truth of the Bible and fail to see the connection it has to the culture.

In other words, parents in the home and leaders in the church have failed to build a firm foundation for the next generation. Instead of equipping them with credible answers about the truth of the Bible, Christian leaders have turned to entertainment and superficial answers that offer no real substance or hope.

That being said, we've put together an acrostic that shows the BIBLE can be trusted based on its *brand, inspiration, background, literature,* and *errorless teaching.*

Brand: Continuity of the Bible

An absolutely amazing feature of the Bible is the basic continuity within the biblical accounts of creation, fall, redemption, and final consummation of the new heaven and new earth. This high level of accuracy in a collection of sixty-six books by forty authors whose occupations ranged from peasant, prophet, fisherman, statesman, poet, plowman, to king is remarkable. Moreover, those forty authors lived across a span of sixteen hundred years and in different locations, and they spoke and wrote in different languages. Yet they pieced the story together just the way the Holy Spirit spoke it through them (2 Pet. 1:20–21). By comparison, a medical manual written by forty doctors from different countries over sixteen hundred years would be a bundle of major contradictions.

> **Inspiration**
> **2 Peter 1:20–21**
>
> God's inspiration—revealed the Word.
> The Holy Spirit's instrumentation—carried the Word.
> Man's dictation—recorded the Word.

Inspiration: Authority of the Bible

The phrase "inspiration of God" comes from two Greek words: *theos* ("God") and *pneustos* ("to breathe"). When combined, the two words form *theopneustos*, which means "God-breathed." This is found in 2 Timothy 3:16: "All Scripture is *breathed out by God* and profitable for teaching, for reproof, for correction, and for training in righteousness" (ESV). Reading or hearing the Word of God exposes your heart and mind to the very breath of God. The Bible is his breathed-out words—his truth. That's how intimately powerful the Word of God is (John 17:17; Heb. 1:1–2). Jesus said, "Every word . . . comes from the mouth of God" (Matt. 4:4; see 5:17–18) and "cannot be broken" (John 10:35 ESV).

Moreover, the Bible is the inspired, inerrant, and infallible Word of God. It's *inspired* because God spoke it, *inerrant* because the original text had no errors or mistakes, and *infallible* because nothing can destroy God's eternal Word (John 10:35).

Background: Canonicity of the Bible

The word *canon* simply means "measuring rod." Thus, canonicity has to do with the *rule* or *norm* of what the Bible states to be doctrinal truth. Centuries later, the word *canon* became known to mean "the rule of faith" because it summarized the beliefs and teachings of the apostles in the early church.

The church used certain criteria in order to confirm what books God inspired:

- Was it written by a prophet (spokesperson) from God?
- Was that person confirmed as a prophet of God by miracles or other means?
- Is it consistent with other revelations and truths contained in other inspired books?
- Does it reveal the life-changing power of God?
- Did the early church accept and live out its truths?

In the first century, Jewish historians accepted all the Old Testament books as part of the Word of God. By AD 90, Jewish scholars at the Council of Jamnia recognized the Old Testament books as canonical.

Jesus quoted from each section of the "Old Testament," and the New Testament writers accepted the whole Old Testament, citing most of the books as the Word of God (1 Thess. 5:27; Col. 4:16; 2 Pet. 3:15–16), thus confirming the canon.

Throughout the second century, many of the church fathers—such as Clement, Polycarp, Ignatius, Irenaeus, and Justin Martyr—recognized the divine authority of both the Old and New Testaments as inspired books of God and used them as Scripture in the church. And in the third century, Origen (AD 185–254) studied the collective books of the New Testament and underscored that they were inspired by God.

In the fourth century, the bishop of Caesarea and great church historian Eusebius (ca. AD 260–340) in his *Church History* listed as canonical most of the twenty-seven books of the New Testament. It was Athanasius (bishop of Alexandria), however, who catalogued in his thirty-ninth *Festal Letter* (AD 367) the twenty-seven canonical books that make up the New Testament today. By AD 397 the Council of Carthage decreed that the twenty-seven books were divine Scripture. And since that point in church history, most of the Western and Eastern churches have affirmed the New Testament as the canon of Scripture.

Literature: Authenticity of the Bible

The authenticity of the Bible is confirmed by the *accuracy* of the biblical manuscripts. The Bible has earlier, more abundant, and more accurately copied manuscripts than any book from the ancient world. There are currently some fifty-eight hundred manuscripts of the New Testament in Greek (and counting). They are earlier and more accurate than other books from the ancient world with over 99 percent accuracy. In fact, 100 percent of the basic teaching of the Bible is conveyed in these copies.

Errorless Teaching: Reliability of the Bible

While there are minor errors in copies of the Bible, there are no errors in any major teaching of the Bible. Many of the writers were either eyewitnesses or contemporaries of eyewitnesses (Luke 1:1–4; Heb. 2:3–4). Further, much of what they wrote has been confirmed by history and archaeology. Literally hundreds of finds have confirmed the reliability of the Bible. Luke mentions over eighty details just in the book of Acts that have been confirmed to be true.

Application

The Bible is the greatest book of all time. Nothing compares to its message and the veracity of what it teaches. You can say with confidence that "every word of God is pure" (Prov. 30:5 NKJV) and has the power to transform lives (Heb. 4:12; James 1:21). No other book in the world possesses the life-transforming power of the Bible.

Bible References

Isaiah 55:11; Matthew 4:4; 2 Timothy 3:16; Hebrews 4:12; James 1:21; 2 Peter 1:20–21

Books

From God to Us: How We Got Our Bible, by Norman L. Geisler and William Nix

Seven Reasons Why You Can Trust the Bible, by Erwin Lutzer

A Popular Handbook of Archaeology and the Bible, by Norman L. Geisler and Joseph Holden

The Book of Acts in the Setting of Hellenic History, by Colin Hemer

Website

"Is the Bible Myth?," Christian Research Institute, http://www.equip.org/perspectives/bible-myth-is-the-bible-a-myth/

DVD

From God to Us: How We Got the Bible, International Legacy Institute

Online Videos

Norman L. Geisler, "How Do We Know the Bible Is Historically Accurate?," The One Minute Apologist, http://www.oneminuteapologist.com/searchpage#bible-is-historically-accurate

Norman L. Geisler, "Is the Bible Reliable?," The One Minute Apologist, http://www.oneminuteapologist.com/searchpage#is-the-bible-reliable

16 How Did the Bible Come Together?

Answer

Did you know the Bible is the world's bestselling book of all time? To date, the complete Bible has been translated into almost five hundred languages and portions of the Bible into over twenty-five hundred languages. This is an extraordinary accomplishment considering it's been over thirty-five hundred years since Moses began to write the first books of the Old Testament.

Following is a summary of how the Bible came together.

Old Testament

The Old Testament (Hebrew Bible) was completed by 400 BC. From the sixth century AD and well into the tenth century, the Masoretes (Jewish rabbis and scholars) guarded and preserved the Old Testament text as they meticulously transmitted copies of copies. The Septuagint (Greek translation of the Old Testament) was produced in about 250–150 BC.

> **Bible Process**
>
> The word *Bible* comes from *biblos* ("book"), the word for the ancient papyrus plant used to make the scrolls on which it was written. This was a popular use for papyrus until the third century AD. *Parchment* (goat and sheep skin) and *vellum* (calfskin) were later used as pages for the Bible, and they lasted longer.
> *Codex* or *book form* was an easier and more functional way for the Bible to be written down using both sides of the paper.

New Testament

The New Testament was completed within a half century after the death and resurrection of Jesus Christ. In other words, all twenty-seven books of the New Testament (written by nine authors) were written, copied, and distributed before AD 100. Scrolls were transferred to papyrus in the second century.

Complete Bible

The scholars at Jamnia (AD 90–118) gave final affirmation to the thirty-nine books in the Old Testament. The Council of Carthage (AD 397) established the New Testament canon of twenty-seven books.

Translations of the Bible

Then around AD 400, Jerome did something remarkable. He translated the Bible into Latin. The Latin Vulgate was the predominant translation of the Bible in medieval times.

- The Wycliffe Bible was the first English translation (1380–82).
- Gutenberg's Latin Bible was the first produced on a printing press (1455).
- Erasmus's Greek New Testament was completed in 1516.
- Coverdale's was the first complete Bible to be printed in English (1535).

In 1227, Stephen Langton (archbishop of Canterbury) divided the Bible into chapters. In 1551 and 1555, Robert Stephanus added verses to the Bible.

Application

When you consider the meticulous care and great pains people in the ancient world took to preserve the Bible, it makes you appreciate it so much more. The prophet Isaiah declared, "The grass withers and the flowers fall, but the word of our God endures forever" (40:8).

Bible References

Psalm 119; Isaiah 40:8; Matthew 4:4; Luke 24:44; 2 Timothy 3:16; Hebrews 4:12; 2 Peter 1:20–21

Books

From God to Us: How We Got Our Bible, by Norman L. Geisler and William Nix

The Origin of the Bible, by Philip Comfort

Taking a Stand for the Bible: Today's Leading Experts Answer Critical Questions about God's Word, by John Ankerberg and Dillon Burroughs

Website

Norman L. Geisler, "The Dating of the New Testament," BeThinking, http://www.be thinking.org/bible/the-dating-of-the-new-testament

DVD

How We Got the Bible, Paul Maier

Online Video

Norman L. Geisler, "How Can We Be Sure the Right Books Got into the Bible?," The One Minute Apologist, http://www.oneminuteapologist.com/ searchpage#how-can-we-be-sure-the-right-books-got-into-the-bible

17 Can We Trust the English Translations of the Bible?

Answer

I (Jason) remember talking to a college student about the reliability of the Bible. He told me that the Bible isn't true because of all the different English translations. I asked him what he meant by that, and he responded, "If the Bible were true, then there would be only one English translation." It was clear to me this student had no clue what he was talking about. So I proceeded to share with him how translating the Old Testament Hebrew and the New Testament Greek into modern English is considered some of the most scholarly work. Afterward, he thanked me for helping him better understand the Bible and was willing to investigate the claims of Jesus Christ. So let's take a closer look at the trustworthiness of the English translations.

There are essentially two approaches to English translations: (1) *formal equivalence*, which means taking a literal approach to translating the original words and conveyed meaning of the author, and (2) *dynamic equivalence*, which means capturing the historical meaning and style of language in its most natural form.

When it comes to Bible translation, there's no direct word-for-word correspondence between the biblical languages and English. This is one of the great advantages to having different English translations. Some remain extremely sensitive to the nuances of words, while others focus on the heart and meaning. Both aim to get as close to the original language as they can while faithfully conveying the meaning of the text for the reader.

Below is a list of various approaches to translation taken by different Bible versions:

Word-for-word—King James Version (KJV), New American Standard Bible (NASB), Young's Literal Translation (YLT)

Thought-by-thought—New International Version (NIV), Contemporary English Version (CEV)

Both—English Standard Version (ESV), New King James Version (NKJV), New Century Version (NCV), New Living Translation (NLT), Holman Christian Standard Bible (HCSB)

59

Paraphrase—New Living Bible (NLB), The Message

Don't think that because there are many different English translations they are all wrong. As a matter of fact, newer revisions are necessary because they are *improvements* to the English language in general as well as to syntax (structure of words and phrases), spelling, and translation specifically. Many of the English translations of the Bible not only accurately translate the original languages but also offer the reader a clear understanding of the text.

Application

Many Christians have made it their living to translate the Bible, and many even lost their lives over ensuring the Bible was translated into English. Don't forget that, and be grateful for the Bible(s) you have.

Bible References

Psalms 19:7; 119; Proverbs 30:5–6; John 17:17; 2 Timothy 3:16

Books

The Complete Guide to the Bible Versions, by Philip Comfort

How to Choose a Translation for All It's Worth: A Guide to Understanding and Using Bible Versions, by Gordon Fee and Mark Strauss

From God to Us: How We Got Our Bible, by Norman L. Geisler and William Nix

Website

"English Bible History," http://www.greatsite.com/timeline-english-bible-history/

DVD

A Lamp in the Dark: The Untold History of the Bible, Christian J. Pinto, director

Online Video

Bobby Conway, "Can We Trust the English Translations of the Bible?," The One Minute Apologist, http://www.oneminuteapologist.com/searchpage#can-we-trust-the-english-translations

18 How Do I Study the Bible?

Answer

How many times have you attempted to read through the Bible in a year? Or started off strong in a Bible study never to finish it?

When Christians are asked why they have a hard time reading the Bible, 64 percent say they're too busy, while another 80 percent say they don't understand the Bible. These statistics are alarming, but there's one that is even more so. National studies consistently reveal that roughly 95 percent of Christians have never been properly trained in how to study the Bible. That means only 5 percent of all Christians know how to appropriately study the Bible.

This lack of growth in understanding the Bible has wreaked havoc in homes, churches, and, ultimately, our nation. One of the church's primary functions should be to teach and train believers how to study the Bible so they can understand and apply God's truth.

Our prayer is that you grow in your understanding of how to study the Bible for yourself. It is our hope that the advice offered below will be of help to you.

Game Plan

The truth is that you don't need to be an expert in order to read the Bible. All you need is a willingness to learn, a plan to follow, and the drive to get it done. The first thing we recommend is picking a Bible-reading plan. You can choose from any of the plans provided below:

- read the Bible in a year
- read the Bible in chronological order
- read the Old Testament in six months
- read the New Testament in three months
- read two Old Testament chapters, two New Testament chapters, one Psalm, and one proverb each day
- do an inductive study of a particular book (verse by verse)
- do topical study and memorization

Make sure you have a solid study Bible and some additional study tools—such as commentaries, Bible software programs, and websites—to help you in your daily reading (recommended resources are provided at the end). There are many good Bible-reading schedules online that you can print out for your use. We recommend following a plan with a friend, spouse, or church group so you have some added accountability. Remember, it's not how much you read but that you spend quality time reading some of God's Word each day.

Pray

Always make sure you pray before reading the Bible. It's important that you ask the author of the Bible, the Holy Spirit, to open your mind and bring you great faith and conviction as you read. First Corinthians 2:12 says, "What we have received is not the spirit of the world, but the Spirit who is from God, so that we may understand what God has freely given us." David prayed, "Open my eyes that I may see wonderful things in your law" (Ps. 119:18).

Read to Observe—"What's going on?"

As you read the Bible, always be alert to what is happening in the passage. It's so much more enriching when you know the *who*, *what*, *when*, *where*, *why*, and *how* of the particular book you are studying. The more insight you have of the *external* background of the book, the deeper your understanding will be of the *internal* matters within the book. So learning about the author, dates, background, and historical setting and significance will broaden your understanding of the *content* and *context* of the Bible.

Read to Interpret—"What does it mean?"

As you observe what's happening in a passage, the next step is to interpret its meaning. But make sure you don't misinterpret Scripture. Again, ask the Holy Spirit to give you proper guidance (1 Cor. 2:10–12; 1 John 2:26–27) as you begin to dissect the text. Remember, the key to studying the Bible is *context, context, context*.

John MacArthur states that there are four gaps that need to be bridged when studying the Bible:

1. *Language gap*: Seek out the original meaning of the languages the Bible was written in (Hebrew, Aramaic, and Greek).
2. *Culture gap*: Be sensitive to the culture and social structures of the time in the Bible.
3. *Geography gap*: Allow geography to be a road map to help you understand the landscape and environment of the people in those times.

4. *History gap*: Gain a historical perspective that will give you more appreciation of the people and events.

Read to Apply—"What must I do?"

Finally, as you study the Bible, seek to apply and live what you learn. Howard Hendricks had a great way of reminding people how to apply the Bible: *read* to concentrate; *record* to remember; *reflect* to apply.

Application

Be diligent to spend quality time investing in the Bible. Put a game plan together of what to read and when you plan to do it. Keep this up until you have established a routine of spending an hour a day studying the Bible.

Time in the Word of God will help shape your worldview and provide you with the faith and conviction needed to stand against Satan and the evils of the world. James exhorts, "But whoever looks intently into the perfect law that gives freedom, and continues in it—not forgetting what they have heard, but doing it—they will be blessed in what they do" (1:25).

Bible References

Psalms 19; 119; Ephesians 6:17; Colossians 3:16; 2 Timothy 2:15; James 1:25

Books

Living by the Book, by Howard and William Hendricks
How to Study the Bible, by John MacArthur
Know Your Bible, by Paul Kent

Websites

http://www.globible.com
http://www.logos.com
http://www.biblestudytools.com

DVDs

How to Study Your Bible for Kids, Kay Arthur and Janna Arndt
Living by the Book, seven-part condensed series

Online Videos

Bobby Conway, "How to Study the Bible," The One Minute Apologist, http://www.one minuteapologist.com/searchpage#how-to-study-the-bible

Bobby Conway, "How to Develop an Appetite for Bible Study," The One Minute Apologist, http://www.oneminuteapologist.com/searchpage#how-to-develop-an-appetite-for-bible-study

PART 3

Questions about Jesus and the Holy Spirit

19 Who Is Jesus Christ?

Answer

History has witnessed its fair share of great leaders whose influence has left major imprints on the world. Abraham's faith led to the rise of the nation of Israel. Moses commanded the greatest exodus of all time. Alexander the Great conquered the known world in only twelve years. George Washington presided over the making of the United States. Mahatma Gandhi led one of the largest nations on earth to its independence. Martin Luther King Jr. sparked a great civil rights movement that paved the way for freedom for African-Americans. Nelson Mandela helped bring an end to apartheid in South Africa. Yet the historical influence of these leaders (and others) only scratched the surface when compared to the impact of a certain historical figure.

That figure is Jesus Christ.

What professional, religious, and political figures have tried to do in a lifetime, Christ accomplished in three short years. Jesus's life, death, and resurrection have impacted directly or indirectly almost every nation and people group on the planet. Let's take a look at the magnificent person of Christ and learn how his influence in the world has eternal consequences.

Titles of Jesus
Son of God—John 20:30–31; Galatians 4:4–6
Savior—Philippians 3:20; Titus 2:13
Messiah—Matthew 16:16
Son of Man—Daniel 7:13; John 5:27
Emmanuel—Isaiah 9:6; Matthew 1:23
I AM—Exodus 3:14; John 8:58
Holy One—Psalm 16:10 ESV; Acts 3:14

It's important to start with his name. *Jesus* literally means "Jehovah saves," and the name *Christ* is "Messiah" (Hebrew: *Mashiach*; Greek: *Christos*), which means "Anointed One."

By simply piecing together portions of the Bible, we get an excellent picture of the person of Jesus Christ:

1. He existed prior to coming into the world (John 1:1–3; 3:13; Heb. 1:2).
2. He was born of a virgin in approximately 4 BC (Isa. 7:14; Dan. 9:24–26; Luke 1:26–56).
3. He was born in Bethlehem (Mic. 5:2; Matt. 2:1).

4. He grew up in Nazareth in Galilee (Luke 2:39).

5. He was both fully God and fully man (Matt. 16:16; John 8:58).

6. He lived a sinless life (Matt. 27:4, 19, 24; Luke 23:41; John 18:38).

7. He performed many miracles (two examples: Matt. 9:18–26; 12:9–13).

8. He fulfilled prophecy (Isa. 9:6–7; 53:11; Dan. 9:25–26).

9. He forgave people of their sins (Mark 2:1–12; John 3).

10. He accepted worship from his followers (Matt. 8:2; 9:18; John 9:38).

11. He was betrayed, arrested, illegally tried, and crucified on a cross (Matt. 26–27; Mark 14–15; Luke 22–23; John 18–19).

12. He was buried in a borrowed tomb for three days (Matt. 12:40; 28:1; 1 Cor. 15:4).

13. He physically rose from the dead (1 Cor. 15:3–8).

14. He appeared to his followers for forty days, teaching them about his kingdom (Acts 1:3).

15. He ascended bodily into heaven (Acts 1:9).

16. He promised his disciples the coming of the Holy Spirit to empower them to spread his message to all nations (Matt. 28:18–20; Acts 1:8).

17. His followers comprise the largest following of any religion of any time.

18. He inspired a book, the Holy Bible, confirming and fulfilling the Old Testament (Matt. 5:17–18; Luke 24:27; John 10:35) and promising the New Testament (John 14:26; 16:13). The Bible has been the runaway bestseller in the world for many generations.

Application

As demonstrated above, no other figure is as remarkable as Jesus. Not only is he central to Christianity, but he is also central to life! Open the Bible and get to know more about his life, teachings, miracles, death, and resurrection. You will find that the more you discover about Jesus, the more your life will change for the better.

Bible References

Acts 2:36–38; 4:9–12; Romans 1:4; 5:1, 11; 1 Corinthians 1:9, 30; 6:11; 8:6; 2 Corinthians 1:9; 13:14; Ephesians 1:17; 2:6; Philippians 2:5–11; Revelation 1:5, 8; 21:6; 22:13

Books

The Apologetics of Jesus, by Norman L. Geisler and Patrick Zukeran

Christ: The Theme of the Bible, by Norman L. Geisler

Jesus Christ, by John Stott

Website

"Who Is Jesus Christ?," Campus Crusade for Christ, http://www.cru.org/training-and
-growth/classics/10-basic-steps/intro-the-uniqueness-of-jesus/01-who-is-jesus-christ.htm

DVD

The Person of Christ: Understanding the Power, Person, and Place of Jesus Christ in All of Life, Voddie Baucham

Online Video

Bobby Conway, "Is Jesus God?," The One Minute Apologist, http://www.oneminute
apologist.com/searchpage#is-jesus-god

20 How Can Jesus Be Both God and Man?

Answer

If there's one thing true about Americans, it's that we love going to the movies. But in the midst of all the romantic dramas, thrillers, and action-packed films, there's one particular brand of film that tops them all.

According to the box offices, Marvel Comics are a huge hit these days. Every time another one is released, it grosses hundreds of millions of dollars!

But why are movies based on comics so popular? What makes millions of people go crazy and flock to the movie theaters?

Here's why: movies based on comics capture our imagination. They do this by building a plot around two main characters: the villain and the protagonist. The villain (representing evil) is often inspired by anger, jealousy, or lust for more power (all relatable traits). The protagonist (representing good) is often an ordinary person who, by some freak accident, is given incredible superpowers and turns into an extraordinary superhero.

As the battle between good and evil ensues, in the end, the superhero saves the day. This is the message that innately appeals to us: good always triumphs over evil. This message is clearly captured in the superhero film genre.

Unlike a comic-book story, however, which is make-believe, the story of an ordinary carpenter who performed some extraordinary miracles is true. According to Christianity, Jesus was far superior to any fictitious comic-book hero. He was not only *fully human* (human nature), but *fully divine* (divine nature) as well. That is, Jesus was the *God-man*. As God-man, Christ became the perfect person to defeat the power of sin and death on the cross (Heb. 10:1–10; 1 Pet. 2:21)—a victory only Jesus Christ was able to achieve.

Let's take a closer look at the incredible abilities possessed by Jesus Christ and, hopefully, come to understand the God-man mystery a little bit better. Four notable facts will help us make sense of the God-man:

1. Christ has two distinct natures and wills: deity and humanity.
2. There's no mixture or intermingling of the two natures or wills.
3. Both natures are necessary for redemption because as man Jesus acts as our perfect sacrifice (Rom. 3:25) and as God he acts as our High Priest (Heb. 7:26).
4. Christ will forever be the Second Person of the Godhead with two natures perfectly expressed in his eternal being.

In essence, the second nature (humanity) was an addition to the person of Christ, not a subtraction of his deity. Likewise, just as the body of Christ consists of both divine and human natures, so the mind of Christ contains

Jesus: God-Man

Deity of Christ

Preincarnate: Jesus existed prior to coming into the world as a human. He came down to earth from heaven, and he revealed his *heavenly origin* to Nicodemus (John 3:13; see John 1:3; Col. 1:16; Heb. 1:2).
Deity: This is Jesus's divine nature. He is fully God (Ps. 110; John 10:30–33; Col. 2:9).

Humanity of Christ

Incarnation: Jesus came into the world as a newborn baby (Luke 2; Gal. 4:4; Heb. 2:14).
Humanity: Jesus (Second Person of the Trinity) "became flesh and dwelt among us" (John 1:14 ESV). This is Jesus's second nature. He is fully human.

God-Man

Theanthropic: The God-man exists in the *person* of Jesus Christ, and therefore, the two *natures* exist in perfect union in the person of Christ.
Hypostatic union: This means that the person of Jesus possesses two distinct natures—divine and human—yet remains unified completely and perfectly.

a divinely inspired will (John 2:18–19) as well as a humanly felt will (Matt. 26:39).

In becoming human, Jesus exercised his *divine will* (as the Son of God) by relinquishing his glorious estate. He freely chose to live and die for the sins of the world in accordance with his *human will* (Rom. 1:3; 2 Cor. 8:9; 1 Tim. 3:16). Hence, every time Christ employed a divine or human attribute, he first willed it from either his divine nature or his human nature.

If both natures were to comingle, then humanity would become eternal and deity would become noneternal, which would be a contradiction because God cannot be transported to man or vice versa (Phil. 2:5–11). Hence, when Jesus became a human, he neither diminished his deity or infinite will nor manipulated his humanity or finite will.

This was a necessary process for Jesus to save us. The Bible affirms, "Since the children have flesh and blood, he too shared in their humanity so that by his death he might break the power of him who holds the power of death—that is, the devil—and free those who all their lives were held in slavery by their fear of death" (Heb. 2:14–15).

Some critics believe it is a contradiction to be both God and man at the same time. But it is not a contradiction because Jesus's two natures are not one and the same. Just as a stick has two different ends without a contradiction, even so, Jesus has two different natures represented in one person without contradiction.

Application

Paul writes, "For you know the grace of our Lord Jesus Christ, that though he was rich, yet for your sake he became poor, so that you through his poverty might become rich" (2 Cor. 8:9). How amazing it is to know that Jesus didn't come to be served (Matt. 20:28) but to humble himself to the point of death on the cross (Heb. 12:2). You can relate to Jesus because he is human, but you can also worship him because he is God.

Bible References

John 10:30–33; Galatians 4:4; Philippians 2:7–8; Colossians 2:9; 1 Timothy 3:16; Hebrews 2:14–15

Books

Jesus Christ Our Lord, by John Walvoord

Basic Theology, by Charles Ryrie

Website

Kenneth Samples, "Thinking about the Incarnation: The Divine Word Became Flesh," Reasons to Believe, http://www.reasons.org/articles/thinking-about-the-incarnation-the-divine-word-became-flesh

DVD

The Real Jesus: A Defense of the Historicity and Divinity of Christ, Apologetic Group

Online Video

Bobby Conway, "How Can Jesus Be Both God and Man?," The One Minute Apologist, http://www.oneminuteapologist.com/searchpage#how-can-jesus-be-both-god-and-man

21 Why Did Jesus Have to Die?

Answer

Mel Gibson's movie *The Passion of the Christ* sent shockwaves around the world. The depiction of Christ's willingness to lay down his life for the world brought many to their knees. Yet *The Passion of the Christ* captured only a glimpse of the brutal torture and excruciating death of Jesus on the cross. The very thought of the cross makes people wonder if there was some other way for God to save us.

The direct answer is no. Peter states it clearly: "He [Jesus] bore our sins in his body on the cross, so that *we might die to sins and live for righteousness*; by his wounds you have been healed" (1 Pet. 2:24). The writer of Hebrews explains that Christ "has appeared once for all at the culmination of the ages *to do away with sin* by the sacrifice of himself" (9:26; see 5:7–10; 9:28).

Jesus came into the world to die for the sins of the world. This was necessary because God is holy; he is absolutely perfect (Matt. 5:48) and cannot tolerate any sin in his presence. God cannot even look upon sin with approval (Hab. 1:13). The angels in his presence sing, "Holy, holy, holy is the LORD of hosts" (Isa. 6:3 ESV).

Further, all sin must be punished, for "the wages of sin is death" (Rom. 6:23). Our sin has put us in debt to God—and that debt must be paid. The choice is clear: *either we pay for it ourselves or someone else must pay for it.* But another sinner cannot satisfy our sins to God. Only someone who is sinless can do that. Of all human beings, only Jesus is absolutely sinless (Heb. 4:15; 1 Pet. 3:18; 1 John 3:5).

Moreover, not only is Jesus a perfect man, but he is also God. Thus, as the God-man (see question 20, *How can Jesus be both God and man?*), he alone is in a position to reconcile both God and man. "For there is one God and one mediator between God and mankind, the man Christ Jesus" (1 Tim. 2:5). Paul describes this mediation between God and humans in Romans 5:12–21:

> Therefore, just as sin entered the world through one man, and death through sin, and in this way death came to all people, because all sinned—To be sure, sin was in the world before the law was given, but sin is not charged against anyone's account where there is no law. Nevertheless, death reigned from the time of Adam to the time of Moses, even over those who did not sin by breaking a command, as did Adam, who was a pattern of the one to come.
>
> But the gift is not like the trespass. For if the many died by the trespass of the one man, how much more did God's grace and the gift that came by the grace of the one man, Jesus Christ, overflow to the many! Nor can the gift of God be compared with the result of the one man's sin: The judgment followed one sin and brought condemnation, but the gift followed many trespasses and brought justification. For if, by the trespass of the one man, death reigned through that one man, how much more will those who receive God's abundant provision of grace and of the gift of righteousness reign in life through the one man, Jesus Christ!
>
> Consequently, just as one trespass resulted in condemnation for all people, so also one righteous act resulted in justification and life for all people. For just as through the disobedience of the one man the many were made sinners, so also through the obedience of the one man the many will be made righteous.
>
> The law was brought in so that the trespass might increase. But where sin increased, grace increased all the more, so that, just as sin reigned in death, so also grace might reign through righteousness to bring eternal life through Jesus Christ our Lord.

Only Jesus could give his life as a payment of our debt to God. Paul articulated in his writings that God is just and justifier of the unjust (Rom. 3:26)—and the just one (Christ) died for the unjust (1 Pet. 3:18). Paul further explains, "God made him who had no sin to be sin for us, so that in him we might become the righteousness of God" (2 Cor. 5:21). Christ paid our debt that we may by faith be justified (without sin) in the eyes of God. Christ's sacrifice satisfied God's justice and made way for him to release his grace on us (1 John 2:2).

Application

There was no other way possible. Jesus had to die on the cross for your sins. Paul writes emphatically, "For what I received I passed on to you as of first importance: that *Christ died for our sins according to the Scriptures*" (1 Cor. 15:3). Stop and think about that for a moment. Jesus Christ freely chose to die on the cross for your sins. And he did that not only for you but also for all humankind! John the apostle expressed the unfathomable sacrifice of Jesus Christ by writing, "See what great love the Father has lavished on us, that we should be called children of God" (1 John 3:1). Oh, what a friend you have in Jesus!

Bible References

Romans 3:20–24; 2 Corinthians 5:21; 1 Timothy 2:5; 1 Peter 2:24; 3:18

Books

The Life of Jesus: His Life, Death, Resurrection and Ministry—Matthew through John, by Henrietta C. Mears

The Cross of Christ, by John Stott

Website

Mark Driscoll, "Why Jesus Died on the Cross," http://www.pastormark.tv/2012/03/27/why-jesus-died-on-the-cross

DVD

The Case for Christ, Lee Strobel

Online Video

Bobby Conway, "Why Did Jesus Have to Die?," The One Minute Apologist, http://www.oneminuteapologist.com/searchpage#why-did-jesus-have-to-die

22 How Do We Know Jesus Rose from the Dead?

Answer

Maybe Jesus didn't die. Or if he did die, maybe he didn't rise from the dead.

These are common speculations some people have about the resurrection of Jesus Christ. Many Muslims, for example, believe Jesus didn't die on the cross but that someone else (such as Judas) replaced him (Sura 4:157). Many liberals believe Jesus died but that he didn't rise from the dead. There are various explanations for the empty tomb: (1) someone stole Jesus's body; (2) the disciples were hallucinating; (3) it was a case of mistaken identity; or (4) Jesus's followers went to the wrong tomb. But consider the evidence in support of the physical death and resurrection of Jesus Christ.

Jesus Died a Physical Death

1. The nature of the crucifixion assures death. Jesus was on the cross from 9 a.m. (Mark 15:25) until just before sunset. He bled from wounded hands and feet as well as from the thorns that pierced his head. What is more, crucifixion demanded that he constantly pull himself up in order to breathe, thus causing more excruciating pain from the nails. Failure to do so meant the person would eventually die of asphyxiation.

2. Jesus's death cry was heard by those at the cross. He declared, "Father, into your hands I commit my spirit! And having said this he breathed his last" (Luke 23:46 ESV; see Matt. 27:45–50).

3. The piercing of Jesus's side with the spear is proof that he had physically died before the piercing. This is because "blood and water" came out (John 19:34), which is medical proof (*pericardial effusion*—"fluid around the heart") that Jesus had already died (see John 19:33). But if that wasn't enough, the spear to Jesus's heart was!

4. The professional Roman executioners pronounced Jesus dead. They were so convinced that Jesus was dead that they did not break his legs, which was a common practice to speed death by making it no longer possible for the person to lift himself up to breathe (John 19:33).

5. Pilate double-checked to make sure Jesus was dead before he gave the corpse to Joseph to be buried. "Summoning the centurion, he asked him

if Jesus had already died. When he learned from the centurion that it was so, he gave the body to Joseph" (Mark 15:44–45).

6. Jesus was wrapped in about seventy-five pounds of cloth and spices and placed in a sealed tomb for three days (Matt. 27:60; John 19:39–40). If he wasn't dead by then, which he clearly was, he would have died from lack of food, water, and medical treatment.

7. The earliest Christian writers after the time of Christ affirmed his death on the cross by crucifixion. Polycarp, a disciple of the apostle John, spoke of "our Lord Jesus Christ, who for our sins suffered even unto death." Ignatius (AD 30–107), a friend of Polycarp, affirmed, "He really suffered and died, and rose again." Josephus, the Jewish historian at the time of Christ, wrote, "Pilate, at the suggestion of the principal men amongst us, had condemned him to the cross."[3]

Jesus Rose from the Dead Physically

Not only is the evidence for Jesus's death unquestionable, but the evidence for his resurrection is indisputable. Consider the following:

1. Jesus's grave and grave clothes were left empty three days later (John 20:1–10).

2. Over five hundred eyewitnesses testified to seeing the resurrected Christ (1 Cor. 15:6).

3. Jesus was seen on twelve separate occasions, by different people, and in different circumstances. Some were women and some were men. Some saw Jesus alone, while others saw him in groups. There were small groups and even large crowds. Some were in the city and others were in the country. Some were believers and others were unbelievers.

4. Jesus appeared to unbelievers such as his brother (John 7:5; 1 Cor. 15:7) and Saul, the Pharisee (Acts 9).

5. Jesus appeared to Thomas, a doubting disciple, and convinced him (John 20:26–29).

6. Jesus taught his disciples about the kingdom of God over a forty-day period of time (Acts 1:3).

7. Jesus showed them physical evidence of his resurrection, like the crucifixion scars (John 20:27), as well as his "flesh and bones" (Luke 24:39).

8. Jesus turned his scared, scattered, and skeptical disciples into the world's greatest missionary society almost overnight as a result of his appearances to them.

9. Within a matter of a few weeks, thousands in the same city were converted through the preaching of his resurrection (Acts 2–4).

10. Within a short time in the same city, a great number of Jewish priests were converted to Christ (Acts 6:7).[4]

Application

There is absolutely no denying the resurrection of Jesus Christ. What a tremendous blessing to know that he came into the world to die for the sins of all humankind—and that he defeated sin by rising from the dead. Hence, the splendor of Paul's words: "And if the Spirit of him who raised Jesus from the dead is living in you, he who raised Christ from the dead will also give life to your mortal bodies because of his Spirit who lives in you" (Rom. 8:11).

Bible References

Matthew 27–28; Mark 15–16; Luke 22–24; John 19–21; 1 Corinthians 15

Books

The Battle for the Resurrection, by Norman L. Geisler

The Case for Christ, by Lee Strobel

Is Jesus Alive Today?, by Lee Strobel, Gary Habermas, and Hank Hanegraaff

Website

Brett Kunkle, "Did Jesus Really Rise from the Dead?," Stand to Reason, http://www.str.org/articles/did-jesus-really-rise-from-the-dead#.U1VuCvldX74

DVD

Did Jesus Really Rise from the Dead?, Ignatius Press

Online Video

Gary Habermas, "Did Jesus Rise from the Dead or Are We Delusional?," The One Minute Apologist, http://www.oneminuteapologist.com/searchpage#did-jesus-rise-from-the-dead

23 Where Did Jesus Go between His Death and Resurrection?

Answer

The Bible isn't very clear about where Jesus went during the three days his body was in the tomb. It's almost like he played the greatest hide-and-seek game ever. Because not much is known as to the hidden location of Jesus during the three days, several theories have taken shape in an attempt to provide a satisfactory answer.

A popularized teaching is that Jesus went to hell during the three days he was buried in the tomb. This is based on several references:

1. "He was not abandoned to Hades [hell]" (Acts 2:31 ESV) but came back to life three days later.
2. Peter speaks about Jesus preaching "to the spirits in prison" (1 Pet. 3:18 NKJV).
3. Ephesians speaks about Christ leading "captivity captive" when he left "the lower parts of the earth" (Eph. 4:8–9 NKJV). At the same time, some believe that Christ brought all the believing souls from their place in Sheol (taking it to mean hell) and took them to heaven with him because they had to wait for his death and resurrection before they could enter heaven (1 Cor. 15:20).
4. Some appeal to the Apostles' Creed, which declares that Jesus "descended into hell."
5. Some claim that no one could enter into heaven until Jesus first died, rose, and ascended (1 Cor. 15:20; John 14:3).
6. Some Word-Faith teachers have added unorthodox teaching to this view, claiming that Jesus defeated Satan in hell, and afterward Jesus was born again.

Other Bible scholars believe that when Jesus died on the cross, his spirit went directly to heaven to be with the Father for three days before he was resurrected and returned to earth. They base their view on the following texts:

1. Jesus said clearly on the cross that he was going to be with the Father when he died, declaring, "Father, into your hands I commit my spirit" (Luke 23:46).

2. Jesus told the thief on the cross that he would be with him in "paradise" that very day (Luke 23:43), and paradise is the "third heaven," or the very presence of God (2 Cor. 12:2).

3. The spirits of Moses and Elijah appeared from heaven when Jesus was on the Mount of Transfiguration (Matt. 17:1–8).

4. In the Old Testament, Enoch was taken up into heaven at the end of his life (Gen. 5:24; Heb. 11:5).

5. Likewise, when Elijah departed from this life, he was taken up into heaven (2 Kings 2:1).

In response to the first view, the following can be pointed out:

1. The "lower parts of the earth" (Eph. 4:9 NKJV) does not refer to hell (which is "under the earth" [Phil. 2:10]) but to the grave where his body was—and thus not to where his spirit was, heaven.

2. The Apostles' Creed was not inspired by the Holy Spirit, but even so, the earliest form of the creed did not contain the phrase "descended into hell."

3. The word *hell* is not an accurate translation of the term "grave" used in Psalm 16:10–11 and Acts 2:31. Peter uses this verse to proclaim the resurrection of Christ's body from the grave (Sheol), not to proclaim that his spirit went to hell.

4. When Paul says Jesus "led captivity captive" (Eph. 4:8–9 NKJV), he could not be referring to taking souls to heaven since believers are not captives in heaven. He is referring to Christ defeating the devil and demons (see Col. 2; Heb. 2) and proclaiming his victory to the spirit world *after* his resurrection (1 Pet. 3:18).

5. Jesus defeated Satan at his death (Heb. 2:14) and resurrection (Rom. 4:25), not in hell. Looking forward to the cross, Jesus said, "Now is the time for judgment on this world; now the prince of this world will be driven out" (John 12:31). Then on the cross he declared, "It is finished" (John 19:30; see Heb. 1:3).

6. No one could get a resurrection body and go to heaven in it until after Jesus was resurrected (1 Cor. 15:20). But this does not mean that people's spirits could not go to heaven before the resurrection. After all, Christ is the Lamb slain from the foundations of the earth (Rev. 13:8; see Eph. 1:4). In the mind of God, salvation was already an accomplished fact,

even before Jesus actually died, since God knows "the end from the beginning" (Isa. 46:10).

7. Peter's reference to Jesus speaking to the spirits in prison does not refer to the time between his death and resurrection. The text says clearly it was after he was "made alive in the Spirit [resurrected]" (1 Pet. 3:18) that he spoke to these spirits, and it was probably to declare his victory over the devil and the demons (see Eph. 4:8; Col. 2:15).

Application

Though no one knows for certain where Jesus went, one thing is for sure: Jesus destroyed sin and death. Paul affirms, "And having disarmed the powers and authorities, he made a public spectacle of them, triumphing over them by the cross" (Col. 2:15).

Bible References

Luke 23:42–43; John 20:17; 1 Peter 3:18–20

Books

When Critics Ask: A Popular Handbook on Bible Difficulties, by Norman L. Geisler and Thomas A. Howe

Basic Theology, by Charles Ryrie

Website

"Where Did Jesus Go after He Died on the Cross?," Christian Apologetics & Research Ministry, http://www.carm.org/christianity/christian-doctrine/where-did-jesus-go-after-he-died -cross

DVD

Jesus: Fact or Fiction?, Peter Sykes, director

Online Video

Norman L. Geisler, "Where Did Jesus Go between His Death and Resurrection?," The One Minute Apologist, http://www.oneminuteapologist.com/searchpage#where-did-Jesus-go -between-his-death-and-resurrection

24 What Kind of Body Did Jesus Have after His Resurrection?

Answer

It is a scientific fact that everyone will die. But Christians aren't to fear death, for death brings life. The day will come when believers will receive their resurrected bodies after the rapture. This is the same body as Jesus received at his resurrection. Paul anticipates, "But our citizenship is in heaven. And we eagerly await a Savior from there, the Lord Jesus Christ, who, by the power that enables him to bring everything under his control, will transform our lowly bodies so that they will be like his glorious body" (Phil. 3:20–21). (See question 55, *What is going to happen in the end times?*)

Jesus's body that died on the cross was the same body of flesh and bones that was resurrected. If the body that died did not come to life again, then there is no resurrection. And if there is no resurrection, then there is no salvation. As the apostle Paul said, "If Christ has not been raised, your faith is futile; you are still in your sins" (1 Cor. 15:17). But Christ did rise from the dead. This is evident for many reasons:

1. Jesus said his resurrection body was the same body in which he died: "Destroy this temple [body], and I will raise it [the same body] again in three days" (John 2:19). John adds, "But the temple he had spoken of was his body" (John 2:21).

2. Speaking of the same body that was crucified, Jesus said to his disciples, "Look at my hands and my feet. It is I myself! Touch me and see; a ghost does not have flesh and bones, as you see I have" (Luke 24:39).

3. The apostle Paul spoke of the resurrection as what will "give life to your mortal bodies" (Rom. 8:11). Jesus's body was not a *replacement* body. He experienced a *resurrection* of his mortal body.

4. Jesus proved his body was physical by being touched (Matt. 28:9; John 20:17) and offering himself to be handled (John 20:27).

5. Jesus also ate on several occasions (Luke 24:41–43; Acts 10:41).

6. Jesus proved he had risen in the same physical body by showing his crucifixion scars on two occasions (Luke 24:40; John 20:27).

There is in fact no other way Jesus could have proven to his disciples that he had risen in the same physical body in which he had died. Of course, Jesus did supernatural things in his resurrection body like entering locked rooms (John 20:19), but this does not prove his body was not physical any more than walking on water before his resurrection (John 6:16–21) proved his body was not physical. He could appear and disappear quickly, but Philip did this in his natural body (Acts 8:39–40).

To be sure, Jesus's resurrection body was changed to one that is immortal (1 Cor. 15:53), but it was not changed into an immaterial body. When Paul said the resurrection body would be a *spiritual body*, he meant a *Spirit-dominated, physical body*. He also referred to literal "spiritual food . . . spiritual drink," and a "spiritual rock" (1 Cor. 10:3–4) as having a spiritual source. In the same sense, the Bible is a spiritual book, but it is not immaterial; it is physical. Likewise, Jesus's resurrection body was a *Spirit-dominated*, physical body—the same body that died on the cross.

Application

Jesus gave this promise to his followers: "Because I live, you also will live" (John 14:19). As a believer, your hope is to be united with Christ in your resurrected body. Paul writes that Christ "will transform our lowly bodies so that they will be like his glorious body" (Phil. 3:21). Keep looking for the return of Christ, and anticipate receiving a resurrected body.

Bible References

Acts 1:11; 1 Corinthians 1:7; 15:35–58; Philippians 3:20–21

Books

The Battle for the Resurrection, by Norman L. Geisler
Jesus Christ Our Lord, by John Walvoord

Website

"Did Jesus Have the Same Physical Body after His Resurrection?," http://www.apologetics press.org/apcontent.aspx?category=6&article=673

DVD

The Real Jesus: A Defense of the Historicity and Divinity of Christ, Apologetics Group

Online Video

Norman L. Geisler, "What Kind of Body Did Jesus Have after His Resurrection?," The One Minute Apologist, http://www.oneminuteapologist.com/searchpage#what-kind-of-body-did-jesus-have-after-his-resurrection

25 Isn't It Intolerant to Say Jesus Is the Only Way to God?

Answer

It's funny how people who, claiming tolerance, are intolerant of the claims made by Jesus Christ (e.g., John 14:6, "No one comes to the Father except through me."). You may know people like that. They get uptight about the exclusivity of Jesus Christ while at the same time exclusively claiming their own personal view.

What these people don't realize is that truth is narrow. For example, 3 + 3 = 6. *Is that intolerant?* Out of all the infinite numbers, there is only one right answer—the number 6. This is narrow, but it is not narrow-minded.

Take the parable of the six blind men and the elephant. Each blind man touches a different part of the elephant and interprets what he thinks it is. The first blind man takes hold of the tail and thinks it's a rope. The second blind man holds the trunk and thinks it's a big snake. Still another blind man feels the flapping ears and thinks it's a fan. The fourth blind man touches the side of the elephant and thinks it's a wall. The fifth blind man grabs hold of a leg and thinks it's a log. Finally, the sixth blind man reaches out and touches the tusk of the elephant and believes it's a spear.

The point is that none of the blind men are correct—they are all wrong. There is only one true answer, and the one telling the story knows it. It's an elephant!

Equally, there are not many ways to God. Only those blinded by sin think so (2 Cor. 4:3–4).

Not all views can be true (see question 2, *Whose truth is true?*). Religions have opposite views, and opposites cannot both be true. But neither can all views be false; at least one view must be true. Jesus claimed to be that truth.

Jesus said, "I am the way and the truth and the life. No one comes to the Father except through me" (John 14:6). Paul said, "There is one God and one mediator between God and mankind, the man Christ Jesus" (1 Tim. 2:5). The apostles declared, "Salvation is found in no one else, for there is no other name under heaven given to mankind by which we must be saved" (Acts 4:12). Indeed, Jesus said, "I told you that you would die in your sins; if you do not believe that I am he, you will indeed die in your sins" (John 8:24; see John 3:36).

Thus, Jesus claimed to be the only way of salvation. But did he offer any evidence to support his claim? Yes, he did. Jesus did three things to prove his right to be the only way to God:

1. He fulfilled prophecy.
2. He lived a sinless and miraculous life.
3. He predicted and accomplished his resurrection from the dead.

Since we've already addressed the last two above (see question 19, *Who is Jesus Christ?* and question 22, *How do we know Jesus rose from the dead?*), we will simply note here that Jesus fulfilled nearly one hundred Old Testament predictions made hundreds of years in advance regarding where he would be born (Mic. 5:2), how he would be born (Isa. 7:14), how he would suffer and die (Isa. 53), and when he would die (Dan. 9:24–27). No other religious leader has fulfilled these specific predictions made hundreds of years in advance. Only Jesus literally fulfilled them; hence, only Jesus is the way to God.

Application

Jesus is the only figure in history who claimed to be the Son of God and the only way to God and proved it in many miraculous ways. As Nicodemus, a Jewish leader, said to Christ, "Rabbi, we know you are a teacher who has come from God. For no one could perform the signs [miracles] you are doing if God were not with him" (John 3:2).

Bible References

John 8:24; 10:9; 11:25; 14:6; Acts 4:12; 1 Timothy 2:5–6; 1 John 5:20

Books

Jesus among Other Gods, by Ravi Zacharias
Fabricating Jesus: How Modern Scholars Distort the Gospels, by Craig Evans
No Other Name: An Investigation into the Destiny of the Unevangelized, by John Sanders

Website

"Only One Way to Heaven? Is Jesus Christ the Only Means to Reach God?," Leadership University, http://www.leaderu.com/theology/onlyoneway.html

DVD

Jesus among Other Gods, Ravi Zacharias

Online Videos

Bobby Conway, "Is Jesus the Only Way?," The One Minute Apologist, http://www.one minuteapologist.com/searchpage#is-jesus-the-only-way

Greg Koukl, "Intolerance," The One Minute Apologist, http://www.oneminuteapologist.com/searchpage#intolerance

Josh McDowell, "Tolerance Is Unbiblical," The One Minute Apologist, http://www.one minuteapologist.com/searchpage#tolerance-is-unbiblical

26 Who Is the Holy Spirit?

Answer

There are many false views of the Holy Spirit. Islam teaches that the Holy Spirit is not a person but merely a creation of Allah. Jehovah's Witnesses believe the Spirit is an active force of power. The Mormons explain the Holy Spirit as the presence of Elohim (God). And spiritists hold that the Spirit is merely a manifestation of a holy person. But according to the Bible, the Holy Spirit is much more than what these opposing views claim he is.

The Holy Spirit Is God

The Bible teaches that the Holy Spirit is the Third Person of the Trinity and coequal with the Father and the Son (see question 4, *Who made God?*). Therefore, the Holy Spirit is God (Heb. 9:14). Paul writes, "And that is what some of you were. But you were washed, you were sanctified, you were justified in the name of the Lord Jesus Christ and by the *Spirit of our God*" (1 Cor. 6:11; see Matt. 28:19–20; 2 Cor. 13:14).

The Holy Spirit Is . . .

God—1 Corinthians 3:16
Eternal—Hebrews 9:14
Omniscient—1 Corinthians 2:10–11
Omnipresent—Psalm 139:7
Omnipotent—Genesis 1:2
Holy—Ephesians 4:30

Names of the Holy Spirit

Spirit of Grace—Hebrews 10:29
Spirit of Truth—John 14:17; 15:26
Spirit of Life—Romans 8:2
Spirit of Promise—Ephesians 1:13
Spirit of God—1 Corinthians 3:16
Helper, Comforter, or Advocate—John
 14:16, 26; 16:7

Representations of the Holy Spirit

Dove—Matthew 3:16
Wind—John 3:8
Fire—Matthew 3:11
Oil—2 Corinthians 1:21; 1 John 2:27
Water—John 3:5
Seal—Ephesians 1:13
Streams of living water—John 7:38
Deposit—2 Corinthians 1:22

The Holy Spirit Is a Person

The Holy Spirit possesses a personality (Rom. 15:30) that exhibits *intelligence* (1 Cor. 2:10–11), *feelings* (Eph. 4:30), and a *will* (Acts 16:6–11). The Holy Spirit *grieves* (Eph. 4:30), *can be lied to* (Acts 5:3), *resists* (Acts 7:51), *can be insulted* (Heb. 10:29), and *can be quenched* (1 Thess. 5:19).

Application

It is important to realize that the Holy Spirit is not only a person but also God. And because he is God, you are to depend on the power, direction, and filling of the Holy Spirit every moment of every day. The Holy Spirit was present at creation (Gen. 1:2) and now resides in each believer (1 Cor. 3:16) as he or she waits for the return of Christ (1 Cor. 1:7).

Bible References

John 14:16, 26; 16:7; 1 Corinthians 2:9–11; 3:16; 6:11; Ephesians 4:30; 1 Thessalonians 5:19; Hebrews 9:14

Books

The Holy Spirit: Activating God's Power in Your Life, by Billy Graham

His Intimate Presence: Experiencing the Transforming Power of the Holy Spirit, by Bill Bright

Website

Bill Bright, "Who Is the Holy Spirit and Why Did He Come?," Campus Crusade for Christ, http://www.cru.org/training-and-growth/classics/10-basic-steps/3-the-holy-spirit/index.htm

DVD

Basic: Holy Spirit, vol. 3, Francis Chan

Online Video

Jason Jimenez, "Who Is the Holy Spirit?," The One Minute Apologist, http://www.one minuteapologist.com/searchpage#who-is-the-holy-spirit-jason

27 What Does the Holy Spirit Do?

Answer

The Holy Spirit is often the least recognized and appreciated person of the Trinity. The Father gets the recognition and praise as Creator, and Jesus the Son receives the glory as Redeemer for conquering sin and death. But what about the Holy Spirit?

Think of it this way. Without the work of the Holy Spirit the universe never would have been created (Gen. 1:2; Ps. 33:6), salvation never would have been given (Eph. 1:13–14), the Bible never would have been written (2 Pet. 1:20–21), the church never would have started (Acts 1:8), and spiritual gifts never would have been bestowed (1 Cor. 12:11).

As you can see, the contributions of the Holy Spirit are invaluable. Jesus promised his disciples the gift of the Holy Spirit at his departure (John 16:5–11). That's a big promise, and one Jesus fulfilled.

The Works of the Spirit
Teaches—John 14:26
Testifies—John 15:26
Convicts—John 16:8
Guides—John 16:13
Empowers—Acts 1:8
Performs miracles—Acts 8:39
Appoints—Acts 20:28
Indwells—Romans 8:9; 1 Corinthians 3:16
Intercedes—Romans 8:26; Hebrews 7:25
Leads—Romans 8:14
Sanctifies—Romans 15:16
Gives gifts—1 Corinthians 12:11
Regenerates—Titus 3:5
Inspires—2 Peter 1:20–21
Speaks—Revelation 2:7

Jesus's Teaching about the Holy Spirit

1. The Holy Spirit *gives life* to the sinner.

> Very truly I tell you, no one can enter the kingdom of God unless they are born of water and the Spirit. Flesh gives birth to flesh, but the Spirit gives birth to spirit.
>
> John 3:5–6

2. The Holy Spirit *teaches* and *reminds* the believer.

> But the Advocate, the Holy Spirit, whom the Father will send in my name, will teach you all things and will remind you of everything I have said to you.
>
> John 14:26

3. The Holy Spirit *testifies* about Jesus.

> When the Counselor comes, whom I will send to you from the Father—the Spirit of truth who goes out from the Father—he will testify about me.
>
> John 15:26

4. The Holy Spirit *convicts* the world of sin, righteousness, and judgment.

> When He has come, He will convict the world of sin, and of righteousness, and of judgment: of sin, because they do not believe in Me; of righteousness, because I go to My Father and you see Me no more; and of judgment, because the ruler of this world is judged.
>
> John 16:8–11 NKJV

5. The Holy Spirit *guides* and *proclaims* Christ's truth to the glory of God.

> But when he, the Spirit of truth, comes, he will guide you into all truth. He will not speak on his own; he will speak only what he hears, and he will tell you what is yet to come. He will glorify me because it is from me that he will receive what he will make known to you. All that belongs to the Father is mine. That is why I said the Spirit will receive from me what he will make known to you.
>
> John 16:13–15

Paul's Teaching about the Holy Spirit

1. The Holy Spirit has *poured out the love of God* to believers.

> Now hope does not disappoint, because the love of God has been poured out in our hearts by the Holy Spirit who was given to us.
>
> Romans 5:5 NKJV

2. The Holy Spirit *sets sinners free* from the law of sin and death.

> Through Christ Jesus the law of the Spirit who gives life has set you free from the law of sin and death.
>
> Romans 8:2

3. The Holy Spirit *makes dead people alive.*

> If the Spirit of him who raised Jesus from the dead dwells in you, he who raised Christ Jesus from the dead will also give life to your mortal bodies through his Spirit who dwells in you.
>
> Romans 8:11 ESV

4. The Holy Spirit *intercedes* for humankind.

> Likewise the Spirit helps us in our weakness. For we do not know what to pray for as we ought, but the Spirit himself intercedes for us with groanings too deep for words. And he who searches hearts knows the mind of the Spirit, because the Spirit intercedes for the saints according to the will of God.
>
> Romans 8:26–27 ESV

5. The Holy Spirit *gives hope.*

> May the God of hope fill you with all joy and peace as you trust in him, so that you may overflow with hope by the power of the Holy Spirit.
>
> Romans 15:13

Application

It is of the utmost importance that you remain under the power and influence of the Holy Spirit. Paul says, "Walk by the Spirit, and you will not gratify the desires of the flesh" (Gal. 5:16). Without the conviction of the Holy Spirit, there is no way for you to overcome the temptations of the world and the devil. Pray daily for the empowerment of the Holy Spirit and see to it that God's will is fulfilled in your life.

Bible References

John 3:5–6; 14:26; 15:26; 16:8–11; Romans 5:5; 8:2, 11, 26–27; 15:13; Galatians 5:16

Books

The Holy Spirit, by Charles Ryrie
The Counselor: Straight Talk about the Holy Spirit, by A. W. Tozer
The Holy Spirit, by John Walvoord

Website

Charles Swindoll, "The Spirit Who Is Not a Ghost," Insight for Living, http://www.insight.org/resources/articles/theology/the-spirit-who-is-not-a-ghost.html

DVD

Forgotten God, Francis Chan

Online Video

Jason Jimenez, "What Does the Holy Spirit Do?," The One Minute Apologist, http://www.oneminuteapologist.com/searchpage#what-does-the-holy-spirit-do

28 What Is the "Filling" of the Holy Spirit?

Answer

The ministry of the Holy Spirit is the single most important aspect of the Christian life. Sadly, however, many movements misinterpret the Bible and, therefore, misrepresent the activity of the Holy Spirit in people's lives. The Pentecostal/Charismatic movement is the most popular. It teaches that Christians can and do experience a repeated *baptism of the Holy Spirit*. However, some (not all) in the Pentecostal/Charismatic movement believe a sign of being baptized in the Spirit includes speaking in tongues, being *slain* or *drunk* in the Spirit, and even performing signs and wonders.

But the Bible teaches something quite different from what is being taught by the "Word of Faith" movement. The Bible never demonstrates or supports the claim of being drunk or out of control by the filling of the Holy Spirit. Ephesians 5:18 reads, "Do not get drunk on wine, which leads to debauchery. Instead, be filled with the Spirit." Paul contrasts the consumption of alcohol with the filling of the Holy Spirit. A drunken person lives an out-of-control life compared to a Spirit-filled life. Paul stresses that a Christian ought to be constantly, moment by moment, under the influence of the Holy Spirit. The more a person is *filled with* or *under the control of* the Holy Spirit, the more he or she will manifest the fruit of the Spirit (Gal. 5:22–23).

That's why Jesus told his disciples to wait in Jerusalem for the gift of the Holy Spirit: "You will receive power when the Holy Spirit comes on you; and you will be my witnesses in Jerusalem, and in all Judea and Samaria, and to the ends of the earth" (Acts 1:8, see 1:4–8). Jesus was saying that the Holy Spirit would make his followers dynamite witnesses. The testimony of Peter holds to this truth. One moment Peter was denying Jesus (Mark 14:66–72), then all of a sudden at Pentecost, he was boldly proclaiming the gospel to thousands (Acts 2). What made the difference? Peter was filled with the power of the Holy Spirit!

The Bible contains many other occurrences of Christians being filled with the Holy Spirit: Stephen (Acts 7:55), Barnabas (Acts 11:24), Paul (Acts 13:9), and the disciples (Acts 13:52).

The Indwelling and Filling of the Holy Spirit

There is a huge difference between the *indwelling* and the *filling* of the Holy Spirit. The indwelling takes place at the moment of salvation (regeneration), and the filling is an ongoing or repeated action controlled and empowered by the Holy Spirit.

At Salvation

Indwelling of the Spirit—John 7:37–39; Romans 5:5; 8:9; 1 Corinthians 6:19–20

Sealing of the Spirit—2 Corinthians 1:22; Ephesians 1:13; 4:30

Baptism of the Spirit—1 Corinthians 12:13; Galatians 3:27

After Salvation

Filling of the Spirit—Acts 6:15; Ephesians 5:18; 6:18

Walking in the Spirit—Galatians 5:16, 22–25; Romans 12:9–21

Empowering of the Spirit—Zechariah 4:6; Romans 8:13

Gifting of the Spirit—1 Corinthians 12:4, 7–11; Ephesians 4:11; 1 Peter 4:10

Application

Every day is a new day to be filled with the Holy Spirit. Not only will he give you the power to overcome sin, but he will also make you more like Christ. The filling of the Holy Spirit will also give you great boldness to share the gospel with others (Acts 2:4, 41; 4:24; 6:3). Therefore, pray in the Spirit (Eph. 6:18) each day and ask for more love, joy, peace, patience, kindness, goodness, faithfulness, gentleness, and self-control in your life (Gal. 5:22–23).

Bible References

Genesis 1:2; Judges 3:10; John 14:26; 16:8–11; Acts 6:15; 7:55; 11:24; 13:9, 52; Ephesians 5:18; 6:18

Books

Living Water: The Power of the Holy Spirit in Your Life, by Chuck Smith
How You Can Be Filled with the Holy Spirit, by Bill Bright
Embraced by the Spirit, by Charles R. Swindoll

Website

Bill Bright, "What Does It Mean to Be Filled with the Holy Spirit?," Campus Crusade for Christ, http://www.cru.org/training-and-growth/classics/transferable-concepts/be-filled-with-the-holy-spirit/04-what-does-it-mean-to-be-filled.htm

DVD

Forgotten God, Francis Chan

Online Video

Hank Hanegraaff, "What Is the Difference between the Infilling and the Indwelling of the Holy Spirit?," The One Minute Apologist, http://www.oneminuteapologist.com/searchpage#what-is-the-difference-between-the-infilling-and-the-indwelling-of-the-holy-spirit

PART 4

Questions about Sin and Salvation

29 Why Are We Born into Sin?

Answer

Our culture rejects the notion that humans are born into sin. Modern psychology considers it taboo to explain people's problems as being the result of sin. And yet a failure to diagnosis the real problem caused by sin will never lead to proper treatment. The Bible makes it clear: "For there is no one who does not sin" (1 Kings 8:46). King David openly confessed, "Surely I was sinful at birth, sinful from the time my mother conceived me" (Ps. 51:5).

This is known as *original sin*. Adam's free choice was self-determined (Gen. 2:16; see Rom. 5:12) and became the root whereby the entire human race inherited a sinful nature (Rom. 3:20–23; 1 Cor. 15:21–22).

Before it came to earth, sin originated with Lucifer in heaven. God created Adam and Eve as two perfect human beings (Gen. 1:26–28, 31; 2:7, 15–17, 21–25). But Satan entered the Garden of Eden and tempted Eve to partake of the forbidden fruit (Gen. 3:1–5; 2 Cor. 11:3). Eve gave in and ate the forbidden fruit and offered it to Adam (Gen. 3:6). Rather than rebuke Eve for her sin, Adam freely chose to disobey God, and he also ate from the tree of the knowledge of good and evil (Gen. 2:9; 3:7, 11).

Application

Since you were born into sin, you will do things that are displeasing to God. Paul writes, "For I know that good itself does not dwell in me, that is, in my sinful nature. For I have the desire to do what is good, but I cannot carry it out. For I do not do the good I want to do, but the evil I do not want to do—this I keep on doing" (Rom. 7:18–19). When temptations come knocking, put on Jesus Christ so you don't fulfill the lusts of the flesh (Rom. 13:14).

Bible References

Genesis 2:17, 25; 3:1–24; Psalm 51:5; John 8:44; Romans 5:12; 2 Corinthians 11:3; 1 Timothy
2:14

Books

Systematic Theology: In One Volume, by Norman L. Geisler

Fallen: A Theology of Sin, by Christopher W. Morgan and Robert A. Peterson

Website

"Survey of Bible Doctrine: Man and Sin," Bible.org, http://www.bible.org/seriespage/
survey-bible-doctrine-man-and-sin

DVD

Christian Essentials Made Easy: Key Christian Beliefs in 20 Minutes, Rose Publishing

Online Video

Hank Hanegraaff, "What Is Sin?," The One Minute Apologist, http://www.oneminute
apologist.com/searchpage#what-is-sin

30 Are Humans More Than a Body?

Answer

You've heard the adage "you are what you eat." But what exactly is the body
made up of?

The body is a living organism with many parts consisting of some sixty
chemical elements. Over 90 percent of body mass is made up of six key elements: oxygen (66 percent), carbon (18 percent), hydrogen (10 percent), nitrogen (3 percent), calcium (1.5 percent), and phosphorus (1.0 percent). The
most common chemical compound in the body is water. So in a way, we can
say humans are a body of water.

According to Charles Darwin, the complexity of the human body evolved through random mutations and natural selection. But as we answered earlier (see question 11, *Is evolution a viable option?*), evolution is not a viable option to explain the origin of life.

What does the Bible have to say about the human body? According to the Bible, humans are made in the image and likeness of God (Gen. 1:26–27). That means God has given us both a *body* that is material (physical dimension) and a *soul/spirit* that is immaterial (spiritual dimension). As human beings, we have a mind (intellect), feelings (emotions), choices (free will), and moral convictions (conscience). The differentiation between soul and body is shown in 1 Thessalonians 5:23: "May your whole *spirit, soul* and *body* be kept blameless at the coming of our Lord Jesus Christ."

The word *body* (Hebrew: *basar*; Greek: *soma*) refers to the material aspect of the human being. James 2:26 states that the body is dead without the spirit. Thus, to be alive, a human must have a body and a spirit. The word *spirit* (Hebrew: *ruach*; Greek: *pneuma)* literally means, "the immaterial (nonphysical) aspect of a human being." The word *soul* (Hebrew: *nephesh*; Greek: *psuche*) generally means "life."

Application

According to the Bible, your purpose in life is to glorify God. Isaiah declares that God calls to himself "everyone who is called by my name, whom I created for my glory, whom I formed and made" (43:7). The Westminster Shorter Catechism reads, "What is the chief end of man? Man's chief end is to glorify God, and to enjoy him forever." Thus, make it your goal in life to fulfill the holy calling God has called you to (2 Tim. 1:9).

Bible References

Body/Flesh: Matthew 10:28; Romans 12:1–2; 1 Corinthians 15:39, 42–44, 53; Hebrews 5:7
Soul/Spirit: Genesis 35:18; Psalm 43:5; Ecclesiastes 12:7; John 19:30; Acts 2:27

Books

Systematic Theology: In One Volume, by Norman L. Geisler
A Survey of Bible Doctrine, by Charles Ryrie

Website

Hank Hanegraaff, "Body and Soul: A 'Whole' in One," Christianity.com, http://www.chris
tianity.com/theology/body-and-soul-a-whole-in-one-11644102.html

DVD

Christian Essentials Made Easy: Key Christian Beliefs in 20 Minutes, DVD Bible Study, Rose
Publishing

Online Video

Bobby Conway, "Are Humans More Than a Body?," The One Minute Apologist, http://www.
oneminuteapologist.com/searchpage#are-humans-more-than-a-body

31 Did God Pick Me or Did I Choose Him?

Answer

Throughout the pages of Scripture, the doctrine of free choice is repeatedly
demonstrated from the Garden of Eden (Gen. 2) to the final judgment of God
on his throne (Rev. 22). This is evident in the fact that Adam and Eve were
free to choose to eat or not to eat the forbidden fruit (Gen. 2:16–17) and had
the choice to obey or rebel against the clear command of God. Several lines
of evidence support the concept of free choice.

First, several key passages in the Bible reveal the tension between *God's
sovereign will* and *human free will*. Jesus taught, "All that the Father gives me
will come to me, and whoever comes to me I will never cast out" (John 6:37
ESV). Luke records Peter preaching, "This Jesus, delivered up according to
the definite plan and foreknowledge of God, you crucified and killed by the
hands of lawless men" (Acts 2:23 ESV). Thus, Scripture teaches that God is
sovereign over the salvation of all people (John 6:44). At the same time, people
are morally free agents who are responsible for the choices and actions they
make (John 1:12; Rom. 10:9–10).

Second, God is the *author of salvation* (Isa. 12:2; Jon. 2:9), and we are
the *beneficiaries of salvation*. This is a relationship between two parties, not
a manipulation of our will. God does not coerce or override the free will of

humans; it is not in his nature to violate the freedom he gave us (Mal. 3:6–7; Heb. 6:18). He freely offers his unconditional love and irresistible grace to the willing (elect), but he never forces them on the unwilling. Thus, God predetermined to save humans from sin and death, but it's up to the individual to decide if he or she wants to receive God's salvation.

Third, just because God knows the end from the beginning (Isa. 46:10) doesn't mean humans have no free will. The free actions of humans do not take place because God foresees them; God foresees them because he knows they will take place. Though God knows the future, he predetermined that the future take place according to human freedom. Thus, our choices are made "according to the foreknowledge of God" (1 Pet. 1:2).

Fourth, the fact that God desires for all people to be saved but knows that not all will choose salvation reveals the difference between God's *desired* (preferred) will and his *determined* (sovereign) will. The Bible affirms that God desires for all people to repent (2 Pet. 3:9) and to come to the knowledge of the truth (1 Tim. 2:4), but he knows not all will come to salvation. On the other hand, Scripture also stresses God's determined (sovereign) will, which cannot be stopped (Job 42:2) and will come to pass (Isa. 46:10). Thus, the salvation of all humankind is God's *desired* (preferred) will, and the return and reign of Jesus Christ is God's *determined* (sovereign) will.

Finally, God chose us before we chose him (Eph. 1:4). He loved us before we loved him (1 John 4:10, 19). And he sought us before we sought him. But God foreknew and determined from all eternity that those he foreknew and fore-loved who accept his love would be saved (John 1:12–13).

Application

Despite the tension between and the confusion regarding sovereign will and free will, it's amazing to know that God loves unconditionally and made a way to save his people from their sins (Heb. 9:28; 1 Pet. 2:24–25).

Bible References

Genesis 2:16–17; 3:13; John 12:37–40; Acts 7:51; Romans 1:18–20; 2 Thessalonians 2:13; 2 Peter 3:9

Books

Chosen but Free, by Norman L. Geisler

Christian Theology, by Millard Erickson

God's Strategy in Human History, by Roger Forster and Paul Marstrom

Website

"The Five Points of Calvinism: Contrasting Extreme versus Moderate Calvinistic Positions," http://www.4himnet.com/bnyberg/tulip.html

DVD

Why I Am Not a Five Point Calvinist, Norman L. Geisler

Online Video

Norman L. Geisler, "Did God Choose Me or Did I Choose Him?," The One Minute Apologist, http://www.oneminuteapologist.com/searchpage#did-god-choose-me-or-did-i-choose -him

32 What Is the Gospel?

Answer

Everyone loves a good story—especially when the story line is about redemption. And the greatest redemptive story of all time is found in the gospel of Jesus Christ.

The Gospel of . . .
The kingdom of God—Matthew 4:23
God—Romans 1:1; 15:16
Jesus Christ—Mark 1:1
Your salvation—Ephesians 1:13
God's grace—Acts 20:24

The word *gospel* is from the Greek noun *euangelion* ("good news") and the verb *euaggelizō* ("to announce good news"). Paul puts forth the essential elements that make up the gospel in 1 Corinthians 15:1–8. He lists the death, burial, resurrection, and resurrected appearances of Jesus Christ. Without each of these, there would be no gospel. Therefore, the message of the gospel is clear: *God sent his only begotten Son into the world to live a sinless life, die for our sins on the cross, and defeat sin and death at his resurrection so that we might have eternal life in the power of the Holy Spirit.*

No one can receive the gospel without faith (John 1:12; Rom. 10:17; Eph. 2:8–9). But the gospel isn't just a message; it's a way of life (Eph. 4–6). We are commanded by Jesus Christ to go wherever, whenever, and to whomever to share the *good news* (Matt. 28:19–20). And as we go out proclaiming the good news of our Lord, we are not to be ashamed of the message of Christ but believe in its power (Rom. 1:16–17), which comes from the Holy Spirit (1 Thess. 1:4–5).

Application

Paul articulates the heart of the gospel in 2 Corinthians 5:21: "God made him who had no sin to be sin for us, so that in him we might become the righteousness of God." To know that Jesus took your sins and replaced them with his righteousness should give you complete assurance and confidence that you have eternal security in Christ (John 10:28; Rom. 8:28–39; Eph. 1:13).

Bible References

Matthew 4:23; Mark 1:1; John 1:12; Acts 20:24; Romans 1:1; 10:17; 15:16; 1 Corinthians 15:1–8; Ephesians 2:8–9

Books

Gospel: Rediscovering the Power that Made Christianity Revolutionary, by J. D. Greear

What Is the Gospel?, by Greg Gilbert and D. A. Carson

Website

"What Is the Gospel?," Bible.org, http://www.bible.org/article/what-gospel

DVD

Christian Essentials Made Easy: Key Christian Beliefs in 20 Minutes, DVD Bible Study, Rose Publishing

Online Video

Bobby Conway, "Can We Repackage the Gospel?," The One Minute Apologist, http://www.oneminuteapologist.com/searchpage#can-we-repackage-the-gospel

33 What about Those Who Never Heard the Gospel?

Answer

This is a difficult question, and it is one of the top questions asked by unbelievers. It implies not only a level of unfairness but also an uncomfortable feeling of injustice. The argument often goes something like this: Suppose there's a remote tribe deep in the Brazilian rain forest that never hears the gospel? What if no missionaries are ever successful in sharing the gospel with them? What happens to them when they die? Do they go to hell even if they never had the chance to hear and receive the gospel? If so, that's unfair!

This argument is often hard to refute. It can plant doubt in people's minds, causing them to walk away from the faith. So here are six important things to remember as you seek to answer this question:

1. *God is holy and just.* Moses claimed, "Who among the gods is like you, LORD? Who is like you—majestic in holiness, awesome in glory, working wonders?" (Exod. 15:11). God would never condemn someone to hell without giving him or her the chance to hear the gospel. Abraham declared, "Shall not the Judge of all the earth do what is just?" (Gen. 18:25 ESV).

2. *God is all-powerful (omnipotent) and all-knowing (omniscient).* Paul preached at Mars Hill: "From one man he made all the nations, that they should inhabit the whole earth; and he marked out their appointed times in history and the boundaries of their lands. God did this so that they would seek him and perhaps reach out for him and find him, though he is not far from any one of us" (Acts 17:26–27). As Creator of the universe, God has absolute authority over and knowledge of the whereabouts and activities of his people. No one is beyond his power to reach and to save.

3. *God has revealed himself in nature (natural revelation).* Paul makes this point clear in Romans 1:20: "For since the creation of the world God's invisible qualities—his eternal power and divine nature—have been clearly seen, being understood from what has been made, so that people are without excuse." In Romans 2:15, he further points out that the "requirements of the law are written on their hearts." Therefore, no one is without an excuse before he or she dies.

4. *God has also revealed his truth through the Bible (special revelation) and calls all people to repent* (Acts 17:30). Again, Paul argued this point at Mars Hill: "In the past God overlooked such ignorance, but now he commands all people everywhere to repent. For he has set a day when he will judge the world with justice by the man he has appointed. He has given proof of this to everyone by raising him from the dead" (Acts 17:30–31).

5. *Jesus made it clear that he is the only way to God* (John 10:1, 9; 14:6) *and that without him no one can be saved* (John 3:18, 36; 8:24; see Acts 4:12). Jesus sacrificed himself on the cross as a payment for the penalty of all sin, and he offers salvation to anyone who is willing to trust in him (Heb. 11:6). Second Thessalonians 1:8 reads, "He will punish those who do not know God and do not obey the gospel of our Lord Jesus. They will be punished with everlasting destruction and shut out from the presence of the Lord and from the majesty of his power." Again, no one can be sent to hell without first having the opportunity to *reject* the truth of God revealed to him.

6. *The Bible makes it clear that all who seek God will find him.* Peter said, "I now realize how true it is that God does not show favoritism but accepts from every nation the one who fears him and does what is right" (Acts 10:34–35). The book of Hebrews adds, "Without faith it is impossible to please God, because anyone who comes to him must believe that he exists and that he rewards those who earnestly seek him" (11:6).

Therefore, according to these scriptural arguments, every person on the planet who truly seeks God will be given the message necessary to save him or her. While God's choice is to give the truth through a missionary (Rom. 10:14–17), he is not limited to that means. He has revealed himself through the Bible, tracts, dreams, visions, and even an audible voice (Heb. 1:1). And he promised that he will reveal the truth to all who seek it: "You will seek me and find me when you seek me with all your heart" (Jer. 29:13).

Application

There are still billions of people all over the world who have never heard the gospel. It is God's command that you reach them with the gospel (Matt. 28:18–20). You are privileged to be the "jars of clay" (2 Cor. 4:7) that God has shaped for his purposes. This ought to motivate you not to waste any time in sharing the gospel with your unsaved family members and friends. Paul asks these convicting questions: "How, then, can they call on the one they have not believed in? And how can they believe in the one of whom they have not heard? And how can they hear without someone preaching to them?" (Rom. 10:14).

Bible References

Genesis 18:25; Deuteronomy 32:4; Psalm 98; Matthew 28:19–20; Acts 4:12; 17:27–31; Romans 1:20–21; 2:14–15

Books

Sense and Nonsense about Heaven and Hell, by Kenneth Boa and Robert Bowman Jr.
Eternity in Their Hearts, by Don Richardson

Website

Norman L. Geisler, "Salvation of the Heathen," John Ankerberg Show, http://www.jashow.org/wiki/index.php?title=Salvation_of_the_Heathen

DVD

The Uniqueness of Christ in World Religion, Ravi Zacharias

Online Video

Bobby Conway, "What about Those Who've Never Heard?," The One Minute Apologist, http://www.oneminuteapologist.com/searchpage#what-about-those-who've-never-heard

34 Can I Lose My Salvation?

Answer

Of all the questions, this one has certainly sparked some of the biggest debates in the church, and it is often to blame for much of the division among denominations. We can testify to this and, regrettably, have seen the damage it has done to Christians in general.

In this short response, it is our hope not to be a discouragement but to encourage believers with the assurance that they are secure in Christ. There are several reasons Christians can't lose their salvation.

For starters, God is the source of salvation (Jon. 2:9) and offers it as a free gift (Rom. 6:23) to as many who will freely receive it (John 1:12; 11:25). Salvation isn't something we earn on our own (Gal. 2:16; Eph. 2:8–9; Titus 3:5–6) but something offered and provided by God. The Bible teaches that "God's gifts and his call are irrevocable" (Rom. 11:29) and that "no purpose of [God's] can be thwarted" (Job 42:2).

Furthermore, Jesus revealed the unmatched love of the Godhead to assure and secure salvation when he said, "My sheep listen to my voice; I know them, and they follow me. I give them eternal life, and *they shall never perish*; no one will snatch them out of my hand. My Father, who has given them to me, is greater than all; *no one can snatch them out of my Father's hand*" (John 10:27–29). Thus, the Christian has the assurance that God is bound by his covenant of redemption and is faithful to keep and complete it (2 Tim. 2:13).

Moreover, when a person puts his or her faith in Jesus Christ, that person becomes part of the body of Christ (1 Cor. 12:13) and is "marked" by the Holy Spirit (Eph. 1:13) until the day of redemption (Eph. 4:30). That's why Paul boldly declared, "For I am convinced that neither death nor life, neither angels nor demons, neither the present nor the future, nor any powers, neither height nor depth, nor anything else in all creation, will be able to separate us from the love of God that is in Christ Jesus our Lord" (Rom. 8:38–39).

Does *eternal security* mean *eternal carnality*? No. If someone is truly saved, he or she will not feel comfortable in sin. As John said, "No one born of God makes a practice of sinning, for God's seed abides in him, and he cannot keep on sinning because he has been born of God" (1 John 3:9). To illustrate, if you put a pig and a lamb in a mud puddle, the pig will want to stay there and the lamb will want to get out. Those who continually practice sin are like the pigs (unbelievers), not the lambs.

Therefore, like Paul, Christians can rest assured that they have eternal security in Christ Jesus.

Application

No matter what you are going through, always remember that God's love and forgiveness are greater than your sin or doubt. Jude 24–25 reads, "To him who is able to keep you from stumbling and to present you before his glorious presence without fault and with great joy—to the only God our Savior be glory, majesty, power and authority, through Jesus Christ our Lord, before all ages, now and forevermore! Amen."

Bible References

John 5:24; 6:37–40; 10:27–28; 17:9–24; Romans 4:5–6; 8; Ephesians 1:4–5, 13; 2:5–6; 2 Timothy 1:12; 1 Peter 1:5

Books

Chosen but Free, by Norman L. Geisler

Systematic Theology: In One Volume, by Norman L. Geisler

Is Jesus the Only Savior?, by Ronald Nash

Website

"Is My Salvation in Christ Secure, or Can I Lose My Salvation?," Back to the Bible, http://www.backtothebible.org/index.php/Q-Is-my-salvation-in-Christ-secure-or-can-I-lose-my-salvation.html

DVD

Why I Am Not a Five Point Calvinist, Norman L. Geisler

Online Video

Hank Hanegraaff, "Can a Christian Lose Their Salvation?," The One Minute Apologist, http://www.oneminuteapologist.com/searchpage#can-a-christian-lose-their-salvation

35 Is Baptism Necessary for Salvation?

Answer

Baptism is not necessary for salvation. If it were, then salvation would not be a *free gift* received by grace through faith (Eph. 2:8–9) but a *works-based achievement* that runs contrary to the teachings of John the Baptist, Jesus Christ, and the apostles of the church.

Paul writes, "To the one who *does not work but trusts* God who justifies the ungodly, their *faith* is credited as righteousness" (Rom. 4:5). Think about the thief on the cross. Jesus told him he would be with him in paradise (Luke 23:43). But how is that possible if the thief was never baptized? Simple. All that was required of the thief was for him to put his faith in Jesus (Luke 23:42). This is true to the message of Jesus Christ (John 1:12; 3:16; 5:24; 6:40; 7:37–38).

Further, the Bible declares that baptism is a work of righteousness (Matt. 3:15). Paul declared that salvation is not by "works of righteousness . . . but according to [God's] mercy" (Titus 3:5–7 NKJV). And he told the Ephesians that "it is by grace you have been saved . . . not by works" (Eph. 2:8–9).

Peter affirmed that one receives the Holy Spirit before baptism (Acts 10:47). And even in Acts 2, salvation did not come as a result of baptism (as some infer from verse 38); rather, "those who accepted his message were baptized" (Acts 2:41). The first thing people have to do is believe in their hearts that Christ died for them and rose again, and they will be saved (Rom. 10:9–10).

Though baptism was an important Christian practice of Jesus's disciples (John 4:1–2) and the early church (Acts 2:38; 8:12–13), nowhere does the Bible indicate that baptism is needed prior to salvation. The biblical pattern is that Christians were baptized after believing in Jesus Christ as Savior. Peter said, "*Repent* and be baptized" (Acts 2:38). Acts 8:12 reads, "But *when they believed* Philip as he proclaimed the good news of the kingdom of God and the name of Jesus Christ, *they were baptized*, both men and women." And later we read, "*Believe* in the Lord Jesus, and you will be saved" (Acts 16:31). Notice that the order isn't *baptism* and then *conversion*.

Finally, *baptism* (Greek: *baptizo*) simply means "immersion." When a Christian is baptized (immersed in water), he or she is performing an *outward act* of the *inward fact* of receiving salvation. Thus, baptism symbolizes the death and resurrection of Jesus Christ. The old life is buried with Christ (in the water), and the new life (coming out of the water) is resurrected with Jesus Christ (Rom. 6:1–4). Again, it isn't the *act* of baptism that saves a person but the *fact* of simply putting his or her faith in the finished work of the death and resurrection of Jesus Christ (Eph. 2:8–9; see Rom. 10:9–10).

Application

It's comforting to know that you don't need to be baptized to wash away your sin. All you need is the shed blood of Jesus Christ (Heb. 9:24–26; 1 Pet. 1:18–19).

Bible References

Acts 2:38; Romans 6:1–4; Titus 3:5–6; Hebrews 9:24–26; 1 Peter 1:18–19

Books

So Great Salvation, by Charles Ryrie

Why Grace Changes Everything: The Key That Unlocks God's Blessings, by Chuck Smith

Website

Greg Koukl, "Is Baptism Necessary for Salvation?," Stand to Reason, http://www.str.org/articles/is-baptism-necessary-for-salvation-2

DVD

How to Tell the Truth, Dr. David Jeremiah

Online Video

Bobby Conway, "Is Baptism Necessary for Salvation?," The One Minute Apologist, http://www.oneminuteapologist.com/searchpage#is-baptism-necessary-for-salvation

36 How Does One Become a Christian?

Answer

When was the last time you shared the gospel with someone? Or when have you had the wonderful opportunity of leading someone to Christ?

If you can't recall the last time you shared the gospel or have never experienced the power of the Holy Spirit in your life while leading someone to Christ, you are missing out. A big part of the Christian life is sharing with others the good news of Jesus Christ.

It's humbling to know that each of us is a sinner (Isa. 64:6; Rom. 3:23; 1 John 3:4) and in need of a Savior. We know that we aren't the answer (Jer. 17:9; Rom. 3:10) but that Jesus Christ is. And yet, how often do we proclaim this message to those who are dead in their sin?

All you need to do is share with people that God loves them and offers a way for them to be free from sin and death. You can do this by telling people to *admit* their sin to God and to *believe* that the Lord Jesus Christ died and rose again for their sin (Acts 16:31). Here's how the Bible explains it.

Admit—Romans 6:23

Paul writes, "For the wages of sin is death, but the gift of God is eternal life in Christ Jesus our Lord" (Rom. 6:23). According to Scripture, the payment for our sin is death. Death is something we deserve because of our sinful nature and rebellion (Rom. 5:12; 7:13). But by the grace of God, he offers us eternal life through Christ Jesus. Therefore, the first thing a person needs to do is admit that he or she has sinned against God (Ps. 51:4) and repent of that sin (Luke 13:3; Acts 3:19; 1 John 1:9). Acts 3:19 says, "Repent, then, and turn to God, so that your sins may be wiped out."

Believe—Romans 10:9–10

The second thing a person needs to do is believe that Jesus is the Son of God, who died for his or her sins and rose again. Paul writes, "If you declare with your mouth, 'Jesus is Lord,' and *believe* in your heart that God raised him from the dead, you will be saved. For it is with your heart that you *believe* and are justified, and it is with your mouth that you profess your faith and are saved" (Rom. 10:9–10). Therefore, putting your faith in the unconditional grace of Jesus Christ is necessary to receive salvation (Eph. 2:8–9).

Application

It is wonderful to see a person come to Christ, but it's also your Christian duty to make sure that new believer is discipled in the Word of God and finds a great, Bible-teaching church. A Christian is to be committed to the daily tasks of *praying* in the Spirit (Eph. 6:19), *being filled* with the Holy Spirit (Eph. 5:18), *performing* good works (James 2:14–26), *meditating* on the Word of God (Ps. 1; 2 Tim. 2:15), *exercising* spiritual gifts (Rom. 12:3–8), and *serving* others (Phil. 2:1–4).

Bible References

John 1:12; 3:16–17; Romans 1:16; 3:23; 6:23; 7:24–25; 10:9–10; Galatians 3:26; 1 John 5:13

Books

Becoming a Contagious Christian, by Bill Hybels and Mark Mittelberg

Knowing Jesus Christ, Studies in Christian Living Series, book 6

Website

David Jeremiah, "Becoming a Christian," Turning Point, http://www.davidjeremiah.org/site/about/becoming_a_christian.aspx

DVD

Lost Boy: The Documentary, New Revolution

Online Videos

Hank Hanegraaff, "What Must I Do to Be Saved?," The One Minute Apologist, http://www.oneminuteapologist.com/searchpage#what-must-I-do-to-be-saved

Erwin Lutzer, "Know for Sure That You Are Going to Heaven," The One Minute Apologist, http://www.oneminuteapologist.com/searchpage#know-for-sure

PART 5

Questions about Heaven and Hell

37 What Is Heaven Like?

Answer

There are scores of books about people's dreams or visions of heaven. Heaven is fascinating not only because of its mysteriousness but also because everyone wants to go there. Although we are unable to wrap our limited minds around heaven (Deut. 29:29), God has provided enough details for now.

The Bible talks about three heavens. The first heaven is the *sky* (earth's atmosphere, Matt. 6:26). The second heaven is the *stars* (the realm of space, Jer. 8:2). And the third heaven is *God's abode*, where he sits on his throne (Ezra 1:2; Matt. 6:9; 2 Cor. 12:2). David declares, "The LORD is in his holy temple; the LORD is on his heavenly throne" (Ps. 11:4). But the fact that God *dwells* in the third heaven doesn't mean he is contained or limited to space. God is infinite and everywhere all at once. Solomon remarks, "But will God really dwell on earth? The heavens, even the highest heaven, cannot contain you" (1 Kings 8:27).

Heaven is also where Jesus sits "at the right hand of the Majesty" (Heb. 1:3). Peter says that Jesus has "gone into heaven and is at the right hand of God, with angels, authorities, and powers having been subjected to him" (1 Pet. 3:22 ESV). Jesus reminded Mary Magdalene, "Do not hold on to me, for I have not yet returned to the Father. Go instead to my brothers and tell them, 'I am ascending to my Father and your Father, to my God and your God'" (John 20:17). In addition, heaven is where angels dwell (Matt. 18:10; Mark 13:32). Nehemiah describes it as a place where the "multitudes of heaven worship [God]" (9:6).

Heaven is a place of bliss ("paradise," 2 Cor. 12:4; see vv. 1–4) for departed spirits of believers (Gen. 5:24; 2 Kings 2:11; Luke 23:43). Paul describes heaven as being "away from the body" and "at home with the Lord" (2 Cor. 5:8). It is a place of unimaginable peace, joy, splendor, beauty, rest, and abundance of life (Ps. 16:11; 1 Tim. 4:8; Rev. 14:13; 21:18–21). The location of heaven is unknown. It is either in a far corner of the universe or part of the multi-dimensional world where it seems the resurrected body of Jesus went to and from (Luke 24:31; John 20:26).

Another amazing fact about heaven is that it's a place where there is no sin or death (Isa. 25:8; Rev. 21:4). People will no longer be given in marriage (Matt. 22:30; Rom. 7:2–3), for Christ is the Bridegroom (Matt. 25:1–13; Mark 2:19), and believers will forever be his bride (John 3:29; Eph. 5:22–33; Rev. 22:17).

Heaven is the final destiny of every believer in Jesus Christ (Matt. 5:17–20; 2 Pet. 3:13). Christians are commanded to set their hearts and minds on heaven (Col. 3:1–4) by storing up "treasures in heaven" (Matt. 6:20) and will receive their eternal rewards and inheritance kept in heaven (Matt. 25:14–30; 1 Pet. 1:4).

Jesus said he is preparing many rooms in his Father's house for his followers (John 14:2). Sometime after the second coming of Christ, heaven (the Holy City) will become the new heaven and new earth (2 Pet. 3:12–13; Rev. 21:1–2), and every believer will dwell there in their physical, resurrected bodies (John 5:28–29; Phil. 3:21).

Application

Heaven is absolutely beautiful because an absolutely perfect and loving Savior dwells there and waits to be reunited with you, his bride. Therefore, set your heart and mind on heaven (Col. 3:1–4).

Bible References

Isaiah 65:17; 66:22; John 14:2; 2 Peter 3:10–13; Revelation 5:9–13; 21:1–27

Books

Heaven, by Randy Alcorn

The Little Book about Heaven, by Ron Rhodes

Website

"What Is Heaven Like?," BibleStudyTools.com, http://www.biblestudytools.com/bible-study/topical-studies/what-is-heaven-like-11636670.html

DVD

Heaven Small Group Study, Randy Alcorn

Online Video

Bobby Conway, "What Is Heaven Like?," The One Minute Apologist, http://www.oneminuteapologist.com/searchpage#what-is-heaven-like

38 Is There Really a Hell?

Answer

The doctrine of hell has certainly been a hot topic for many centuries. But just because something seems harsh or is difficult to comprehend doesn't exclude it from being real (see question 9, *Would a loving God send people to hell?*).

The reality is that hell is as real as the fact that you are reading this book right now. Jesus took hell seriously, so much so that he talked more about hell than he did about heaven. He wanted people to know the truth about hell so they would be driven to want heaven (see question 37, *What is heaven like?*).

The nature of hell is horrific. The Bible describes it with these terms: "outer darkness" (Matt. 8:12); "weeping and gnashing of teeth" (Matt. 22:13); "eternal fire" (Matt. 25:41); "torment" (Luke 16:23); "under the earth" (Phil. 2:10); "Death and Hades" (Rev. 1:18). Hell is eternal separation from God (2 Thess. 1:7–9).

Hell is not a torture chamber where God gets his kicks seeing the people who rejected him undergo suffering. Rather, hell is a designated place for those who *willfully* rejected *eternal life* in favor of *eternal separation* from God, which results in *eternal torment*. The "eternal fire" (Matt. 25:41) in hell is real but not physical. This is how hell can be both "outer darkness" and "eternal fire" (Matt. 8:12; 25:41).

Hell

Old Testament

Sheol (Hebrew)—"unseen world"; refers to the grave of unseen spirits (Ps. 9:17; Isa. 66:22–24; Dan. 12:2).

New Testament

Hades (Greek)—where "departed wicked spirits" went (Matt. 5:29–30; Luke 16:19–31).
Gehenna (Hebrew, Greek)—often translated as *hell*. It comes from the Valley of Hinnom, a putrid landfill of trash set on fire outside Jerusalem (Matt. 13:42, 50; Mark 9:43). This is the everlasting punishment for the wicked and Satan's remaining demons (Matt. 25:41).
Tartarus (Greek)—abode where fallen angels were sent (2 Pet. 2:4).

There are three theological bases for the existence of hell:

1. *God's holiness demands it.* Habakkuk 1:13 says, "Your eyes are too pure to look on evil; you cannot tolerate wrongdoing." God cannot and will

not tolerate evil, and he executes his perfect justice on all wrongdoing (Gen. 18:25).

2. *Satan's rebellion compels it.* Satan is the originator of sin (Ezek. 28:16–17; Rev. 12:4). Jesus stated that hell was made for Satan and his fallen angels (Matt. 25:41).

3. *People's sinfulness requires it.* A just sentence for the wicked (Rom. 3) against an eternal God (Ps. 90:1–4) is an eternal punishment (Matt. 25:46). Hell fits that punishment.

Application

Since hell is real and people who reject Jesus go there, be more diligent to share the gospel with those who have never put their trust in Jesus Christ.

Bible References

Matthew 5:29–30; 8:12; 22:13; 25:41; Luke 16:24–25; 2 Thessalonians 1:5–9; Jude 12–13; Revelation 14:11; 19:20; 20:10

Books

Erasing Hell: What God Said about Eternity, and the Things We've Made Up, by Francis Chan and Preston Sprinkle

Is Hell for Real or Does Everyone Go to Heaven?, by Timothy Keller, Albert Mohler Jr., and J. I. Packer

The Great Divorce, by C. S. Lewis

Website

"Hell: Answers to Questions about God's Judgment on Those Who Reject His Forgiveness," Always Be Ready Ministry, http://www.alwaysbeready.com/hell

DVD

One Minute after You Die: 8 Transformational Teachings on Eternity, Erwin Lutzer

Online Video

Bobby Conway, "What Is Hell in a Nutshell?," The One Minute Apologist, http://www.one minuteapologist.com/searchpage#hell-in-a-nutshell

39 Can a Good Person Get into Heaven?

Answer

No. There is no such thing as a "good person." Before God, "there is none who does good, no, not one" (Rom. 3:12 NKJV). Nothing in the Bible speaks of a person being good enough (on his or her own) to get into heaven.

Humans are born in sin (Ps. 51:5) and commit acts that break the laws of God (1 John 3:4). Paul admitted, "For all have sinned and fall short of the glory of God" (Rom. 3:23). Solomon expressed, "Indeed, there is no one on earth who is righteous, no one who does what is right and never sins" (Eccles. 7:20 ESV).

The Bible describes humans as haters of God (Rom. 1:30); lawbreakers (Rom. 2:23); liars and unrighteous (Rom. 3:4, 10); powerless, ungodly, and sinners (Rom. 5:6–8); dead in transgressions and sins, and disobedient (Eph. 2:1–2). It doesn't sound like the Bible agrees there are *good people*.

The problem with those who believe they will get into heaven on *good behavior* is that they have to weigh all their *bad behavior* as well. The book of James tells us that sin comes from our lusts and from our failure to love or to do good to others (1:15; 2:8–9; 4:17). So at what point does someone determine their *good* outweighs their *bad*? The fact is that the person claiming to be good is making a judgment that is neither objective nor just.

No matter how good a person tries to be, his or her good deeds or works are as "filthy rags" to God (Isa. 64:6). The book of Proverbs poses the question, "Who can say, 'I have kept my heart pure; I am clean and without sin'?" (Prov. 20:9). Jesus said, "No one is good—except God alone" (Mark 10:18). For that reason, a *good God* made a way for *sinful humans* to get into heaven: through Jesus Christ (Acts 4:12), not by any other way.

Application

God keeps watch over you and is ready and willing to forgive you of your sins and cleanse you from all unrighteousness (1 John 1:9). The Bible says, "The eyes of the LORD are everywhere, keeping watch on the wicked and the good" (Prov. 15:3).

Bible References

Psalms 32; 51; Proverbs 20:9; Ecclesiastes 7:20; Isaiah 64:6; Mark 10:18; Romans 3; Ephesians 2:1–2

Books

How Good Is Good Enough?, by Andy Stanley

Not a Fan: Becoming a Completely Committed Follower of Jesus, by Kyle Idleman

Website

"Are You Good Enough to Go to Heaven?," Living Waters, http://www.wayofthemaster.com/goodperson.shtml

DVD

BIO: How to Become an Authentic Disciple of Jesus, Living on the Edge

Online Video

Bobby Conway, "Can a Good Person Get into Heaven?," The One Minute Apologist, http://www.oneminuteapologist.com/searchpage#can-a-good-person-get-into-heaven

40 Do Near-Death Experiences Really Happen?

Answer

People are intrigued by the unexplainable. Some of the most interesting stories come in the form of near-death experiences. This is evidenced by the number of bookstores filled with books on this topic and the number of talk shows and news outlets that interview people who have had near-death experiences. Near-death experiences bring proof to the believer and bewilderment to the skeptic. But no matter how real the experiences may seem, are all near-death experiences really of God?

Multiple reports and experiences have been well documented and studied in recent years. Many people have experienced leaving their bodies and returning.

Some people have experienced heaven—while others have experienced hell. So there is no doubt that people have had these experiences. There are, however, many questions that can be raised about the reality of these experiences. We will discuss six such issues:

1. Some of the experiences are contradictory, and contradictions cannot both be true. One can experience almost anything, but not everything experienced is real. There are dreams, illusions, and delusions that have no basis in reality.

2. Some of the experiences are contrary to the teachings of the Bible and thus must be rejected by biblical Christians. For example, near-death experiences can be used to claim there is nothing to fear in death for anyone. Of course, this is true for Christians, but non-Christians definitely should fear death since the Bible teaches, "It is appointed for men to die once, but after this the judgment" (Heb. 9:27 NKJV).

3. An out-of-body experience (where the person leaves and then comes back into his or her body) cannot be true for a Christian. The Bible teaches that when the soul leaves the body, that person is dead. When a Christian is "absent from the body" he or she is "present with the Lord" (2 Cor. 5:8 NKJV; see Phil. 1:23). If the out-of-body experience was real and the body was really dead, then the coming back of the soul to the body would be a resurrection. Since resurrection is an act of God, then God would be miraculously confirming an error, but this is contrary to God's nature (John 3:2; Heb. 2:3–4).

4. In some of these experiences, people claim to have seen God. But the Bible teaches that no mortal human can see God and live (John 1:18). Only immortal men and women in the next life (after permanent death and resurrection) can see God and live. Once they have seen God face-to-face (called the *beatific vision*), they can no longer sin or return to this life (1 Cor. 13:12; Rev. 22:4).

5. Not everything one experiences as real is real; there are false experiences. All out-of-body or near-death experiences should be measured against the standard of God's infallible Word (John 10:34–35). We should never use our experiences to interpret the Bible; instead, we should use the Bible to interpret our experiences.

6. This raises the question of the source of near-death and out-of-body experiences. Basically, there are three possible sources: God, the demons (2 Cor. 11:13–14), and psychological deception. How do we know which it is? Obviously, one needs an objective source of truth to judge these experiences. For a Christian, it is the Word of God. Thus, a person's *vision* or *experience* should never contradict or add to what the Word

of God has already revealed to the church. Christians aren't to follow or rely on someone's controversial experience as they would the Bible.

The apostle Paul had an experience during which he was "caught up to the third heaven" (2 Cor. 12:2). Rather than speak about it, however, Paul said the experience was too great to tell (2 Cor. 12:3–5). That should say something.

So in brief, any near-death or out-of-body experience that is contrary to the Word of God is false (see Deut. 13:1–3; 18:20–22; 1 John 4:1–6).

Application

It's not an out-of-body or near-death experience you should yearn for but instead to someday see God face-to-face (1 John 3:1–3).

Bible References

2 Corinthians 5:8; Philippians 1:23; 3:20–21; Hebrews 9:27

Books

Journey into the Light, by Richard Abanes
Deceived by the Light, by Douglas Groothuis

Website

"The Near Death Experience Archive," Christian Research Institute, http://www.equip.org/category/near-death-experience/

DVD

One Minute after You Die: 8 Transformational Teachings on Eternity, Erwin Lutzer

Online Videos

Gary Habermas, "Are Near Death Experiences Possible?," The One Minute Apologist, http://www.oneminuteapologist.com/searchpage#are-near-death-experiences-possible

Hank Hanegraaff, "Afterlife: Near Death Experiences," The One Minute Apologist, http://www.oneminuteapologist.com/searchpage#afterlife

PART 6

Questions about Angels and Demons

41 Who Are Angels and What Do They Do?

Answer

Angels are fascinating creatures. They have captured the human imagination for centuries. There have been many attempts by artists and producers to capture an accurate picture or film about angels. Some of the most popular imagery of angels shows them as babies with wings, while others portray them as magnificent beings that shine with glory and might.

But what is the truth about angels and what they do?

Angels are spiritual creatures ("sons of God," Job 2:1 ESV; see also 1:6) who were created by God before the creation of the world (Job 38:6–7; Ps. 148:2, 5; Col. 1:16). They are immortal spirit beings (Heb. 1:14) who possess personalities (intellect, emotion, and will, 1 Pet. 1:12; 2 Pet. 2:4) and have great power, knowledge, and abilities (Ps. 103:20; 2 Pet. 2:11). Some angels have taken on bodily forms (Gen. 18; 19; Heb. 13:2), but this doesn't mean they have material bodies. Angels are incorporeal (no physical existence). They do not marry or procreate (Matt. 22:30), and they do not die (Luke 20:36), but they are not infinite like God. They are created beings. Though made lower than angels (Ps. 8:5), humans will be crowned with greater glory (Heb. 2:17) and will one day judge angels (1 Cor. 6:3).

Angels
Serve and praise God—Psalms 103:21; 148:2
Execute God's judgments—2 Samuel 24:16–17
Act as messengers of God—Daniel 4:17
Serve as guardians of people—Matthew 18:10; Hebrews 1:14
Protect God's glory—Genesis 3:22–24

Angels have also played an important role in God's redemptive plan for the world. The angel Gabriel revealed to Mary that she would give birth to the Messiah (Luke 1:26–38); angels warned Joseph in a dream of Herod's deadly plot (Matt. 2:13, 20); they ministered to Jesus after the wilderness temptation (Matt. 4:11) and in the Garden of Gethsemane (Luke 22:43); and they announced the resurrection of Jesus (Matt. 28:5–7).

The most well-known angels are Michael the archangel, whose name means "who is like God?" (see Dan. 10:13; Jude 9); Gabriel, "devoted to God" (see Dan. 9:21–22; Luke 1:11–13, 26–33); and Lucifer, "son of the morning" (Isa. 14:12 NKJV), who rebelled against God and became the devil (1 Tim. 3:6; Rev. 12:3–4).

Application

Don't underestimate the power and beauty of angels. God created them not only to glorify him (Rev. 4:11) but also to provide protection for his children (Matt. 18:10).

Bible References

Ranks of angels: archangel (1 Thess. 4:16); chief princes (Dan. 10:13); rulers (Rom. 8:38; Eph. 3:10); authorities (Eph. 6:12; Col. 2:10); dominions (Col. 1:16; Jude 8 KJV); cherubim (Gen. 3:24; Ezek. 28:14, 16); seraphim (Isa. 6:2–7)

Books

Angels, by Billy Graham

Angels: Who They Are and How They Help—What the Bible Reveals, by David Jeremiah

Angels among Us, by Ron Rhodes

Website

"Angels," BibleGateway, http://www.biblegateway.com/resources/dictionaries/dict_meaning.php?source=1&wid=T0000240

DVD

Angels: The Angelic Realm, vol. 1, Chuck Missler

Online Video

Bobby Conway, "Who Are Angels and What Do They Do?," The One Minute Apologist, http://www.oneminuteapologist.com/searchpage#who-are-angels-and-what-do-they-do

42 Who Are Demons and What Do They Do?

Answer

There is a lot of speculation about demons. Simply put, demons are fallen angels (see question 41, *Who are angels and what do they do?*). The Bible sheds light on the fall of Lucifer and a third of the angels who fell with him (Heb. 12:22; Rev. 12:3–9). "How you have fallen from heaven, morning star, son of the dawn! You have been cast down to the earth, you who once laid low the nations!" (Isa. 14:12). Peter says some angels sinned (2 Pet. 2:4), and Jude states they didn't "keep their positions of authority but abandoned their proper dwelling" (1:6).

Demons
Disrupt God's purposes—Daniel 10:10–14; Revelation 16:13–16
Advance darkness—Ephesians 6:11–12
Inflict diseases—Matthew 4:24; 9:32–33; 17:15
Possess unbelievers and animals—Matthew 4:24; Mark 5:13
Oppress people—Matthew 8:16
Promote evil teachings—1 Timothy 4:1–3; 1 John 4:1–4
Stifle spiritual growth—Ephesians 6:12; 1 John 2:18–19
Promote idolatry—Deuteronomy 32:17; Revelation 9:20
Pervert marriage and sex—Romans 1:26–27; 1 Timothy 4:1–3

We can be quite certain that the fall of Lucifer and a third of the angels occurred prior to the fall of Adam and Eve. John tells us in Revelation 12:9, "The great dragon was hurled down—that ancient serpent called the devil, or Satan, who leads the whole world astray. He was hurled to the earth, and his angels with him." Some angels have been kept in prison (2 Pet. 2:4; Jude 6), while others are free to rule in the midst of this dark world (Eph. 6:12) and to do the work of Satan (Matt. 12:24). Demons are not the "elect angels" (1 Tim. 5:21) because they chose to rebel against God and are unredeemable (Matt. 25:41). On many occasions, demons are referred to as "unclean spirits" (Matt. 10:1; Mark 1:23; Luke 4:33; Acts 5:16; Rev. 18:2 ESV).

Demons know and fear Jesus Christ (Mark 5:7; Acts 19:15; James 2:19) and ultimately know their doom is coming (Matt. 8:29; Rev. 12:12).

Application

You don't have to worry or be paranoid about demons. Though they are powerful and cause much havoc among Christians, Jesus is the King of kings and Lord of lords (Rev. 19:16). No demon can overpower Jesus Christ (Mark 1:25–26; 3:11; 5:8–13; 6:7; 9:25).

Bible References

Matthew 10:1; Mark 1:23; 5:1–20; Acts 16:16–18; Ephesians 6:10–18; Hebrews 12:22; 2 Peter 2:4; Revelation 12:3–9

Books

The Strategy of Satan: How to Detect and Defeat Him, by Warren W. Wiersbe

Spiritual Warfare: The Battle for God's Glory, by Jerry Rankin

The Invisible War: What Every Believer Needs to Know about Satan, Demons, and Spiritual Warfare, by Chip Ingram

Spiritual Warfare: How to Stand Firm in the Faith, by Ray Stedman

Website

"What Does the Bible Say about Demons?," Worldview Ministries, http://www.seanmcdowell .org/index.php/theology/what-does-the-bible-say-about-demons/

DVD

Angels and Demons, Ligonier Ministries

Online Video

Bobby Conway, "What Are Demons and What Do They Do?," The One Minute Apologist, http://www.oneminuteapologist.com/searchpage#what-are-demons-and-what-do-they-do

43 What Kind of Power Does Satan Have?

Answer

The Bible provides many insights into the fall and destructive behaviors of Satan. But before he was Satan (adversary), he was Lucifer (morning star, son of the dawn, Isa. 14:12), a beautiful and holy cherub (Ezek. 28:12–15). Lucifer's pride made him corrupt and resulted in his being kicked out of heaven (Isa. 14:12–14; Ezek. 28:17).

Old Testament Descriptions of Satan's Power

The Bible describes Satan as a "serpent" who is "more crafty than any of the wild animals the LORD God had made" (Gen. 3:1). He is powerful enough that he "incited David to take a census of Israel" (1 Chron. 21:1). Satan is permitted to roam "throughout the earth, going back and forth on it," and then to enter the presence of God (Job 1:6–7), standing as the "accuser" of the brethren (Ps. 109:6; Rev. 12:10; see Zech. 3:1–2).

Names of Satan
Devil—Matthew 4:1
Evil one—John 17:15
Great dragon—Revelation 12:3–4, 7–9
Abaddon—Revelation 9:11
Adversary—1 Peter 5:8 ESV
Beelzebub—Matthew 12:24
Father of lies—John 8:44
Tempter—Matthew 4:3

New Testament Descriptions of Satan's Power

Jesus refers to Satan as the "prince of this world" (John 14:30) and the "prince of demons" (Matt. 9:34). Paul says he is the "god of this age" (2 Cor. 4:4) and the "ruler of the kingdom of the air" (Eph. 2:2). John pronounces that the "whole world is under the control of the evil one" (1 John 5:19). The archangel Michael "did not dare to condemn him for slander" (Jude 9), knowing his power and deception (2 John 7; Rev. 12:10).

Satan does many things as ruler of this world. He

- "masquerades as an angel of light" (2 Cor. 11:14);
- "prowls around like a roaring lion looking for someone to devour" (1 Pet. 5:8);
- "tempts" people to sin (Matt. 4:1–2; see 1 John 2:16–17);
- leads others astray (2 Cor. 11:13);
- is "the accuser of our brethren" (Rev. 12:10 NKJV);
- performs counterfeit miracles (2 Thess. 2:9);
- "deceives those who are perishing" (2 Thess. 2:10);
- promotes "deceiving spirits and things taught by demons" (1 Tim. 4:1–3; see Rev. 2:24);
- "blind[s] the minds of unbelievers" (2 Cor. 4:4);
- plants weeds (Matt. 13:38–39);
- "takes away the word that was sown" (Mark 4:15);
- hinders Christian ministry (1 Thess. 2:18);
- enters unbelievers (Luke 22:3);
- "lies" (John 8:44);

- "deceives the whole world" (Rev. 12:9 NKJV);
- causes believers to "suffer persecution" (Rev. 2:10);
- "comes only to steal and kill and destroy" (John 10:10).

In the end, however, Satan is powerful, but only God is all-powerful. Satan is a finite creature; only God is the infinite Creator. Satan can do supernormal things, but only God can do the supernatural. Satanic "displays of power through signs and wonders" are false miracles (2 Thess. 2:9); only God can do true miracles. Satan is a super scientist and master magician, but he cannot create, resurrect the dead, or bring about truly supernatural events.

Application

Satan is a powerful foe, but he is also a defeated foe (Rev. 12:12). John reminds believers that Jesus "destroy[ed] the devil's work" (1 John 3:8), and Paul confirms that the death of Jesus Christ "disarmed the powers and authorities" of Satan (Col. 2:15). Jesus prayed to the Father, asking him to "protect [his children] from the evil one" (John 17:15), and he continues to "make intercession for us" in heaven (Rom. 8:34 NKJV). Therefore, "submit yourselves, then, to God. Resist the devil, and he will flee from you" (James 4:7).

Bible References

Genesis 3:1–5; John 8:44; Hebrews 2:14–15; 1 Peter 5:8

Books

The Strategy of Satan: How to Detect and Defeat Him, by Warren W. Wiersbe
Spiritual Warfare: The Battle for God's Glory, by Jerry Rankin
The Invisible War: What Every Believer Needs to Know about Satan, Demons, and Spiritual Warfare, by Chip Ingram
Spiritual Warfare: How to Stand Firm in the Faith, by Ray Stedman

Website

"What Does the Bible Say about Satan?," American Family Association, http://www.afa.net/Blogs/BlogPost.aspx?id=2147502271

DVD

The Invisible War, Living on the Edge

Online Video

Jason Jimenez, "What Kind of Power Does Satan Have?," The One Minute Apologist, http://www.oneminuteapologist.com/searchpage#what-kind-of-power-does-satan-have

44 Can a Christian Be Demon Possessed?

Answer

Horror films are a huge hit among moviegoers. The scarier the film is, the better the ratings will be. The more popular horror films usually have an element of demon possession that is meant to inflict fear on the moviegoer (e.g., *The Exorcist, Paranormal Activity, The Amityville Horror,* and *The Shining*).

Even though most of the horror films in Hollywood are fictional, that doesn't mean demon possession doesn't happen. There is no doubt that a person can be demon possessed. The question, however, is whether Christians can be possessed by demons. Of course, opinions vary greatly on this issue, so a clear understanding of what the Bible teaches is in order.

The first thing to point out is that there is no direct example in the Bible of a Christian being possessed (inhabited or indwelt) by a demon. As a matter of fact, Paul provides a direct response:

> What harmony is there between Christ and Belial? Or what does a believer have in common with an unbeliever? What agreement is there between the temple of God and idols? For we are the temple of the living God. As God has said: "I will live with them and walk among them, and I will be their God, and they will be my people."
>
> 2 Corinthians 6:15–16

The apostle John writes:

> The one who does what is sinful is of the devil, because the devil has been sinning from the beginning. The reason the Son of God appeared was to destroy the devil's work.
>
> 1 John 3:8

It is clear from these two passages that demons cannot inhabit a believer's body because it is the temple of God and also because Jesus reigns victoriously in a believer's life (1 John 5).

Furthermore, Satan isn't strong enough to overpower God's protection over his people (1 Pet. 1:5). The apostle John declares, "The One who was born of God keeps them safe, and the evil one cannot harm them" (1 John 5:18). Christians "have been brought to fullness. [Christ] is the head over every power and authority" (Col. 2:10). Jesus "disarmed the powers and authorities . . . triumphing over them by the cross" (Col. 2:13).

Elsewhere, the Bible gives Christians the promise that we are "God's children" (Rom. 8:16), who are also called "children of light" (Eph. 5:8). We have been "redeemed from the hand of the foe" (Ps. 107:2), are "more than conquerors" (Rom. 8:37), and are able to "overcome all the power of the enemy" (Luke 10:19).

Nonetheless, even though believers cannot be *indwelt* by demons, they can be *influenced* by them. Believers who do not have on the armor of God (Eph. 6:11–17) can be deceived and derailed in their spiritual lives (1 Pet. 5:8–9). Thus, it's important that every Christian submit himself or herself to God and resist the devil (James 4:7).

Application

There is so much false teaching about demon possession that incites fear in the hearts of Christians. But don't worry; all you need to do is put your faith in the power and authority of Jesus Christ and make sure to "put on the full armor of God, so that you can take your stand against the devil's schemes" (Eph. 6:11).

Bible References

Luke 10:19; 2 Corinthians 6:14–15; Ephesians 6:10–19; Colossians 2:12–15; 1 John 3:8

Books

The Strategy of Satan: How to Detect and Defeat Him, by Warren W. Wiersbe

Spiritual Warfare: The Battle for God's Glory, by Jerry Rankin

The Invisible War: What Every Believer Needs to Know about Satan, Demons, and Spiritual Warfare, by Chip Ingram

Spiritual Warfare: How to Stand Firm in the Faith, by Ray Stedman

What Demons Can Do to Saints, by Merrill Unger

Website

"Can Christians Be Demon Possessed?," ChristianAnswers.net, http://www.christiananswers .net/q-esp/esp-demonpossession.html

DVD

The Invisible War, Living on the Edge

Online Video

Bobby Conway, "Can a Christian Be Demon Possessed?," The One Minute Apologist, http:// www.oneminuteapologist.com/searchpage#can-a-christian-be-demon-possessed

45 Can Christians Cast Demons Out of People?

Answer

It's strange how so many Christians are interested in the power of Satan and his legions yet, at the same time, are curious to know what kind of authority Christians have over them. The bottom line is that Christians have no authority on their own to cast out demons. The authority given comes from the name of Jesus Christ (Mark 9:38). He, and he alone, has complete authority over Satan and his legions. Luke records an incident when Jesus was confronted with an evil spirit and cast it out:

> In the synagogue there was a man possessed by a demon, an impure spirit. He cried out at the top of his voice, "Go away! What do you want with us, Jesus of Nazareth? Have you come to destroy us? I know who you are—the Holy One of God!"
>
> "Be quiet!" Jesus said sternly. "Come out of him!" Then the demon threw the man down before them all and came out without injuring him.
>
> All the people were amazed and said to each other, "What words are these! With authority and power he gives orders to impure spirits and they come out!" And the news about him spread throughout the surrounding area.
>
> Luke 4:33–37

During the ministry of Jesus, he gave special gifts to the apostles, including the authority to cast out demons (Matt. 10:1; Luke 9:1). Mark 6:13 reads, "They drove out many demons and anointed many sick people with oil and healed them." Jesus also sent out the seventy-two disciples, and upon their return they said, "Lord, even the demons submit to us in your name" (Luke 10:17). As Jesus said, casting out demons comes with the faith to move mountains (Matt. 17:20–21) and with much prayer (Mark 9:29). But we do not have all the gifts the apostles had (2 Cor. 12:12).

The best approach for a believer is to put on the whole armor of God (Eph. 6:11). And in dealing with demonic influence in an unbeliever's life, the best tactic is to bring the person to Christ. Light casts out darkness. If a person is truly saved, Satan cannot indwell him or her (see question 44, *Can a Christian be demon possessed?*). Christians who claim to be harassed by demons should be taught that Satan is a defeated foe (Eph. 6; Col. 2; Heb. 2). He may roar like a lion (1 Pet. 5:8), but he has been defanged and declawed by the cross. Believers can claim this victory and be delivered from the dominion of darkness.

Application

It's more important for you to remain alert to Satan's lies and be quick to forgive (see question 66, *How can I forgive someone who has hurt me deeply?*) than to look for ways to cast out demons. Paul writes, "I have forgiven in the sight of Christ for your sake, in order that Satan might not outwit us. For we are not unaware of his schemes" (2 Cor. 2:10–11). Christ is victorious and has given you victory over Satan. Claim this victory in your life and see God use you in mighty ways (1 John 5:4).

Bible References

Matthew 10:1; Mark 3:15; 6:13; Luke 9:1; 10:17–19; 2 Corinthians 2:10–11; Ephesians 6:10–19

Books

The Strategy of Satan: How to Detect and Defeat Him, by Warren W. Wiersbe

Spiritual Warfare: The Battle for God's Glory, by Jerry Rankin

The Invisible War: What Every Believer Needs to Know about Satan, Demons, and Spiritual Warfare, by Chip Ingram

Spiritual Warfare: How to Stand Firm in the Faith, by Ray Stedman

What Demons Can Do to Saints, by Merrill Unger

Website

"Casting Out Demons," GreatBibleStudy.com, http://www.greatbiblestudy.com/casting_out_demons.php

DVD

The Invisible War, Living on the Edge

Online Video

Jason Jimenez, "Can Christians Cast Demons Out of People?," The One Minute Apologist, http://www.oneminuteapologist.com/searchpage#cast-demons-out

PART 7

Questions about the Church and End Times

46 What Is the Church?

Answer

The organized church is a dying breed in America. The majority of Christians who fill the seats every Sunday don't have a clue what church really is. If you ask the average Christian, you may get a response like: "The church is a building." "The church has music and Bible programs." "The church is a place Christians go on Sunday mornings to hear the pastor preach a sermon."

All these answers are correct to a certain degree, but they don't come close to defining the church. According to the Bible, the church is the body of Christ (1 Cor. 12:13)—of which Christ is the head (Eph. 1:22; Col. 1:18; 2:19). The church is also referred to as the "bride of Christ" (Rev. 19:7–8), and Christ is the Bridegroom (Matt. 25:6; Eph. 5:25). This description not only reflects the *rulership of Christ* but also reveals the *relationship of Christ* to his church.

The meaning of the word *church* (Greek: *ekklesia*) is "those called out" or "an assembly." In the New Testament, the church became known as the gathering of believers (Acts 16:31; Titus 3:5–6) who worship and serve Christ (Acts 2:1; Heb. 10:25).

To get a better understanding of the church, it's necessary to examine it in two ways: *local* (visible) and *universal* (invisible). Simply put, the *local* church is the *visibility* of gathered believers all over the earth (1 Cor. 1:2; 1 Thess. 1:1). The *universal* church is the *invisibility* of all believers, both on earth and in heaven. This is known as the *totality* of the church because it represents the spiritual body of Jesus Christ. This is demonstrated in Hebrews 12:23: "To the *church of the firstborn*, whose names are written in heaven. You have come to God, the Judge of all, to the spirits of the righteous made perfect."

The apostle Paul was privileged by God to reveal many mysteries of the church:

> Consequently, you are no longer foreigners and strangers, but fellow citizens with God's people and also members of his household, built on the foundation of the apostles and prophets, with Christ Jesus himself as the chief cornerstone.

In him the whole building is joined together and rises to become a holy temple in the Lord. And in him you too are being built together to become a dwelling in which God lives by his Spirit.

Ephesians 2:19–22

Listed below are six insights about the church found in this passage:

1. The church is made up of "fellow citizens" who are "God's people" and are considered "members of God's household" (v. 19).
2. The church is built on the doctrine of the apostles and prophets (v. 20).
3. The church has Jesus Christ as its "chief cornerstone" (v. 20).
4. The church is joined together by Christ (v. 21).
5. The church is the "holy temple of the Lord" (v. 21).
6. The church is where the Holy Spirit dwells (v. 22).

The church is an organism that has many members who are diverse in function (Eph. 4:16) yet united as one body (1 Cor. 12:12–13; Eph. 4:3). Paul writes, "There is one body and one Spirit, just as you were called to one hope when you were called; one Lord, one faith, one baptism; one God and Father of all, who is over all and through all and in all" (Eph. 4:4–6).

Application

In essence, the church is you. And when the various roles and gifts are instituted, the work and edification of the church expand and grow (Eph. 4:12). That's why the Bible teaches us not to neglect assembling together with other believers (Heb. 10:25). The body needs its members (1 Cor. 12:14–26). Thus, make sure you are actively involved in growing and serving in a Christ-centered church.

Bible References

Romans 12; 1 Corinthians 12; Ephesians 2:19–22; 4:12; Hebrews 10:25

Books

Systematic Theology: In One Volume, by Norman L. Geisler

Simple Church: Returning to God's Process for Making Disciples, by Thom Rainer and Eric Geiger

What the Spirit Is Saying to the Churches, by Henry Blackaby

Website

"What Is the Church?," Focus on the Family, http://www.focusonthefamily.com/faith/the_study_of_god/why_study_god/what_is_the_church.aspx

DVD

Transformational Church, LifeWay

Online Video

Bobby Conway, "What Is the Church?," The One Minute Apologist, http://www.one minuteapologist.com/searchpage#what-is-the-church

47 How Can I Know a Good Church from a Bad One?

Answer

The late, great Charles Spurgeon once preached a sermon entitled "Feeding Sheep or Amusing Goats?" That title implies that even back then Christians were measuring a *good* church on the basis of *entertainment* rather than *substance*. But there's so much more to church than entertaining people and making them feel comfortable (see question 46, *What is the church?*).

The truth is church isn't about the individual; it's about the person of Jesus Christ. But many people today have made church into a social club and are more concerned with image and size than about the gospel of Christ. People want churches that are like a theme park, offering them more choices than they can ever dream of and keeping their families entertained with fun activities week in and week out.

But don't be fooled. Such churches may attract a large crowd and keep them preoccupied, but they certainly do not train up Christians and send them out to reach the world with the gospel.

Here's a biblical checklist of things to look for in a good church:

Pure worship of God—Psalm 145
> Put aside the style of music and simply focus on whether the worship is about the people on stage or about the God of heaven.

139

Preaching and teaching of the Word of God—Acts 6:2
> The purpose and responsibility of any church is to stay true to the message of Christ and to the Word of God.

Faithful shepherding and leading of the people—1 Peter 5:1–4
> Pastors are to love and care for the people God has given them by faithfully teaching, protecting, and shepherding their flock.

Promotion of unity in diversity—1 Corinthians 12:12–13
> A sign of a healthy church is that it is built on a strong and unified team of leaders.

Family-basis—Deuteronomy 6:6–7; Ephesians 6:4
> It's not about programs; it's about people! Parents and grandparents need to be trained so they can be the most effective with their families.

Discipling and sending out of believers for local and global missions—Matthew 28:19–20
> The job of the church is to equip the saints for the work of the ministry. Christ commanded that we go and reach the nations in his name.

Application

Don't test churches the way you would a restaurant or a place of business. Remain open and objective and seek to always support and not offend. There are solid churches out there that will love you and your family and will equip you for the work of ministry (Eph. 4:12).

Bible References

Deuteronomy 6:6–7; Psalm 145; Matthew 28:19–20; Acts 6:2; 1 Corinthians 12; Ephesians 6:4; 1 Peter 5:1–4

Books

Simple Church: Returning to God's Process for Making Disciples, by Thom Rainer and Eric Geiger

What the Spirit Is Saying to the Churches, by Henry Blackaby

Website

"Finding a Good Church," Billy Graham Evangelistic Association, http://www.billygraham.org

DVD

It: How Churches and Leaders Can Get It and Keep It, Craig Groeschel

Online Video

Hank Hanegraaff, "How Do I Find a Good Church?," The One Minute Apologist, http://www.oneminuteapologist.com/searchpage#find-a-good-church

48 How Can I Get My Family Involved in Church?

Answer

Parents are struggling with this more than ever. It seems most Christian families can no longer agree on what kind of church to attend. Usually when a family does get to church, the kids run off to their Sunday school classes, the teens to their respective cool zones, and mom and dad to their age-specific classes.

Whether divorced, single, or married, parents are finding it difficult to commit to a church where every member of the family feels connected and fulfilled. The big problem is that most families miss the whole purpose of church. Why? Because they are more concerned about the quality of music than the humility of worship. They are more anxious to hear a podcast than to grow deeper in the Word of God. Parents are more worried about what their kids think of church than about keeping their focus on God.

So what's a family to do?

The first thing is to get your family together and pray and learn what the Bible has to say about the church. (See question 46, *What is the church?* and question 47, *How can I know a good church from a bad one?*)

Once your family understands the purpose of church, the next step is to focus on spiritual gifts and acts of service (Rom. 12:3–8; 1 Cor. 12; Eph. 4:7–16). The Holy Spirit has given each member of the church a gift, and it is the Holy Spirit's desire that we use those gifts according to their proper role. Church is more about *giving* than it is about *receiving*. Therefore, help foster one another's spiritual gifts and seek out church leadership if you have any questions.

Then seek out ways to use your gifts in the various ministries and activities offered by your church. Don't just look for opportunities to serve alone but be proactive to engage your whole family. Set up an appointment with your pastor and talk about the church, the spiritual gifts in your family, and ways you and your family can get involved.

Application

There is so much more to the church than you can ever know. Don't just sit around and be a sponge in your church. Get involved by serving others with the gifts God has given you.

Bible References

Romans 12:3–8; 1 Corinthians 12; Ephesians 4:7–16

Books

Discover Your Spiritual Gifts: Identify and Understand Your Unique God-Given Spiritual Gifts, by C. Peter Wagner

You Lost Me: Why Young Christians Are Leaving Church . . . and Rethinking Faith, by David Kinnaman and Aly Hawkins

Sticky Faith: Everyday Ideas to Build Lasting Faith in Your Kids, by Kara Powell and Chap Clark

Website

Jim Burns, "Getting Kids Involved at Church," Christian Broadcasting Network, http://www.cbn.com/family/parenting/getting-kids-involved-at-church-burns.aspx

DVD

They Like Jesus but Not the Church: Six Sessions Responding to Culture's Objections to Christianity, Dan Kimball

Online Video

Jason Jimenez, "How Do I Get My Family Involved in Church?," The One Minute Apologist, http://www.oneminuteapologist.com/searchpage#involved-in-church

49 Why Are Churches So Divided?

Answer

Did you know that the number one reason Christians leave the church is because someone in the church wounded them? That's heartbreaking, isn't it? The one place where Christians should feel safe and encouraged has become a battlefield for many.

God makes it perfectly clear that he loves when his church is united. Psalm 133:1 reads, "How good and pleasant it is when God's people live together in unity." Unfortunately, pride within the pastorate and an unwillingness to relinquish power have created a chasm among church denominations, resulting in public division and internal criticisms. Poll after poll shows that the number of wounded Christians who are no longer attending church is growing daily.

Think about that. The very people the church reaches with the gospel are the same ones the church hurts in the end. Something is very wrong with this picture.

That's why the Bible deals extensively with division and its potential dangers. Division in the church is never good. It's damaging not only to the organization but also, most importantly, to the body of Christ. Division sends a bad message to the rest of the world. But what causes division in the church?

Division is created when people teach contrary doctrine (Rom. 16:17), quarrel over affiliations (1 Cor. 1:10), harbor jealousy (1 Cor. 3:3), show favoritism (Jude 16 ESV), or think more highly of themselves than they ought to (Gal. 6:3).

Oftentimes, a church may seem warm and inviting, but once inside, you quickly realize the discord within the church—nothing but bickering over the style of music, judging others' appearances, disputing over doctrinal issues, disagreeing over philosophy of ministry, and gossiping and complaining about leadership.

And there is the always growing problem of arrogant pastors leading churches today. This, of course, makes it extremely difficult for churches to partner with one another or to even meet the needs of their own flocks.

These (and other reasons) are why the church breaks off into smaller denominations, each germinating its own membership and culture of worship.

In due time, these break-off denominations start to have their own set of disagreements.

Despite the divergence of opinions, however, the church is to achieve a "unity of the Spirit in the bond of peace" (Eph. 4:3 ESV), reflecting the union shared with its Savior. The Bible is quick to remind Christians that "there should be no division in the body, but that its parts should have equal concern for each other" (1 Cor. 12:25). Jesus said these words in Matthew 12:36: "But I tell you that everyone will have to give account on the day of judgment for every empty word they have spoken."

Application

If Christians humbly lived out Romans 12:9–16, all disputes and divisions within the church would come to an end. As for you, don't seek to divide the church but remain a member of it. If, perhaps, someone in the church hurts you, get godly counsel and seek to make things right with that brother or sister.

Bible References

Romans 12:9–21; Ephesians 4:3–13; Philippians 1:3–11; 2:1–5; Titus 3:9–11

Books

Complete Guide to Christian Denominations: Understanding the History, Beliefs, and Differences, by Ron Rhodes

I Am a Church Member: Discovering the Attitude that Makes the Difference, by Thom Rainer

What the Spirit Is Saying to the Churches, by Henry Blackaby

Website

Ray Stedman, "Behind Divisions," Authentic Christianity, http://www.raystedman.org/new-testament/1-corinthians/behind-divisions

DVD

Complete Kit for Christian History Made Easy, Timothy Paul Jones

Online Video

Jason Jimenez, "Why Is the Church So Divided?," The One Minute Apologist, http://www.oneminuteapologist.com/searchpage#why-is-the-church-so-divided

50 Can Protestants and Catholics Agree on Anything?

Answer

Roman Catholicism is one of the world's most recognizable religious organizations. There are over a billion adherents of the Catholic faith. Over time, the institutionalization of Roman Catholicism took shape based on growing traditions (especially after the East-West schism in 1054).

It's best to describe Catholicism as a combination of some basic Christian doctrine, a Roman hierarchical structure, a Jewish ritualistic form, and what many believe are pagan, idolatrous practices. However, it varies from country to country as to which of these characteristics are more dominant.

What Evangelical Protestants and Roman Catholics Agree On

1. *The Bible is the Word of God.*
2. *The canon of Scripture is closed*: There are no new revelations from God.
3. *The Trinity*: There are three persons in one eternal essence of God: Father, Son, and Holy Spirit.
4. *Jesus Christ*: He is both God and man (two natures united in one person).
5. *Virgin birth*: Jesus was miraculously conceived in Mary's womb, without a biological father.
6. *Atonement*: Jesus alone paid the price for our salvation from the guilt and eternal consequences of our sins.
7. *The Resurrection*: Jesus arose from the dead in the same body in which he died.
8. *The Ascension*: Jesus ascended physically into heaven in the same body in which he was raised immortal.
9. *The church*: There is a universal, spiritual body of Christ to which all the saved belong regardless of their earthly denomination.
10. *The second coming*: Jesus will return to earth physically to judge the wicked.
11. *Heaven and hell*: There is a place of eternal, conscious bliss for the saved and another place of eternal, conscious woe for the unsaved.

In addition, evangelical Protestants and Roman Catholics agree on the two ordinances of baptism and communion, the existence of absolute truth and moral absolutes, and pro-family and pro-life issues.

Most orthodox Christian groups confess one Bible, two Testaments, three creeds (Apostles', Nicene, Athanasian), and four councils at Nicea (AD 326), Constantinople (381), Ephesus (431), and Chalcedon (451) during five centuries.

How Evangelical Protestants Differ from Roman Catholics

After laying out the shared beliefs between evangelicals and Catholics, it's important to dig deeper to reveal the doctrinal differences. Evangelicals, in contrast to Roman Catholics, believe in

1. the Bible alone (*sola Scriptura*) as the sole written authority for faith;
2. Christ alone (*sola Christa*) as the only redeemer;
3. grace alone (*sola gratia*) apart from works as the sole means of salvation;
4. faith alone (*sola fide*) as the sole means of receiving God's gift of salvation.

Roman Catholics believe in the *necessity* of grace but not the *exclusivity* of grace (since they believe good works are also necessary for salvation).

Evangelical Protestants Reject These Distinctive Doctrines of Roman Catholics

1. Roman Catholics added *eleven books of the Apocrypha* to the Bible (1546).
2. They pronounced the pope *infallible* (1870) when speaking officially (*ex cathedra*) on matters of faith and practice.
3. They added *works to grace* as a condition of salvation.
4. They added *works to faith* as a means of receiving salvation.
5. They added *Mary to Christ* as a means of mediating salvation.
6. They added *purgatory to the cross* for completing salvation (from the temporal consequences of sin).
7. They added belief in the *immaculate conception* of Mary (1854).
8. They added the *bodily assumption of Mary* (1950) to the bodily assumption of Christ.
9. They added the *institutional church to Christ* as a means of dispensing grace that brings salvation.

Evangelicals, in contrast to Roman Catholics, believe the institutional church has only a *ministerial* role, not a *magisterial* role, in the life of believers. Thus, the church is the *servant* of the canon of Scripture, not the *master* of it.

Evangelical Protestants Reject These Practices of Roman Catholics

1. Roman Catholics added the *veneration of Mary* to the worship of God.
2. They added the *veneration of images* to the worship of God.
3. They added the *worship of the consecrated host* to the worship of God.
4. They added *prayers to dead saints* to prayers to the living God.
5. They added *prayers for the dead* (people in purgatory) to prayers for the living.
6. They added *priests* as means to approach God.
7. They added the *practice of penance* to grace to gain the favor of God.
8. They added the practice of *confession of sin to a priest* to confession to God.

In summary, Roman Catholicism is *a* Christian church—in that it confesses many basic Christian doctrines—but it is not *the* Christian church. Many other confessions of Christianity are less polluted with false doctrine and pagan practices.

Application

Contrary to the doctrine of Roman Catholicism, the Word of God teaches that salvation is only by grace through faith. Ephesians 2:8–9 reads, "For it is by grace you have been saved, through faith—and this not from yourselves, it is the gift of God—not by works, so that no one can boast." Elsewhere, Paul explained to the Romans that they have "been justified by [Jesus's] blood" (Rom. 5:9), and he explained to Titus that "[God] saved us, not because of righteous things we had done, but because of his mercy" (Titus 3:5). Peter wrote, "[Jesus] bore our sins in his body on the cross, so that we might die to sins and live for righteousness" (1 Pet. 2:24). Thus, Roman Catholics have it wrong when they teach that a person must do good works in order to be saved. Therefore, as a Christian, be thankful that your salvation isn't dependent on good works but simply on the goodness of God.

Use the material below to become more familiar with Roman Catholicism, and make an effort to share Christ with Catholics.

Bible References

Matthew 16:23; Romans 4:5; Galatians 2:11–14; Ephesians 2:8–9, 20

Books

Reasoning from the Scriptures with Catholics, by Ron Rhodes

The Gospel according to Rome: Comparing Catholic Tradition and the Word of God, by James McCarthy

Roman Catholics and Evangelicals: Agreements and Differences, by Norman L. Geisler and Ralph MacKenzie

Website

"Witnessing Effectively to Roman Catholics," John Ankerberg Show, http://www.jashow.org/wiki/index.php?title=Witnessing_Effectively_to_Roman_Catholics

DVD

Roman Catholicism: A Look into the Teachings of the Roman Catholic Church, Charlie Campbell

Online Video

Norman L. Geisler, "What Do Catholics Believe?," The One Minute Apologist, http://www.oneminuteapologist.com/searchpage#what-do-catholics-believe

51 Is Tithing 10 Percent Enough?

Answer

This question is often asked because people are either confused about the biblical methods of tithing or struggle to give back to God. Either way, the Bible makes a strong case that "God loves a cheerful giver" (2 Cor. 9:7).

So how much are we expected to give in order to be considered a cheerful giver? It's not *how much we give* but *how we give* that matters. Tithing is more than just giving money. It also has to do with giving our time, sharing resources to benefit others (Matt. 25:34–40), and utilizing our spiritual gifts to enhance the body of Christ (Rom. 12:6–8).

The word *tithe* simply means "tenth." That's why most people believe tithing 10 percent of their income is the standard when giving to the local church and other parachurch ministries (biblical examples include Abraham, Gen. 14:20; Jacob, Gen. 28:22; the Pharisee, Luke 18:12). Though 10 percent is commonly considered the standard, the truth is that the majority of Christians don't give at all!

Paul implies that Christians should tithe to support their ministers in the same way they did in the Old Testament (1 Cor. 9:13–14). Can you imagine if Christians decided to start giving 10 percent of their income to the church? It would make a huge difference in the church.

Tithe

Old Testament

War tithe—Genesis 14:20
Land tithe—Leviticus 27:30–33
Priestly tithe—Numbers 18:21
Temple tithe—Deuteronomy 12:2–7; 14:22–29
Charity tithe—Deuteronomy 26:12
Faithful tithe—Malachi 3:8–10

New Testament

Hypocritical tithe—Matthew 23:23
Church offering—1 Corinthians 16:1–2
Relief offering—Acts 11:27–39

The New Testament makes it clear that we are to give as we are able. Paul argues, "Each of you should give what you have decided in your heart to give, not reluctantly or under compulsion, for God loves a cheerful giver" (2 Cor. 9:7). Jesus watched as the rich man gave extravagantly in public, but then a poor woman dropped in two small copper coins. Jesus said, "This poor widow has put in more than all the others. All these people gave their gifts out of their wealth; but she out of her poverty put in all she had to live on" (Luke 21:3–4). The point Jesus was making is that it's not your *standard of living* that counts but the *standard of giving* you are willing to invest that matters for all eternity.

That is the measure in which we are to give. Although giving comes from *natural* means, it ultimately comes from God's *supernatural* hands. Therefore, be generous, as God has been generous to you.

Application

Life on earth is not about taking all you can get but about giving back all you have. Seek to give toward ministries that advance God's work and meet the needs of those who are less fortunate. Pray and ask God *where* you should give, and he will tell you *how much* to give.

Bible References

Proverbs 21:13; Matthew 5:42; 6:1–4, 19–24; 25:14–46; Luke 3:10–14; Acts 2:44–45; 1 Timothy 5:17–18; 1 John 3:17

Books

The Treasure Principle: Unlocking the Secret of Joyful Giving, by Randy Alcorn

Giving and Tithing: Includes Serving and Stewardship, by Larry Burkett

Website

Randy Alcorn, "43 quotes from *The Treasure Principle: Discovering the Secret of Joyful Giving*," Eternal Perspectives Ministries, http://www.epm.org/resources/2010/Feb/3/43-quotes-treasure-principle-discovering-secret-jo/

DVD

The Treasure Principle Video Workshop, Randy Alcorn

Online Video

Jason Jimenez, "Is Tithing 10 Percent Enough?," The One Minute Apologist, http://www.oneminuteapologist.com/searchpage#tithing

52 Why Is Biblical Prophecy Important?

Answer

Where has God revealed an account from the beginning of time all the way to things to come? The Bible.

The Bible is a divine book. It is made up of sixty-six books—divided into the Old Testament (thirty-nine books) and the New Testament (twenty-seven books). It took a span of over fifteen hundred years and some forty authors to write and complete the Bible. Out of the thirty-nine books in the Old Testament, seventeen are prophetic books (Isaiah, Jeremiah, Lamentations, Ezekiel, Daniel, Hosea, Joel, Amos, Obadiah, Jonah, Micah, Nahum, Habakkuk,

Zephaniah, Haggai, Zechariah, and Malachi). In the New Testament, major sections of the four Gospels and Pauline Epistles are directly related to prophecy. The last book of the Bible (Revelation) is completely devoted to prophecy. That means roughly 30 percent of the Bible is made up of prophecy! That's saying something.

What God is pointing out is that prophecy is extremely important to the fate of the world as well as to the Christian life. That's why Christians need to pay close attention to prophecy and try to understand it better.

Prophecy is the declaration of things to come and is closely related to eschatology, the study of things to come. Revelation 19:10 reads, "For the testimony of Jesus is the spirit of prophecy" (ESV). Thus, prophecy is important because its central figure is Christ and the final focus is on his glorious reign (John 5:46; Rev. 22:16). Furthermore, prophecy is important because it not only confirms the infinite knowledge of God (past, present, and future) but also details future events that have not yet taken place.

Listed below are reasons why Christians should find biblical prophecy important:

1. Prophecy validates biblical inspiration of God's divine revelation (Isa. 46:9–13; Zech. 7:12).
2. Prophecy provides a proper and complete interpretation of the Bible (Luke 24:45–47).
3. Prophecy reveals God's secrets (Amos 3:7).
4. The testimony of Jesus Christ is the key to prophecy (Rev. 19:10).
5. Prophecy acts as a guide to the meaning of history (Isa. 46:9–10).
6. Prophecy gives comfort and hope (Rom. 15:4).
7. Awaiting the return of Christ helps purify the soul (Titus 2:11–13; 1 John 3:1–3).
8. God blesses those who read prophecy and take it to heart (Rev. 1:3).
9. A proper understanding of prophecy motivates Christians to share the gospel (2 Thess. 2).
10. Focusing on God's prophetic Word keeps Christians from falling into deceptive doctrine (2 Pet. 2).

Application

In 1 Corinthians 1:7–8, Paul encourages Christians with these words: "Therefore you do not lack any spiritual gift as you eagerly wait for our Lord Jesus Christ to be revealed. He will also keep you firm to the end, so that you will be blameless on the day of our Lord Jesus Christ." Devote time to study prophecy (see question 55, *What is going to happen in the end times?*). It will definitely give you a better perspective on life.

Bible References

Isaiah 46:9–13; Amos 3:7; Zechariah 7:12; Romans 15:4; 1 Corinthians 1:7–8; Titus 2:11–13; 2 Peter 2; 1 John 3:1–3; Revelation 1:3, 9–11; 19:10; 22:16

Books

Every Prophecy of the Bible: Clear Explanations for Uncertain Times, by John Walvoord

The End Times in Chronological Order: A Complete Overview to Understanding Bible Prophecy, by Ron Rhodes

The End: A Complete Overview of Bible Prophecy and the End of Days, by Mark Hitchcock

Things to Come, by J. Dwight Pentecost

Website

John F. Walvoord, http://www.walvoord.com

DVD

The Coming Economic Armageddon, David Jeremiah

Online Video

Jason Jimenez, "Why Is Biblical Prophecy Important?," The One Minute Apologist, http://www.oneminuteapologist.com/searchpage#biblical-prophecy

53 Is America Mentioned in Prophecy?

Answer

Most Americans are perplexed as to why there isn't any direct mention of the United States in prophetic Scripture. It's hard to imagine the most powerful nation in history not being a prime player in the future world order. This leads many to think that certain catastrophic events are destined that will result in the destruction of the United States.

Let's consider the text of Scripture and examine the *supposed* mention of the United States in the Bible.

Many students of prophecy argue that key passages in the Bible refer to the United States. Some hold that the destruction mentioned in Isaiah 9:10–11 is a hidden reference to America. Others interpret the phrase "divided by rivers" in Isaiah 18:1–7 to mean the Mississippi River. Moreover, there are those who believe America is disguised in Ezekiel 38:13. They interpret the "merchants of Tarshish, and all their young lions" (NKJV) as the Western powers (i.e., the United States). And, finally, the "great city that rules over the kings of the earth" (Rev. 17:18) is perhaps a direct reference to New York City.

It is clear from a proper reading of each text provided above, however, that the United States is not even remotely implied in these passages of Scripture. The bottom line is that the Bible does mention major countries—but the United States is not one of them. The Bible mentions Israel, Iraq (Babylon), Egypt, Sudan, Jordan, Russia (Rosh), Iran (Persia), Europe (United Roman Empire), Syria, Greece, Saudi Arabia, Lebanon, and China (kings of the East). Yet there is no mention of the United States of America.

The reason America is not mentioned in prophecy is quite simple. It doesn't carry any significant weight from either a historical perspective or a prophetic one. Many other nations are not mentioned specifically (Japan, India, and Australia).

Furthermore, the United States is gradually declining as a superpower. America's trillions of dollars in debt and fragile economy, the rise of hostility among states, and the growing acts of terrorism in America are all tell-tale signs of an impending collapse. In addition, imagine how many Christians in America will be taken at the rapture. America will lose more Christians per capita than any other nation. This will have a dramatic effect on the United States. This single event will cripple America's ability to function and maintain its influence around the world. And because of its downgraded status, America may lend itself to the future support and aid of the Antichrist as part of his Western confederacy of nations.

Application

The focus of prophecy is not so much on the nations involved but on waiting for the coming reign of Christ to rule the nations on earth. The church will soon be raptured (1 Thess. 4:13–18), and the nation of Israel will embrace

Jesus Christ as the Messiah (Matt. 23:37–39). The nation you should pay close attention to is Israel (see question 54, *Should Americans care about Israel?*).

Bible References

Isaiah 43:5–6; Jeremiah 30:3; Daniel 9:24–27; Matthew 24; Mark 13; Luke 21

Books

The Late Great United States: What Bible Prophecy Reveals about America's Last Days, by Mark Hitchcock

101 Answers to the Most Asked Questions about the End Times, by Mark Hitchcock

Implosion: Can America Recover from Its Economic and Spiritual Challenges in Time?, by Joel Rosenberg

Website

"Is America in Bible Prophecy?," Pre-Trib Research Center, http://www.pre-trib.org/articles/view/is-america-in-bible-prophecy

DVD

Israel, Iran, and America in Bible Prophecy, Greg Laurie

Online Video

Jason Jimenez, "Is America Mentioned in Prophecy?," The One Minute Apologist, http://www.oneminuteapologist.com/searchpage#america-in-prophecy

54 Should Americans Care about Israel?

Answer

It's quite amazing how God chose to use a small region of the world with little prestige to champion his cause—even to the bitter end (see Rom. 9:21–23).

It all started long ago when God elected Abraham and gave him three everlasting promises: *land*, *seed*, and *blessing*.

> Go from your country . . . to the land that I will show you. And I will make of you a great nation, and I will bless you and make your name great, so that you will be a blessing. I will bless those who bless you, and him who dishonors you I will curse, and in you all the families of the earth shall be blessed.
>
> Genesis 12:1–3 ESV

The extent of the blessing not only applied to Abraham (personally) but also extended to Israel (nationally)—and to the whole world (Gal. 3:8, 16). From Abraham's descendants would eventually come the Messiah, Jesus Christ (Matt. 1:1; Rom. 9:5), who would take away the sins of his people (Matt. 1:21; John 1:29; 1 John 3:5). Moreover, it was through Israel that "the oracles of God" were given to the world (Rom. 3:2 ESV). These two great blessings—the *living* Word (the Savior) and the *written* Word (the Scriptures)—came through Abraham's descendants.

Subsequently, not only was Abraham blessed but so were the nations who blessed him. Historically, America has been one of those nations.

Deuteronomy 7:7–9 reveals why God chose Israel:

Covenants

Abrahamic Covenant

God chooses a nation and makes an everlasting covenant with Abraham (Gen. 12:1–3, 7; 13:14–16; 15:4–18; 17:1–9, 21; Heb. 6:13–18).

Mosaic Covenant

God gives the law to Moses and establishes a conditional covenant with Israel (Exod. 20:1–17; Leviticus; Deut. 5–26; Gal. 3:17–25).

Davidic Covenant

God establishes an everlasting throne with David, the king of Israel (2 Sam. 7:11–16; Ps. 89:20–37; Isa. 55:1–3).

> The Lord did not set his affection on you and choose you because you were more numerous than other peoples, for you were the fewest of all peoples. But it was because the Lord loved you and kept the oath he swore to your ancestors that he brought you out with a mighty hand and redeemed you from the land of slavery, from the power of Pharaoh king of Egypt. Know therefore that the Lord your God is God; he is the faithful God, keeping his covenant of love to a thousand generations of those who love him and keep his commands.

In a nutshell, Israel is important because God made it so. God chose Israel to be a model and to proclaim his love and faithfulness to the heathen nations (Exod. 19:3–8; Deut. 4:6–8).

Israel is also important because it plays a significant role in the tribulation period. In a historic and prophetic event, Israel became a sovereign nation on May 14, 1948. Ezekiel prophesied, "I will multiply people on you, the whole house of Israel, all of it. The cities shall be inhabited and the waste places rebuilt. . . . I will take you from the nations and gather you from all the countries and bring you into your own land" (36:10, 24 ESV).

Today, nearly six million Jews live in Israel. More Jews are returning to their homeland as prophesied by the prophets (Ezek. 20:33–38; Isa. 11:11–12). Jews returning to Israel is necessary for the Antichrist to sign a peace treaty with Israeli leaders (Dan. 9:27). But God will use 144,000 messianic Jews from the twelve tribes of Israel (Rev. 7) to spread the gospel all over the world during the tribulation period. Much of Israel will be converted to Christianity prior to the millennium (Joel 2:28–29; Zech. 10:8–12; 12:10; Matt. 24:31).

Hence, the nation of Israel is important because God divinely elected it to represent and extend his glory through the course of history and beyond.

Application

As a Christian, it is important for you to pray daily for the peace and safety of Israel (Ps. 122:6–7). Pray also for more Jews to believe in Yeshua (Jesus) and receive eternal life (1 John 5:11–13).

Bible References

Genesis 12:1–3; Deuteronomy 7:7–9; Psalm 122:6–7; Ezekiel 20:33–38; Daniel 9:24–27; Isaiah 11:11–12

Books

Why Care about Israel? How the Jewish Nation Is Key to Unleashing God's Blessings in the 21st Century, by Sandra Teplinsky and Michael Brown

Epicenter 2.0: Why the Current Rumblings in the Middle East Will Change Your Future, by Joel Rosenberg

Israel under Fire: The Prophetic Chain of Events that Threatens the Middle East, by John Ankerberg, Jimmy DeYoung, and Dillon Burroughs

Website

Christians United for Israel, http://www.cufi.org

DVD

Israel under Fire, John Ankerberg and Jimmy DeYoung

Online Video

Norman L. Geisler, "Should Americans Care about Israel?," The One Minute Apologist, http://www.oneminuteapologist.com/searchpage#americans-care-about-israel

55 What Is Going to Happen in the End Times?

Answer

It's a natural tendency to anticipate and fear what the future holds. That's why everyone has questions about the future. Even the disciples asked Jesus about the future. In the Olivet Discourse (Matt. 24–25, Mark 13, Luke 21), the disciples asked Jesus three prophetic questions:

> When will these things be?
> What will be the sign of your coming?
> What will be the sign of the end of the age?

It's clear that no one knows the day and hour of the return of Christ (Matt. 24:36; Acts 1:7). But Jesus did leave his church with two key warning signs to watch for: (1) the escalation of deception (Matt. 24:4–5), and (2) the rumors of wars (Matt. 24:6–7).

Here's a consolidated outline of end-times events in chronological order.

Heavenly Activity

1. *Rapture of the church* (John 14:1–3; 1 Cor. 15:51–55; 1 Thess. 4:13–18; Rev. 4:1): Many Bible scholars believe the next great event will be the rapture of the church, though some place this later in the tribulation or at the end. The word *rapture* (Greek: *rapturo*) means "caught up" (1 Thess. 4:17). It is referred to as the "blessed hope" (Titus 2:13) and is imminent, or will occur at any moment (Rom. 13:11–12; James 5:7–9). When the last trumpet sounds, Christians will be translated into their resurrection bodies prior to the tribulation period (1 Cor. 15:52–58; 2 Cor. 5:2–4; 1 Thess. 4:16). Christians will not need to endure the tribulation because they are saved from the wrath of God (1 Thess. 5:9; Rev. 3:10),

and furthermore, there is no mention of the church in the tribulation (Jer. 30:4–11; Dan. 8:24–27; Matt. 13:30, 39–42; 2 Thess. 2:1–11; Rev. 4–18).

2. *Judgment seat of Christ* (Rom. 14:10; 1 Cor. 3:9–15; 4:1–5; 9:24–27; 2 Cor. 5:10): Paul taught that every believer will stand before the judgment seat of Christ (*bema*, Rom. 14:10). The purpose is for each person to give account of his or her stewardship on earth (1 Cor. 4:5). Thus, the judgment seat determines the gain or loss of rewards, not of salvation (Rom. 8:1; 1 Cor. 3:9–15).

3. *Marriage of the Lamb* (2 Cor. 11:2; Rev. 19:6–8): The wedding ceremony involves Christ and the church in heaven after the judgment seat. Afterward is the singing of the two songs and Christ, the Lamb, receives the seven sealed scrolls (Rev. 4:1–5:14).

Earthly Activity

1. *Seven-year tribulation* (Dan. 9:24–27; Rev. 4–19): Daniel prophesied that the Antichrist will sign a seven-year peace treaty with Israel (Dan. 9:27), which will signal the start of the tribulation period. The tribulation is broken up into two equal halves of three and a half years.

   a. *First half of the tribulation*: (1) The Jewish temple is rebuilt (Rev. 11:1); (2) a revised Roman Empire emerges (Dan. 2:40–44; 7:7–8, 24); (3) the earth experiences the seven seal judgments and the seven trumpet judgments (read Rev. 6–11:19 for descriptions of the severe desolation); and (4) the 144,000 Jewish evangelists share the gospel.

   b. *Midpoint of the tribulation* (prophetic events mentioned here may not necessarily be confined to this time frame): (1) the Russian-Islamic invasion (Gog and Magog of Ezekiel 38–39) of Israel occurs, but the nations are decimated by God's supernatural power (Dan. 11:40–45); (2) the Antichrist seeks his opening and breaks his covenant with Israel by invading the land (Dan. 11:40–41); (3) the Antichrist desecrates the temple ("abomination of desolation," Dan. 9:27 ESV; see Matt. 24:15; 2 Thess. 2:4; Rev. 13:5); (4) the Antichrist is killed or badly wounded (Dan. 11:45; Rev. 13:3) and seemingly resurrected (Rev. 13:12, 14); (5) Satan delivers massive persecution on Israel (Rev. 12:7–13; 13); and (6) the Antichrist controls the revised Roman Empire (ten-nation confederacy, Dan. 7:24; Rev. 17:12–13).

   c. *Second half of the tribulation*: The remaining "42 months" or "1,260 days" (Rev. 11:2–3) of the "great tribulation" (Matt. 24:21 ESV) or "day of the LORD" (Isa. 2:12 NKJV; Joel 1:15; Zech. 14:1; 1 Thess. 5:2) become the darkest and worst experience, unparalleled in human history (Matt. 24:8, 21, 29; Rev. 6:16). The "labor pain" (1 Thess.

5:3) of the second half increasingly gets worse with the seven bowl judgments (Rev. 15:1–16:21) and the false prophet advancing the mark of the Beast (Rev. 13:11–18) as the Antichrist conquers and rules the world (Dan. 11:42–43; Rev. 13:5, 15–18). The end of the tribulation results in the destruction of Babylon (Rev. 17–18) and the Battle of Armageddon (Rev. 16:16). Christ returns at his second coming and annihilates the armies gathered in Megiddo (Rev. 19:11–16) to establish his millennial kingdom on Mount Zion (Zech. 14:4; Rev. 20:4–6).

2. *Seventy-five-day interval period* (Dan. 12:11–12): There is a seventy-five-day interval between the second coming of Christ (Dan. 12:1–3) and the official start of the millennial kingdom (Ezek. 40–48). This time is necessary to cast the false prophet and the Antichrist into the lake of fire (Rev. 19:20–21), bind Satan in the abyss (Rev. 20:1–3), cleanse the temple (Dan. 12:11; 2 Thess. 2:4), judge Israel and the Gentile nations (Matt. 25:1–46), and resurrect the Old Testament and tribulation saints (Dan. 12:1–3; Rev. 20:4).

3. *Millennial kingdom* (Ps. 2:6; Isa. 2:1–4; 33:5; 35:1–10; Ezek. 48:35; Rev. 20:4–6): With the reign of Christ on earth for a thousand years, there is complete peace throughout the nations, expansion in agricultural wealth in Israel, economic prosperity, longevity of life, and a deliverance from the effects of the fall of man. Christ's reign brings holiness, righteousness, and justice to the world.

4. *Satan's last revolt* (Rev. 20:7–10): Satan is released from the bottomless pit and assembles a massive army to destroy Jesus Christ. But Satan is no match for him and is quickly taken out by fire from heaven and is thrown into the lake of fire with the false prophet and the Antichrist for all eternity (Rev. 20:10).

5. *Great white throne judgment* (Rev. 20:11–15): This is the final judgment for all sinners, both "great and small," who rejected Jesus Christ, and they are thrown into the lake of fire (Rev. 20:12–15).

6. *New heaven and new earth* (Rev. 21–22): The present world, or *old creation*, passes away (Isa. 34:4; Matt. 24:35; 2 Pet. 3:10–12; Rev. 21:1) and the new heaven and new earth (Isa. 65:17; 66:22) are established for all eternity where the righteous dwell (2 Pet. 3:13).

7. *New Jerusalem* (Rev. 21:10–22:5): The New Jerusalem is the capital of the new heaven and new earth and is a place where the glory of God shines forth forever and ever (Rev. 21:11, 23).

Application

What a blessing it is to have this kind of insight into the future! God has revealed these future events to his children so that they remain pure and expand the kingdom of God until Christ returns.

Bible References

Daniel 9:24–27; Matthew 24–25; Mark 13; Luke 21; 1 Thessalonians 4:13–18; Revelation 4–22

Books

Every Prophecy of the Bible: Clear Explanations for Uncertain Times, by John Walvoord

The End Times in Chronological Order: A Complete Overview to Understanding Bible Prophecy, by Ron Rhodes

The End: A Complete Overview of Bible Prophecy and the End of Days, by Mark Hitchcock

Things to Come, by J. Dwight Pentecost

Website

"Biblical Prophecy-Eschatology," Always Be Ready Ministry, http://www.alwaysbeready.com/prophecy-eschatology

DVD

The End Times: In the Words of Jesus, Questar

Online Video

Jason Jimenez, "What's Going to Happen in the End Times?," The One Minute Apologist, http://www.oneminuteapologist.com/searchpage#end-times

56 Who Is the Antichrist?

Answer

In the popular fiction series Left Behind, Tim LaHaye and Jerry Jenkins cast the Antichrist as Nicolae Jetty Carpathia—a former president of Romania who becomes the Supreme Potentate of the Global Community.

Antichrist
The little horn—Daniel 7:8
The king—Daniel 11:36
The man of lawless-ness—2 Thessalonians 2:3 ESV
The wicked one—2 Thessalonians 2:8 KJV
The beast—Revelation 11:7; 13:1, 2, 6

The Left Behind series is, of course, made up of fictitious novels that attempt to imagine what the Antichrist will be like. No one knows for sure *who* the Antichrist will be, but there is information about what *kind of person* he will be.

Although the Bible doesn't directly give the title "Antichrist," it does capture his deceptive agenda on earth as the "false Christ." John announces, "Every spirit that does not acknowledge Jesus is not from God. This is the spirit of the antichrist, which you have heard is coming and even now is already in the world" (1 John 4:3).

Several passages of Scripture reveal characteristics of the Antichrist:

He will be a brilliant person (Dan. 8:3).

He will be a blasphemer (Dan. 11:36; 2 Thess. 2:4; Rev. 13:6).

He will be a political genius (Rev. 17:11–12).

He will be extremely wealthy (Dan. 11:43; Rev. 13:16–17).

He will be a military mastermind (Rev. 6:2; 13:2).

He will be able to perform special signs and wonders (Matt. 24:24; 2 Thess. 2:9).

He will be possessed by Satan (Rev. 13:2–5).

He will arise from the reunited Roman Empire (Dan. 7:8; 9:26).

As you can see, the Antichrist will be an extraordinary figure in the future. No wonder it will be the Antichrist who signs a peace treaty with Israel (Dan. 9:27), leads the whole world to worship and obey him (Rev. 13:3), subdues three nations and takes control of the ten-nation confederacy (Dan. 7:24; Rev. 17:12–13), and gathers the nations to fight against Israel in the Battle of Armageddon (Rev. 16:16; 19:19). In the end, however, he will be destroyed in the lake of fire (Rev. 20:10).

Application

Be encouraged that Christians are not looking for the *rise* of the Antichrist but for the *return* of Jesus Christ. Your hope is not in a false savior but is grounded in the true and living Savior!

Bible References

Daniel 7:8; 8:3; 9:26; 11:36; Matthew 24:24; 2 Thessalonians 2:4, 9; Revelation 13:1–6; 17:11–12

Books

Unmasking the Antichrist: Dispelling the Myths, Discovering the Truth, by Ron Rhodes
Who Is the Antichrist? Answering the Question Everyone Is Asking, by Mark Hitchcock

Website

Ron Rhodes, "Is the Antichrist Alive Today?," excerpt from *Unmasking the Antichrist*, Dallas Theological Seminary, http://www.dts.edu/read/is-the-antichrist-alive-today-rhodes-ron

DVD

The Antichrist Is Coming, David Jeremiah

Online Video

Norman L. Geisler, "Who Is the Antichrist?," The One Minute Apologist, http://www.one minuteapologist.com/searchpage#antichrist

57 Will Christians Face the Great White Throne Judgment?

Answer

The writer of Hebrews aptly warns, "People are destined to die once, and after that to face judgment" (9:27). So it's not a matter of whether a person will be judged but what kind of judgment a person will receive.

According to the Bible, there are different kinds of judgments. In fact, the word *judgment* appears over 260 times in the Bible. Thus, it's safe to say judgment is a very serious matter.

In regard to Christians, they will face the judgment seat of Christ (2 Cor. 5:10), not the great white throne. This will occur immediately following the rapture of the church. It's important to point out that the judgment seat (*bema*) has nothing to do with sin but with the giving of rewards based on the faithful stewardship of the Christian (Rom. 14:10; 1 Cor. 4:5; 2 Cor. 5:9–10).

Unbelievers (those who rejected the gospel), however, will face the great white throne judgment at the end of the millennium and before the eternal state (Rev. 20:11–15). Jesus Christ is the Judge who presides over this final judgment before ushering in the new heaven and new earth (Matt. 19:28; 25:31; John 5:22; Acts 17:31; Rom. 2:5–6; 2 Thess. 1:8–9). Daniel provides this amazing account:

> As I looked, thrones were set in place, and the Ancient of Days took his seat. His clothing was as white as snow; the hair of his head was white like wool. His throne was flaming with fire, and its wheels were all ablaze. A river of fire was flowing, coming out from before him. Thousands upon thousands attended him; ten thousand times ten thousand stood before him. The court was seated, and the books were opened.
>
> Daniel 7:9–10

Graphic words are used to describe where these people come from in order to be judged. John mentions the "sea" and "death and Hades" (Rev. 20:13). The Bible emphatically states that people without Christ are "dead in [their] trespasses and sins" (Eph. 2:1 ESV). Therefore, the unbelievers go to Hades (a place of torment, Luke 16:18–31) after they die and await their final judgment at the great white throne before they are cast into the lake of fire (Matt. 25:41; Rev. 19:20; 20:10, 14–15). The lake of fire is also referred to as "the lake of burning sulfur" (Rev. 19:20; 20:10). It is where the Beast, the false prophet, Satan at his last rebellion, death, Hades, and all those whose names are not found in the Book of Life will be cast. The lake of fire is also called "the second death" (Rev. 20:14) because it is the final destination of the wicked. It is also referred to as the final resurrection because the first resurrection has to do with the righteous (Dan. 12:2; John 5:29; Acts 24:15).

Though the great white throne judgment graphically portrays the reality of the second death, the truth of the matter is that the people who are thrown into the lake of fire *freely* rejected the *free* gift of salvation. The great white throne judgment is such an important part of the chronological sequence of events because it finalizes the end of sin.

Therefore, *believers* will appear before the *judgment seat of Christ* for rewards for service in this life, and *unbelievers* will stand before Christ at the *great white throne judgment* for the pronouncement of their eternal doom.

Application

Paul proclaimed that God "has set a day when he will judge the world with justice by the man he has appointed" (Acts 17:31). Hence, live your life as a good steward, making sure you're not storing up a pile of wood, hay, and stubble that will be burned up at the judgment seat of Christ (1 Cor. 3:9–15).

Bible References

Romans 14:10; 1 Corinthians 3:9–15; 4:5; 2 Corinthians 5:9–10; Hebrews 9:27

Books

The End Times in Chronological Order: A Complete Overview to Understanding Bible Prophecy, by Ron Rhodes

Your Eternal Reward: Triumph and Tears at the Judgment Seat of Christ, by Erwin Lutzer

Facing Your Final Job Review: The Judgment Seat of Christ, Salvation, and Eternal Rewards, by Woodrow Kroll

Website

"Great White Throne Judgment," Rapture Ready, http://www.raptureready.com/abc/great_white_throne.html

DVD

The Judgment Seat of Christ: Your Eternal Rewards, John Ankerberg Show

Online Video

Norman L. Geisler, "Will Christians Face the Great White Throne Judgment?," The One Minute Apologist, http://www.oneminuteapologist.com/searchpage#great-white-throne -judgment

58 What Is the Millennial Kingdom?

Answer

The word *millennium* comes from a Latin term that means "a thousand years," and it is mentioned six times in Revelation 20:1–6. There are several titles for the millennium:

- "the world to come" (Heb. 2:5)
- "the kingdom of heaven" (Matt. 5:10)
- "the kingdom of God" (Mark 1:15)
- "the last day" (John 6:40)
- "the regeneration" (Matt. 19:28 NKJV)

The millennium (or millennial kingdom) is the earthly, physical, and political reign of Christ on earth for a thousand years. He will rule over the whole world from Jerusalem with his apostles and disciples serving him.

In Isaiah, the millennium is described as being in the "mountain of the LORD's temple" (2:2). This is a direct reference to the millennial temple that will exist during the reign of Christ according to Ezekiel 40–43. The millennial temple will be built in Jerusalem and will act as the governmental and political enterprise of Christ's power on earth. The significance of the temple mount in Jerusalem is a major theme of Isaiah's book because of the major prophetic implications it has in the future (Isa. 11:9; 25:6–7; 27:13; 30:29; 56:7; 57:13; 65:11, 25; 66:20). The millennium will be a time of universal peace among all nations and perfect union within the animal kingdom (Isa. 11:1–9; 65:25). It will be a time when the whole world will be "filled with the knowledge of the LORD as the waters cover the sea" (Isa. 11:9; see Jer. 31:33–34).

During the millennium, climatic and geographical changes will enrich the agricultural land (Isa. 35:1–10; Amos 9:13–14), frequent healings of the sick will occur (Isa. 29:18; 33:24; 61:1–2), extended life spans will be more prevalent (Isa. 65:20), and a renewed sense of joy will fill the hearts of Israel (Jer. 31:12–14) while the holiness of the Lord is manifested among his people (Ezek. 40–44; Dan. 7:13–14; Zech. 14:16–19).

Furthermore, no unsaved person will be allowed to enter the millennium (Isa. 35:4; Jer. 31:33–34; Ezek. 20:37; Matt. 25:30, 46). Only the saved will enter the millennium and will repopulate the earth with children who will be raised under the physical rule and reign of Christ. We are told in Isaiah 11:4 and 65:20 (ESV), however, that sin will still be prevalent on the earth, and those who once followed God will later refuse to go up to Jerusalem to worship the Lord (Zech. 14:17–19).

Application

Humans attempt to rule the world with an iron fist, but Jesus Christ will rule the world with his splendor and glory. Don't set your eyes on the kingdom of humans but instead on the millennial reign of Christ. Paul proclaimed boldly that the day will come when "at the name of Jesus every knee should bow, in heaven and on earth and under the earth, and every tongue confess that Jesus Christ is Lord, to the glory of God the Father" (Phil. 2:10–11 ESV).

Bible References

Isaiah 35:4; Jeremiah 31:33–34; Ezekiel 20:37; 40–44; Daniel 7:13–14; Amos 9:13–14; Zechariah 14:16–19; Matthew 25:30, 46; Revelation 20:1–6

Books

Revelation, by John Walvoord

The Millennium, by John Walvoord

The End Times in Chronological Order: A Complete Overview to Understanding Bible Prophecy, by Ron Rhodes

Things to Come, by J. Dwight Pentecost

Website

John Walvoord, "The Prophetic Context of the Millennium," Bible.org, https://bible.org/series/prophetic-context-millennium

DVD

What on Earth Is the Millennium?, David Jeremiah

Online Video

Norman L. Geisler, "What Is the Millennial Kingdom?," The One Minute Apologist, http://www.oneminuteapologist.com/searchpage#what-is-the-millennial-kingdom

59 What Is the New Heaven and New Earth?

Answer

Do you recall experiencing Disneyland for the very first time? Remember how mesmerizing it was to enter the happiest place on earth?

Stepping into Disneyland is like entering a fantasy world—an enchanted place made up of theme parks with loveable cartoon characters, fun rides, and all the delicious treats you can get your hands on. "It's a Small World After All" plays joyously in the background as you explore Pirates of the Caribbean and adventure out on Splash Mountain.

But as charming as Disneyland is, it pales in comparison to what the new heaven and new earth will be like.

According to the Bible, the current heaven and earth will be destroyed (Isa. 34:4; Matt. 24:35; 2 Pet. 3:10–12; Rev. 21:1), and God will consummate the new heaven and new earth (Isa. 65:17; 66:22), where the righteous will dwell with him for all eternity (2 Pet. 3:13; Rev. 21:1). John offers an amazing description of the new heaven and new earth in Revelation 21–22.

In Revelation 21:5, Jesus declares, "I am making everything new!" God promises in Isaiah 65:17, "See, I will create new heavens and a new earth. The former things will not be remembered, nor will they come to mind." The new heaven and new earth will merge and no longer be two separate realms. Therefore, the eternal state of the new heaven and new earth will be a shared experience of absolute perfection bathed in the glory and splendor of God. This is where the redeemed will spend eternity (Heb. 12:22–24).

It's hard to imagine a day when sin and evil will be completely wiped away. Try to imagine a place where you feel no sorrow and experience no pain and

167

where you never again have to face worry of any sort. It is truly mind-boggling! But this will all be true when the day comes when all believers enter the new heaven and new earth.

Application

Soon will be the day when there will be no more sin, sorrow, or death (Rev. 21:4). What hope you have in knowing that Jesus will make all things new someday (Rev. 21:5).

Bible References

Isaiah 34:4; 65:17; 66:22; Matthew 24:35; 2 Peter 3:10–13; Revelation 21:1, 5

Books

Revelation, by John Walvoord

The End Times in Chronological Order: A Complete Overview to Understanding Bible Prophecy, by Ron Rhodes

Things to Come, by J. Dwight Pentecost

Website

"The New Heaven and the New Earth," Bible.org, https://bible.org/seriespage/21-new-heaven -and-new-earth

DVD

The New Heaven and the New Earth, David Jeremiah

Online Video

Norman L. Geisler, "What Is the New Heaven and New Earth?," The One Minute Apologist, http://www.oneminuteapologist.com/searchpage#new-heaven-and-new-earth

PART 8

Questions about the Christian Life

60 How Can I Overcome Sin in My Life?

Answer

Temptation is always lurking. The moment you resist temptation in one area of your life, it comes knocking somewhere else. All it takes is one small slipup, and before you know it, the temptation has given rise to major sin in your life. James writes, "Each person is tempted when they are dragged away by their own evil desire and enticed. Then, after desire has conceived, it gives birth to sin; and sin, when it is full-grown, gives birth to death" (1:14–15). *Sin* is falling short of God's holy standards. There is the sin of *commission* (doing things we shouldn't do, Rom. 7:14–20) and the sin of *omission* (not doing the things we should do, James 4:17). Yet despite the challenges of temptation, there's hope and freedom in Jesus Christ.

So what does a Christian have to do to ensure freedom from sin? The first thing is to confess the *desire* to sin in the first place. Paul contends, "So I say, walk by the Spirit, and you will not gratify the desires of the sinful nature" (Gal. 5:16). Elsewhere Paul writes, "Clothe yourselves with the Lord Jesus Christ, and do not think about how to gratify the desires of the flesh" (Rom. 13:14). If you keep making it a habit to clothe yourself with Christ and be filled with the Holy Spirit (Eph. 5:18), you will live a more holy life. But if your desire is to sin, then sin will overcome you—not the other way around.

Furthermore, as a Christian, you have to realize that you are no longer a slave to sin. Paul writes, "I have been crucified with Christ and I no longer live, but Christ lives in me" (Gal. 2:20). A life that has been crucified with Christ is a free and victorious life. It is not a life that is overcome by evil but a life that overcomes evil with good (Rom. 12:21). Paul described a Christian life as *putting off the old self* and *putting on the new self* (see Eph. 4:17–28). That's why Paul is able to say it's no longer about him (old self is dead) but about his new self (new life in Christ).

The following Scripture passages point out how you can daily overcome sin in your life and train to be godly:

1. Glorify God in all things (1 Cor. 10:31).
2. Ask for the continual filling of the Holy Spirit (Eph. 5:18).
3. Devote your life to daily prayer (Col. 4:2; 1 Thess. 5:17).
4. Grow in the Word of God (2 Tim. 3:16–17; Heb. 4:12).
5. Remain obedient and pure (Rom. 16:19; 1 Tim. 6:11).
6. Evangelize the lost (Matt. 28:19–20).
7. Do good works (Titus 3:8).
8. Advance your spiritual gifts to minister to others (1 Pet. 4:10–11).
9. Stay involved in church (Heb. 10:25).
10. Faithfully await the return of Christ (Titus 2:13).

Application

God will never allow you to face more temptation than you are able to handle (1 Cor. 10:13). Not only has God the Father chosen you to be holy and blameless, but Christ has also redeemed you, and you have been sealed and filled with the Holy Spirit. Thus, receive the promises of God (Heb. 10:35–36) and persevere so that sin will not have a grip on you.

Bible References

Romans 7:14–20; 8:1–17; 13:14; 1 Corinthians 10:13; Galatians 5; James 1:14–15; 4:17; 1 John 3:4–6

Books

Every Man's Battle: Winning the War on Sexual Temptation One Victory at a Time, by Stephen Arterburn, Fred Stoeker, and Mike Yorkey

Respectable Sins: Confronting the Sins We Tolerate, by Jerry Bridges

Cultivating Purity in an Impure World, by Charles Swindoll

Website

Rick Thomas, "3 Ways to Overcome Temptation, Sin, and Sin Patterns," Biblical Counseling Coalition, http://biblicalcounselingcoalition.org/blogs/2013/03/21/3-ways-to-overcome
-temptation-sin-and-sin-patterns

DVD

Gods at War, Kyle Idleman

Online Video

Bobby Conway, "How Do I Overcome Sin?," The One Minute Apologist, http://www.one minuteapologist.com/searchpage#overcome-sin

61 How Can I Grow in My Faith?

Answer

Peter said, "Like newborn babies, crave pure spiritual milk [Word of God], so that by it you may grow up in your salvation" (1 Pet. 2:2). This kind of dependency, however, takes faith and a commitment to want to grow in faith. The Bible makes it clear that it's impossible to please God without faith (Heb. 11:6), and faith is necessary to believe in God (Gen. 15:6) and to receive salvation (Eph. 2:8–9). Paul instructs, "Faith comes from hearing the message, and the message is heard through the word about Christ" (Rom. 10:17). Thus, to grow in your faith you must read, study, and live out the Word of God in your life (Josh. 1:8–9; Ps. 1; James 1:22–25). There is absolutely nothing more important.

God also allows certain trials and tribulations in order to grow your faith (James 1:2–3; 1 Pet. 4:12–13). Peter provides this answer for trials: "These have come so that the proven genuineness of your faith—of greater worth than gold, which perishes even though refined by fire—may result in praise, glory and honor when Jesus Christ is revealed" (1 Pet. 1:7). James says that the "testing of your faith develops perseverance" (1:3).

Inevitably, as you study the Word of God and persevere through various trials, your faith will develop certain qualities. The apostle Peter writes, "For this very reason, make every effort to add to your faith goodness; and to goodness, knowledge; and to knowledge, self-control; and to self-control, perseverance; and to perseverance, godliness; and to godliness, mutual affection; and to mutual affection, love" (2 Pet. 1:5–7). A Christian who doesn't add these qualities to his or her faith is considered "ineffective," "unproductive," "nearsighted," and "blind" (2 Pet. 1:8–9).

Moreover, stay in constant communication with God. Always pray and ask that he will "fill you with the knowledge of his will through all spiritual wisdom and understanding" (Col. 1:9). Paul's prayer points out great truths that will help you grow in your faith. The first is to be filled with the *knowledge of God's will*—that is, to have a completeness and a deep understanding of the Word of God and to walk in obedience to it. The second is to grow in *spiritual wisdom*, which means to live out your life with good judgment and discernment. And third, Paul prays for *spiritual understanding*, which has to do with making good decisions in day-to-day life.

Finally, as you communicate with God, pray that your life is an example of Christ to others. There is no greater exercise of faith than to love others (1 Cor. 13:2). Paul encourages, "Be devoted to one another in love. Honor one another above yourselves" (Rom. 12:10).

Application

Be reminded of Paul's advice: "But as you excel in everything—in faith, in speech, in knowledge, in all earnestness, and in our love for you—see that you excel in this act of grace also" (2 Cor. 8:7 ESV). God desires to see you excel in your faith, speech, and knowledge so that your great witness can impact others.

Bible References

Matthew 13:23; Romans 10:17; 12:9–21; Ephesians 5:18; 6:10–19; Colossians 1:9–14; James 1:2–3; 1 Peter 4:12–13; 2 Peter 1:3–15

Books

Growing Your Faith: How to Mature in Christ, by Jerry Bridges

What Every Christian Ought to Know: Essential Truths for Growing Your Faith, by Adrian Rogers

Conformed to His Image: Biblical and Practical Approaches to Spiritual Formation, by Ken Boa

Website

"10 Ideas: Reflecting the Fruit of the Spirit," Family Life, http://www.familylife.com/articles/topics/faith/essentials/growing-in-your-faith/10-ideas-reflecting-the-fruit-of-the-spirit#.U44DwpRdUX4

DVD

Five Things God Uses to Grow Your Faith, Andy Stanley

Online Video

Jason Jimenez, "How Do I Grow in My Faith?," The One Minute Apologist, http://www.oneminuteapologist.com/searchpage#grow-in-my-faith

62 What Is the Great Commission?

Answer

Jesus called the eleven disciples to meet him in Galilee at the Mount of Olives (Matt. 28:16). It was Jesus's farewell and final commissioning of his disciples before ascending into heaven (Luke 24:51; Acts 1:9). In what is known as the *Great Commission*, he said to them:

> All authority in heaven and on earth has been given to me. Therefore go and make disciples of all nations, baptizing them in the name of the Father and of the Son and of the Holy Spirit, and teaching them to obey everything I have commanded you. And surely I am with you always, to the very end of the age.
>
> Matthew 28:18–20

The message of the Great Commission is one of "repentance and forgiveness of sins" (Luke 24:47), and it is given in the authority of Jesus Christ (Matt. 28:18) and in the power of the Holy Spirit (Acts 1:8). But the Great Commission is more than an evangelistic call to action. Jesus gave the command to "make disciples" (Matt. 28:19). This imperative to make disciples is a command to "go into all the world and preach the gospel to all creation" (Mark 16:15) and to *baptize* and *teach* disciples to follow and obey Jesus Christ.

Thus, to fulfill the Great Commission, Christians must invest time and resources in making disciples of Christ (Heb. 5:12–14)—not just winning souls.

Application

Your responsibility is to make disciples whenever and wherever you go. So the challenge before you is this: Are you doing so?

Bible References

Matthew 28:19–20; Mark 16:15; Luke 24:46–47; Acts 1:8

Books

The Complete Evangelism Guidebook: Expert Advice on Reaching Others for Christ, Scott Dawson, editor

Finding Common Ground: How to Communicate with Those outside the Christian Community . . . While We Still Can, by Tim Downs

The Great Commission: Evangelicals and the History of World Missions, Martin Klauber and Scott M. Manetsch, editors

Website

"The What and Why of the Great Commission," Campus Crusade for Christ, http://www.cru .org/training-and-growth/classics/transferable-concepts/help-fulfill-the-great-commission /03-what-and-why-of-great-commission.htm

DVD

Great Souls: Billy Graham, Tom Ivy and William Paul McKay

Online Video

Bobby Conway, "What Is the Great Commission?," The One Minute Apologist, http://www. oneminuteapologist.com/searchpage#great-commission

63 How Do I Share My Faith?

Answer

There are three main reasons why Christians don't share their faith: (1) fear, (2) ignorance, and (3) rejection. Christians are afraid to speak up because they don't want to be embarrassed by not having the right answers or being rejected by a friend or family member. It boils down to this: *for most Christians, sharing their faith is a risk they are unwilling to take.*

Sound anything like you? If so, please don't let your excuses prevent you from sharing your faith. God has placed you in many lives at work, at school, in your neighborhood, and in your family, and these people need to hear and see the gospel of Jesus Christ. But as long as you don't take the risk to share your faith, they never will.

Can you imagine how many opportunities you have turned down? Or how many souls you have neglected to reach with the gospel?

Jesus gave the mandate to "go and make disciples" (Matt. 28:19). Doing so takes obedience and action on your part to reach people with the truth of the gospel. But as mentioned above, you have to overcome your fears and assumptions and trust the Holy Spirit to empower you (Acts 1:8). Jesus offers these encouraging words: "Do not be anxious about how you should defend yourself or what you should say, for the Holy Spirit will teach you in that very hour what you ought to say" (Luke 12:11–12 ESV). Isn't that comforting to know?

The point is that you don't have to know all the answers to share your faith. But you do have to make sure your conversation conveys truth and is done in love (2 Cor. 2:1–5). Paul writes, "Be wise in the way you act toward outsiders; make the most of every opportunity. Let your conversation be always full of grace, seasoned with salt, so that you may know how to answer everyone" (Col. 4:5–6).

Furthermore, it's not for you to decide *when* and with *whom* to share your faith. Nor is it right for you to assume how a person will respond. This is up to God, not you. All you need to do is have faith in him and trust him to provide a perfect opportunity to share Christ with someone.

When you do get the chance to share Christ with someone and he or she rejects the gospel, it's not your problem to worry about or fix. The person's issue is not with you but with Jesus (John 15:18). Jesus said, "The one who hears you hears me, and the one who rejects you rejects me, and the one who rejects me rejects him who sent me" (Luke 10:16 ESV). In the end, the important thing is not your reputation or the relationship you seek to keep. Trust in the Lord and take risks that will reap eternal rewards in heaven.

Here are some tips for sharing your faith:

1. Pray for opportunities to share your faith.
2. Be open and ready to share your faith.
3. Spark conversations.
4. Ask a lot of questions.
5. Remain attentive.
6. Navigate conversations toward spiritual matters.
7. Share your testimony.
8. Quote the Bible (Romans Road: Rom. 1:16; 2:14–15; 3:23–24; 6:23; 7:24–25; 8:1; 10:9–10; 13:14).
9. Offer an invitation to receive Jesus Christ as personal Lord and Savior.
10. Lead them in a salvation prayer.

11. Help plug them into a church.
12. Follow up in discipleship.

Application

It's easy to sit back and not engage the world for Christ. Sharing your faith isn't easy, but it is certainly the most rewarding thing you can do while on earth. Your decision to share or not share the gospel has eternal consequences. The Bible says, "If you suffer as a Christian, do not be ashamed, but praise God that you bear that name. For it is time for judgment to begin with God's household; and if it begins with us, what will the outcome be for those who do not obey the gospel of God?" (1 Pet. 4:16–17).

So what's it going to be? Are you willing to trust the Holy Spirit to empower you to share the gospel?

Bible References

Matthew 28:19–20; Acts 1:8; Colossians 4:5–6; 1 Peter 3:15; Jude 3

Books

The Complete Evangelism Guidebook: Expert Advice on Reaching Others for Christ, Scott Dawson, editor

Conversational Evangelism, by David Geisler and Norman L. Geisler

Dare 2 Share: A Field Guide to Sharing Your Faith, by Greg Stier

Website

"Sharing Your Faith with Family and Friends," Billy Graham Evangelistic Association, http://billygraham.org/decision-magazine/may-2010/sharing-your-faith-with-family-and-friends/

DVD

How to Share the Gospel: The Ray Comfort Collection

Online Video

Mark Mittelberg, "What Are Some Tips for Sharing the Gospel?," The One Minute Apologist, http://www.oneminuteapologist.com/searchpage#tips-for-sharing-the-gospel

64 How Can I Defend My Faith against Attacks?

Answer

The world is certainly becoming more hostile toward Christianity, which means that Christians need to be more prepared and ready to defend themselves against such attacks.

Peter championed the persecuted church:

> In your hearts revere Christ as Lord. Always be prepared to give an answer [*apologia*] to everyone who asks you to give the reason for the hope that you have. But do this with gentleness and respect, keeping a clear conscience, so that those who speak maliciously against your good behavior in Christ may be ashamed of their slander.
>
> 1 Peter 3:15–16

The word *apologetics* comes from the Greek word *apologia*, which conveys the idea of a person attempting to provide legitimate facts to exonerate the falsely accused (in this case, Christianity). You can break up the word *apologia* into two parts: *apo* ("away") and *logia* ("speech"), meaning "to speak away" an accusation (Acts 22:1; 25:8, 16; 1 Cor. 9:3; 2 Cor. 7:11; Phil. 1:7, 16; 2 Tim. 4:16; 1 Pet. 3:15–16). Thus, apologetics is giving a verbal defense for the Christian faith.

Defending the faith, however, is not always about winning an argument. Apologetics is effective when the character of the apologist does not *contradict* but rather *complements* the clear teachings of the Bible. The aim is to offer a reasonable defense of Christianity and to give an opportunity for people to receive Jesus Christ as Lord and Savior. It's not about setting up barriers between you and a skeptic; it's about removing any obstacles people may have regarding Christ.

Application

To be a fervent defender of the faith, you must follow the acrostic APOLOGIST:

"Always being prepared to make a defense" (1 Pet. 3:15 ESV).
"Put on the Lord Jesus Christ" (Rom. 13:14 ESV).

"Obey God rather than man" (Acts 5:29 ESV).

"Let love be without hypocrisy" (Rom. 12:9 NKJV).

"Obedient in all things" (2 Cor. 2:9 NKJV).

"Give thanks to God always" (2 Thess. 2:13 NKJV).

"Imitators of God" (Eph. 5:1 ESV).

"Speaking the truth in love" (Eph. 4:15).

"Test all things; hold fast to what is good" (1 Thess. 5:21 NKJV).

Bible References

Acts 22:1; 25:8, 16; 1 Corinthians 9:3; 2 Corinthians 7:11; Philippians 1:7, 16; Colossians 4:5–6; 2 Timothy 4:16; 1 Peter 3:15–16

Books

Tactics: A Game Plan for Discussing Your Christian Convictions, by Greg Koukl

Cold-Case Christianity: A Homicide Detective Investigates the Claims of the Gospels, by J. Warner Wallace

Confident Faith: Building a Firm Foundation for Your Beliefs, by Mark Mittelberg

Website

Norman L. Geisler, "The Need for Apologetics," BeThinking, http://www.bethinking.org/apologetics/the-need-for-apologetics

DVD

Foundations of Apologetics, Ravi Zacharias International Ministries

Online Videos

Bobby Conway, "What Is Apologetics?," "Why Is Apologetics Important?," and "Why Is Apologetics Important Now More Than Ever?," The One Minute Apologist, http://www.oneminuteapologist.com/searchpage#what-is-apologetics

65 Why Does God Allow Trials in My Life?

Answer

We don't know the mind of God, so it's challenging to understand why certain tragedies befall some and not others. That makes it tricky to answer such a difficult question.

The reality is that trials come upon everyone. No person is good enough to be above trials. Just take Job, for example. He was the most righteous man, and yet he lost everything in life. What did he do to deserve this? Nothing.

That's the point. You need to come to expect trials, not avoid them. James forewarns, "Consider it pure joy, my brothers and sisters, whenever you face trials of many kinds, because you know that the testing of your faith produces perseverance. Let perseverance finish its work so that you may be mature and complete, not lacking anything" (1:3–4). Rather than being outraged *over the trials*, we need to have an attitude of joy *in the midst of trials.*

Though *answers* are not always well-defined in the midst of trials, the *purposes* of trials are always clear. According to James, trials essentially have four benefits: (1) testing, (2) developing perseverance, (3) leading to maturity and completeness, so that (4) you lack nothing. It is only the purifying effect of trials that can produce good qualities in your life (Luke 8:15; Rom. 8:25). Paul lists these qualities: "suffering produces perseverance; perseverance, character; and character, hope" (Rom. 5:3–4). Paul indeed was familiar with trials in his life (Acts 20:19; 2 Cor. 6:3–13), so he is considered an expert in this field.

Likewise, Peter affirms:

In all this you greatly rejoice, though now for a little while you may have had to suffer grief in all kinds of trials. These have come so that the proven genuineness of your faith—of greater worth than gold, which perishes even though refined by fire—may result in praise, glory and honor when Jesus Christ is revealed.

1 Peter 1:6–7

Later he writes:

> Dear friends, do not be surprised at the fiery ordeal that has come to test you, as though something strange were happening to you. But rejoice inasmuch as you participate in the sufferings of Christ, so that you may be overjoyed when his glory is revealed.
>
> 1 Peter 4:12–13

Peter makes it clear that even as you grieve during various trials you are to rejoice in the midst of them. He further adds that the trials are meant to refine your faith. That's the amazing thing about trials: no one likes to go through them, but sometimes trials are the only way to make you more like Jesus. Indeed, trials have a way of revealing a deeper understanding of the sufferings of Jesus while filling your heart with joy and praise.

Application

Trials are necessary to refine your faith and keep you humble and expectant until the return of Christ. Therefore, rejoice in the participation of Christ's sufferings, because if you "remain steadfast under trial," you will "receive the crown of life" (James 1:12 ESV).

Bible References

John 16:33; Romans 5:2–5; 8:28; 12:22; 1 Peter 1:6–7; 4:12–13; James 1:3–4, 12

Books

The Problem of Pain, by C. S. Lewis
Our Ultimate Refuge: Job and the Problem of Suffering, by Oswald Chambers
The Goodness of God: Assurance of Purpose in the Midst of Suffering, by Randy Alcorn
If God, Why Evil?, by Norman L. Geisler

Website

Michael Youssef, "The Blessings of Trials," Crosswalk.com, http://www.crosswalk.com/faith/spiritual-life/the-blessings-of-trials-1327677.html

DVD

When Life Is Hard, James MacDonald

Online Video

Jason Jimenez, "Why Does God Allow Trials in Our Life?," The One Minute Apologist, http://www.oneminuteapologist.com/searchpage#trials

66 How Can I Forgive Someone Who Has Hurt Me Deeply?

Answer

There's not a single person alive who hasn't been hurt. Many people walk through life wounded and haunted by the memories of battered, broken relationships. Through years of ministry, we each have counseled many Christians who can't seem to forgive others for the pain they intentionally or unintentionally caused.

Forgiving someone is the most difficult thing for any human to do. But forgiveness sets the captive free and brings with it immense healing to the heart and soul. Paul put it like this: "Be kind and compassionate to one another, forgiving each other, just as in Christ God forgave you" (Eph. 4:32).

The truth is that no one can forgive in his or her own strength. If you plan to forgive others, you first must experience the forgiveness of God through the death and resurrection of Jesus Christ (Eph. 1:7; Col. 1:14). Forgiveness is not a *natural* act that springs from the human condition; it is a *supernatural* act that comes from Jesus Christ. It is not until you experience the unconditional love and forgiveness of Christ that you will be able to forgive whatever grievances you may have with unkind people (Col. 3:13). Your motive is not to seek revenge but to obey God's commandments and "live at peace with everyone" (Rom. 12:18–19; see John 14:15).

Jesus presented a compelling case about forgiveness in the Sermon on the Mount: "So if you are offering your gift at the altar and there remember that your brother has something against you, leave your gift there before the altar and go. First *be reconciled* to your brother, and then come and offer your gift" (Matt. 5:23–24). The word *reconciled* strongly conveys an immediate response to make peace with the offended person. According to Jesus, it is the duty of both parties to seek reconciliation. Any wrongful act or behavior needs to be dealt with swiftly; otherwise, reconciliation will never be achieved.

Elsewhere Jesus said, "Forgive and you will be forgiven" (Luke 6:37). The word *forgive* (Greek: *apolyo*) literally means "to set free or release." When you forgive someone, you are setting that person free from the wrong he or she committed. Forgiveness doesn't carry a record of wrongs but rather extends favor and comfort, lest that person "be overwhelmed by excessive sorrow" (2 Cor. 2:7). But to forgive, you must be willing to confront the situation with that person. It's not enough to make blanket statements of apology or accept forgiveness in vague terms. Thus, reconciliation is not just about forgiving those who wronged you; it's also about forgiving those who are unwilling to ask for forgiveness.

Peter came to Jesus and asked him, "Lord, how many times shall I forgive my brother or sister who sins against me? Up to seven times?" (Matt. 18:21). Jesus's response to Peter contained no limit to forgiveness. He gave an example of the unmerciful servant who was forgiven of his massive debt and yet refused to forgive the person who owed him pennies in comparison (Matt. 18:21–35).

The bottom line is that if you don't forgive others for their sins, neither will your heavenly Father forgive you for your sins (see Mark 11:25–26). If you are a follower of Christ, your love will be reflected in how you forgive others (1 Cor. 13:5; 1 John 3:10–17).

Application

1. Confess your sin daily before God (1 John 1:9).
2. Confess any wrongdoing to others (James 5:16).
3. Live free from the guilt of your sin (Ps. 32; Rom. 3:24–25).
4. Don't keep a record of wrongs (1 Cor. 13:5; Phil. 4:8).
5. Avoid retaliating and getting even (Rom. 12:19).
6. Seek to forgive and restore relationships (Matt. 6:14–15; 18:21–35).

Bible References

Matthew 5:23–24; 6:14–15; Mark 11:25–26; Luke 6:27, 37; Ephesians 4:32; Colossians 3:13

Books

The Gift of Forgiveness, by Charles Stanley

Forgiveness: Breaking the Power of the Past, by Kay Arthur, David Lawson, and B. J. Lawson

Website

Ed Chinn, "Learning to Forgive Others," Focus on the Family, http://www.focusonthefamily. com/lifechallenges/relationship_challenges/learning_to_forgive_others.aspx

DVD

Forgive Me, David Jeremiah

Online Video

Jason Jimenez, "How Do We Forgive Someone Who's Hurt Us?," The One Minute Apologist, http://www.oneminuteapologist.com/searchpage#forgive-someone

67 Does God Hear My Prayers?

Answer

It's so important for Christians to know that God loves to communicate with his children and that he cherishes their prayers. A great passage in the Old Testament paints a beautiful picture of prayer: "The priests and the Levites stood to bless the people, and *God heard them*, for their *prayer reached heaven*, his holy dwelling place" (2 Chron. 30:27). Similarly, while Jonah was in the belly of the whale, he prayed, "When my life was fainting away, I remembered the Lord, and my prayer *came to you, into your holy temple*" (Jon. 2:7).

As great as this sounds, it's sometimes hard to believe. We often feel more like the prophet Habakkuk when he cried, "How long, O Lord, must I call for help, but you do not listen?" (Hab. 1:2). But the reason most Christians relate more to Habakkuk's plea than to Jonah's prayer is that either they don't know what to ask God or they lack the faith to be persistent in prayer. Any person can ask God for anything. The real test of faith is whether a person will be persistent in prayer for God to answer that prayer (Matt. 26:41). Jesus said, "Until now you have not asked for anything in my name. Ask and you will receive, and your joy will be complete" (John 16:24). This kind of prayer requires the faith not to give up but to keep on asking, seeking, and knocking. Jesus said, "Ask and it will be given to you; seek and you will find; knock and the door will be opened to you. For everyone who *asks receives*; the one who *seeks finds*; and to the one who knocks, the *door will be opened*" (Matt. 7:7–8).

Prayer has to do with the praise of God and the recognition that it's about his plan and will for our lives (Matt. 26:42). There is no place for a selfish will in prayer. John writes, "This is the confidence we have in approaching God: that if we ask anything *according to his will*, he hears us. And if we know that he hears us—whatever we ask—we know that we have what we asked of him" (1 John 5:14–15). Jesus taught his disciples to pray, "Our Father in heaven, hallowed be your name, your kingdom come, *your will be done*, on earth as it is in heaven" (Matt. 6:10–11).

God doesn't give positive answers to boastful prayers (Luke 18:10–14) or prayers disrupted by willful sin (Ps. 66:18). Nor will God answer prayers that lack faith (Heb. 11:6) or that come from a person who is unwilling to submit to his will (Matt. 6:9–10). God will hear only prayers that honor him and will answer only the prayers that honor his will.

Application

God has four answers to our prayers: (1) yes, (2) no, (3) wait, and (4) here is something better! No good parent always says "yes" to his or her child's requests. "No" is just as much an answer as "yes." We are often too impatient to wait, but as with any child, it is sometimes best for us. When it comes to something better, we sometimes miss out because we wrongly think we know what is better than our infinitely loving heavenly Father does.

Thus, devote your life to prayer (Col. 4:2) and believe in faith that you will "receive from him anything [you] ask, because [you] keep his commands and do what pleases him" (1 John 3:22).

Bible References

2 Chronicles 7:14; 30:27; Psalms 34; 86:7; Matthew 7:7–8; John 15:7; 1 John 3:22–23; 5:14–15

Books

The Practice of the Presence of God, by Brother Lawrence
The Autobiography of George Muller, by George Muller
Draw the Circle: The 40 Day Prayer Challenge, by Mark Batterson

Website

"Does God Answer Our Prayers?," EveryStudent.com, http://www.everystudent.com/wires/prayers.html

DVD

The Prayers of Jesus: Six In-Depth Studies Connecting the Bible to Life, Matt Williams, general editor

Online Video

Hank Hanegraaff, "Why Should I Pray If God Already Knows What I Need?," The One Minute Apologist, http://www.oneminuteapologist.com/searchpage#already-knows

68 How Can I Know God's Will for My Life?

Answer

As pastors always say, if I had a dime every time someone asked me this question, I would be rich! The reason this question is among those most asked by Christians is because it seeks to answer why we are here. Everybody longs to have a purpose—to know God's will and fulfill it. Fortunately, the Bible makes it crystal clear what the will of God is for your life.

Jesus listed two of the greatest commandments: (1) love God with your whole being and (2) love your neighbor as yourself (Matt. 22:37–39; Luke 10:27–28). The first answer to the will of God question is to make sure you love God and his people (1 Cor. 13). God rewards a person who loves him and seeks to serve others (Matt. 16:27; Mark 9:41).

Next, there's a difference between the *sovereign will* of God and the *moral will* of God. The *sovereign will* of God is his ultimate and final authority (Ps. 115:3). There is nothing that can prevent or thwart God's sovereign purposes (Job 42:2), and everything God decrees will come to pass as he perfectly wills it to be (Isa. 46:10). For example, God's act of sending Jesus Christ to die for our sins was part of his sovereign will (Acts 2:23; Gal. 1:4).

The *moral will* of God is about his children living a holy and pure life according to his standards. Listed below are numerous passages of Scripture that lay this out:

> It is God's will that you should be sanctified: that you should avoid sexual immorality.
>
> 1 Thessalonians 4:3

> Offer your bodies as a living sacrifice, holy and pleasing to God—this is your true and proper worship. Do not conform to the pattern of this world, but be transformed by the renewing of your mind. Then you will be able to test and approve what God's will is—his good, pleasing and perfect will.
>
> Romans 12:1–2

> You may live a life worthy of the Lord and please him in every way: bearing fruit in every good work, growing in the knowledge of God.
>
> Colossians 1:10

> Give thanks in all circumstances; for this is God's will for you in Christ Jesus.
>
> 1 Thessalonians 5:18

As for God's *particular will* for your life—such as where to go to school, what occupation to pursue, and whom to marry—the Bible gives only general guidance. For example, you should only marry "in the Lord" (1 Cor. 7:39 ESV). Further, God's will is for you not to live a foolish life but to be wise in taking every opportunity to serve God and others (Eph. 5:15–17).

A good way to determine God's particular will is to recognize the convergence of three circles: the Bible, your gifts, and your circumstances. If you are living according to the Word of God and exercising your gifts in circumstances in which you find yourself, then you are following the will of God at that time and place.

Application

It's not a matter of getting from point A to point B that determines God's plan for your life. Following the will of God has to do with the person you are *in Christ* and how that newness of life impacts those around you with the gospel (Rom. 8:1, 10; 12:5; 15:17; 1 Cor. 1:30). To help you fulfill God's will for your life, seek daily to "be filled with the Spirit, . . . always giving thanks to God the Father for everything" (Eph. 5:18, 20).

Bible References

Matthew 22:37–39; Luke 10:27–28; Romans 12:1–2; Ephesians 5:15–17; Colossians 1:10; 1 Thessalonians 4:3

Books

Discovering God's Will, by Andy Stanley

Decision Making and the Will of God, by Garry Friesen and Robin Maxson

Website

J. Warner Wallace, "The 'Sure' Will of God," Stand to Reason, http://www.str.org/articles/the-%E2%80%9Csure%E2%80%9D-will-of-god#.U160qfldX74

DVD

Discovering God's Will, Andy Stanley

Online Video

Jason Jimenez, "How Can We Know God's Will for Our Life?," The One Minute Apologist, http://www.oneminuteapologist.com/searchpage#god's-will

69 What Are My Spiritual Gifts?

Answer

There is much confusion over the role and purpose of spiritual gifts in the church. Sadly, many Christians go through life without ever knowing what their spiritual gifts are. The failure to know and exercise spiritual gifts has contributed to the decline of the church. If Christians are to build up the body of Christ (Eph. 4:12), then it's essential that they know what their spiritual gifts are and how to exercise them in the church.

Paul says that God has given each person a measure of grace (Eph. 4:7). He also writes in 1 Corinthians 12:7, "Now to each one the manifestation of the Spirit is given for the common good." It is the Holy Spirit who determines what gift each person receives and how he or she ought to use it for the edification of the body of Christ (1 Cor. 12:11; 1 Pet. 4:10). Paul stresses, "Since you are eager for gifts of the Spirit, try to excel in gifts that build up the church" (1 Cor. 14:12). Christians are not to boast about their spiritual gifts or be prideful in their roles at church. Instead, they are to excel in their gifts in hopes of building up the church.

In three separate epistles, Paul lists a total of nineteen spiritual gifts: Romans 12:6–8; 1 Corinthians 12:8–10, 28–31; and Ephesians 4:11.

Romans 12:6–8	1 Corinthians 12:8–10, 28–31	Ephesians 4:11
Prophecy	Wisdom	Apostleship
Service	Knowledge	Prophecy
Teaching	Faith	Evangelism
Encouragement	Healing	Pastoring/Shepherding
Giving	Miracles	Teaching
Leadership	Prophecy	
Mercy	Discernment	
	Administration	
	Tongues	
	Interpretation of Tongues	
	Apostleship	
	Teaching	
	Service/Helping	

It's important that Christians have a better grasp on the spiritual gifts, and so below are the meaning and purpose of each.

Administration: A person with this gift is organized and is able to guide and direct people to an end, as in building up the body of Christ (Eph. 4:13–15; Titus 1:4–5).

Apostleship: This position or office was limited to the twelve apostles under Jesus and to Paul (Mark 3:13–19; Acts 1:21–22; 1 Cor. 9:1; 2 Cor. 12:12).

Discernment: A person with this gift can distinguish between good and evil spirits and judge a person or situation with clarity (Acts 5:3–6; 1 Thess. 5:20–21; 1 John 4:1).

Encouragement: A person with this gift comes alongside to comfort and strengthen others (Acts 4:36; 9:27; 15:32).

Evangelism: Although every Christian is commanded to share his or her faith (Matt. 28:19–20), those with the gift of evangelism are especially gifted to share and proclaim the gospel (Acts 21:8; 2 Tim. 4:5).

Faith: Although every Christian needs faith to be saved (Eph. 2:8–9), there are those who have an incredible amount of faith in God's mighty work and live boldly for him (Acts 3:1–10; 6:5; Heb. 11).

Giving: A person who has this gift loves to share and gives generously to those in need (Acts 4:32–37; 2 Cor. 9:6–15).

Healing: A person with this gift doesn't possess the power to heal but instead is the instrument God uses to supernaturally heal a person. This individual usually possesses great faith in God's healing power and seeks to honor and glorify God—knowing the healing will come only if God wills it (Acts 3:1–10).

Interpretation of tongues: A person with this gift has the ability to interpret a language he or she has never learned (1 Cor. 14:26–28).

Knowledge: A person with the gift of knowledge has the ability to process information, analyze the truth, and offer the best course of action (Luke 1:1–4; Acts 5:1–11).

Leadership: A person who has this gift is able to set goals and lead others to accomplish God's purposes (Acts 6:1–7; Heb. 13:17).

Mercy: A person with this gift has a compassionate heart and is empathetic toward those who are going through a difficult time (Acts 11:28–30; 16:33–34).

Miracles: A person with this gift acts as an instrument whereby God performs a supernatural act (Acts 9:36–42; 20:7–12).

Pastoring/shepherding: This person is gifted in overseeing and caring for a group of believers and shares in the responsibilities of teaching, equipping, and exhorting them (Eph. 4:11–14; 1 Tim. 3:1–7; 1 Pet. 5:1–4).

Prophecy: A person with this gift has a special ability to receive and announce a word from God (Rom. 12:6; 1 Cor. 14:1–40).

Service/helping: This person is passionate about serving the physical needs of people in the church (Acts 6:1–3; Rom. 12:7).

Teaching: This person is gifted in communicating the truths of the Bible and helping others apply them in their lives (Acts 2:14–36; 7:1–53).

Tongues: A person with this gift is able to receive and communicate a message in a different language to edify the church (Acts 2:1–13; 1 Cor. 14:26–28).

Wisdom: A person with this gift has sound judgment and is experienced in offering practical insight and advice that help bring solutions (Acts 20:20–21; 15:13–20).

There is, of course, a great debate about spiritual gifts in the church today. Some hold that the gifts existed only in apostolic times and have all passed away. Others hold that all of these gifts are in existence today and should be exercised, as the New Testament orders. A third group believes that some of these gifts exist today for the continuation of the church while those special apostolic gifts for the establishment of the church have passed away. The bottom line is that every Christian should agree that love is the greatest of all the gifts (1 Cor. 13).

Application

Clearly, there are no apostles in the church today in the sense of the apostles Christ chose to establish his church (Eph. 2:20). To be an apostle, you had to be an eyewitness of the resurrected Christ (Acts 1:22; 1 Cor. 9:1), and it seems as though some special gifts were associated with the office of apostleship (2 Cor. 12:12). But just because you are not an apostle doesn't mean your gifts are any less important. We encourage you to trust in the gifts the Holy Spirit has given you for your kingdom contributions.

Bible References

Romans 12:6–8; 1 Corinthians 12:8–10, 28–31; Ephesians 4:11–13

Books

Finding Your Spiritual Gifts Questionnaire, by C. Peter Wagner

40-Minute Bible Studies: Understanding Spiritual Gifts, by Kay Arthur, David Lawson, and B. J. Lawson

What's So Spiritual about Your Gifts?, by Henry Blackaby and Melvin Blackaby

Signs and Wonders, by Norman L. Geisler

Website

Spiritual Gifts Assessment, Dr. Elmer Towns, http://www.elmertowns.com/?page_id=203

DVD

Your Divine Design, Living on the Edge

Online Video

Bobby Conway, "What Are My Spiritual Gifts?," The One Minute Apologist, http://www.oneminuteapologist.com/searchpage#spiritual-gifts

70 How Can I Set and Accomplish Goals in My Life?

Answer

Setting goals is a great challenge. An even greater challenge is accomplishing them.

I (Jason) remember talking with a waitress at a restaurant. I asked her if she had any big dreams. She told me she did; her goal was to become a registered nurse. But in order for her to accomplish this goal, she needed to work extra jobs to pay for schooling. She shared how she was working long hours each day, but it was well worth it. This waitress was not only committed to her goals but also determined to become a registered nurse. I wouldn't be surprised if she accomplished her dream.

What about you? What are some goals you hope to accomplish in your life? God has given each person specific goals to accomplish, but (as mentioned earlier) for most, it can be a difficult feat to *know* and *accomplish* them.

Most people will say they wish they had more time in the day to get things completed. One of the main reasons people are so overwhelmed is because they have not set wise goals in life. This speaks to all of us in one way or another. As the saying goes, "Aim at nothing, and you will hit it every time."

Some people wish they had more time to spend with their family; others wish they could devote more time to serving in their church. No matter what the case, setting and accomplishing goals in life are important skills everyone should learn to master. The problem is that most never do.

Why is that? It comes down to the difference between an *organized* life and a *disorganized* life. Solomon put it this way: "The plans of the diligent lead to profit as surely as haste leads to poverty" (Prov. 21:5). What Solomon was saying is that people must be strategic in their planning if they hope to earn a profit. The problem is that far too many people fail to plan out their goals—resulting in little to no results. Many people start off with good intentions, but they never seem to accomplish what they set out to do. Whether the blame is put on a lack of drive, distractions, busyness, fatigue, personal letdowns, or financial setbacks, the bottom line is that most people don't accomplish their goals because they are unorganized and lazy. And when laziness begins to take over, quitting is sure to follow. This applies to family, education, job performance, relationships, faith building, diet, and physical fitness and exercise.

Notice what Solomon—the wisest man on the planet—has to say about determination and accomplishing plans: "Finish your outdoor work and get your fields ready; after that, build your house" (Prov. 24:27). "The plans of the diligent lead to profit as surely as haste leads to poverty" (Prov. 21:5).

The apostle Paul wrote to the church of Thessalonica, "Make it your ambition to lead a quiet life. You should mind your own business and work with your hands, just as we told you, so that your daily life may win the respect of outsiders and so that you will not be dependent on anybody" (1 Thess. 4:11–12; see Eph. 4:28). Paul went on to "warn those who are idle" (1 Thess. 5:14) and to say, "The one who is unwilling to work shall not eat" (2 Thess. 3:10). The point Paul was making is that *planning* out your work and *working* out your plan go hand in hand. Setting and accomplishing goals require wise planning and much hard work.

Here are biblical tips to help you set and accomplish goals:

1. *Vision*: Evaluate where you are and determine where you want to be (Prov. 29:18).
2. *Purpose*: Write down the purpose of each goal and make sure it is realistic (Prov. 24:8–9).
3. *Plan*: Write down a detailed plan that shows how you will accomplish your goals (Prov. 21:5).
4. *Counsel*: Seek wise counsel that will give you clarity of insight to accomplish your goals (Prov. 11:14; 15:22; 20:18).
5. *Discipline*: Setting, working toward, and accomplishing goals take a lot of patience and discipline. Don't rush into anything without praying about it, seeking wise counsel, and applying the virtue of patience in your decision making (Prov. 14:16).
6. *Determination*: Whatever you do, don't quit! Keep pursuing your goals and never give up (Prov. 10:4; 12:24; 13:4).

Application

Zig Ziglar had a great way of defining goals with this acrostic: Godly Objectives Assure Lasting Success. If your plans don't align with God's, then your plans will surely fail. Solomon gave this counsel: "Commit your actions to the LORD, and your plans will succeed" (Prov. 16:3 NLT). Stay focused on God's plan for your life and watch as he moves in mighty ways.

Bible References

Proverbs 3:5–7; 6:6–19; 14:12; 16:3; 21:5; 24:27; Luke 14:28; Philippians 3:14; James 4:13–15

Books

Organizing Your Day: Time Management Techniques That Will Work for You, by Sandra Felton and Marsha Sims

The 15 Invaluable Laws of Growth: Live Them and Reach Your Potential, by John Maxwell

The Principle of the Path: How to Get from Where You Are to Where You Want to Be, by Andy Stanley

Website

"How to Set and Reach Your Goals," Christian Post, http://www.christianpost.com/news/how-to-set-and-reach-your-goals-part-one-34221/

DVD

The Power of Momentum Set, Catalyst

Online Video

Jason Jimenez, "How Do I Set and Accomplish Goals in My Life?," The One Minute Apologist, http://www.oneminuteapologist.com/searchpage#goals

Questions about Moral and Ethical Issues

71 Who Determines What Is Morally Right and Morally Wrong?

Answer

There are many opinions floating around about what is right and what is wrong. With all the moral confusion in our society, it's difficult to figure out what people should actually believe. No matter where you go, questions like these arise: Doesn't everyone have the right to determine what is right and wrong for himself or herself? Isn't everything relative to the individual? These questions and others like them are broadcast on blogs and websites and spewed from secular universities.

Without question, relativism is one of the foremost -isms of our time. It claims that there are no absolutes and that anyone who thinks there are absolutes is absolutely wrong (see question 1, *What is truth?*). But isn't this one of the basic problems with relativism? Absolutely. Here are some others.

1. It is self-defeating to claim that one is absolutely certain there are no absolutes. The claim that one should never use the word *never* just used the word *never* in that claim. Likewise, the claim that one should always avoid using the word *always* just used the word *always*. (See question 2, *Whose truth is true?*)

2. The assertion that the world is getting worse (or better) is not possible unless one has a moral absolute to know what is best. Even simple judgments about how good (or evil) the world is depend on some objective standard outside ourselves by which such judgments can be made. Without a moral absolute, all we could say is that things are *changing*. We could not say that more poverty, abuse, exploitation, and slavery would make the world worse, or that more peace, harmony, and love would make it better.

3. Moral comparisons, which we make all the time, depend on moral absolutes (what is the *best?*). How can we say that Jesus Christ is *better* than

Osama bin Laden unless we have some objective standard by which to know which is better?

4. Moral disputes imply universal moral laws. We can't say something is right and something else is wrong unless there is a standard by which to measure them. Thus, there must be an ultimate standard that measures the two so they can be compared.

5. We didn't invent moral laws any more than we invented mathematical or physical laws. Newton did not invent gravity; he merely discovered it. No one invented the laws of logic; they are just part of the furniture of the universe. Likewise, moral laws were not invented; they were discovered.

6. Universal moral guilt shows there are universal moral laws. Why do we make excuses for our faults unless we know we are wrong? C. S. Lewis brilliantly unpacked this truth in his classic book *Mere Christianity*. Lewis points out that we are inclined to behave a certain way to avoid breaking certain moral principles we know are not meant to be broken.[5]

7. Following moral laws cannot be herd instinct since we sometimes choose duty over instinct—as when a person chooses to rush into a burning building to save a child. The ultimate demonstration of this is when a person sacrifices his or her own life to save another.

8. We all find some things evil. For example, genocide, child abuse, and slavery are universally frowned upon. But how do we know they are evil unless there is a moral law that informs us they are wrong?

9. Our real moral principles are not discovered by our actions (but by our reactions) since we are all imperfect and do not always do what we know we ought to do. This is why we can't determine moral laws by *what we do to others*. But there are many things we don't want others to do to us (such as lying, cheating, abusing, and killing). So moral laws are based on *what we want others to do to us*. Jesus said, "Do to others what you would have them do to you" (Matt. 7:12).

10. The same basic moral codes are found in all major cultures. C. S. Lewis made a collection of them in his excellent book on moral absolutes titled *The Abolition of Man*. In the appendix of this book, Lewis collated moral principles from diverse cultures. What he found was that rather than being totally diverse, the moral principles were strikingly similar. This included respect for the property and personhood of others.[6] As the great philosopher Immanuel Kant put it, we should not will anything that cannot be willed universally for all people. This *categorical imperative* includes the prohibition against lying and murder.

Application

In the end, who determines right and wrong? God does. The moral lawgiver determines the moral laws, and they are written in his Word (Exod. 20) and on our hearts (Rom. 2:12–15). Therefore, you are obligated to obey such moral laws.

Bible References

Exodus 20; Matthew 7:12; John 14:15; Romans 2:12–15; 4:5; 2 Timothy 3:15–16; 1 John 1:8

Books

What We Can't Not Know: A Guide, by J. Budziszewski
Written on the Heart: The Case for Natural Law, by J. Budziszewski
Mere Christianity, by C. S. Lewis
The Abolition of Man, by C. S. Lewis
Christian Ethics: Contemporary Issues and Options, by Norman L. Geisler
Right for You but Not for Me: A Response to Moral Relativism, by Steve Garofalo

Website

Norman L. Geisler, "Any Absolutes? Absolutely!" Christian Research Institute, http://www.equip.org/articles/any-absolutes-absolutely

DVD

Doing the Right Thing: Making Moral Choices in a World Full of Options, Chuck Colson, Robert George, and Brit Hume

Online Videos

William Lane Craig, "Are Morals the Result of Social Conditioning?," The One Minute Apologist, http://www.oneminuteapologist.com/searchpage#social-conditioning

Brett Kunkle, "Can Evolution Explain Morality?," The One Minute Apologist, http://www.oneminuteapologist.com/searchpage#can-evolution-explain-morality

Brett Kunkle, "Can We Be Good without God?," The One Minute Apologist, http://www.oneminuteapologist.com/searchpage#good-without-god

72 Should Christians Judge Others?

Answer

Has someone ever said to you, "It's wrong to judge," or "It's wrong to impose your values on others"? It's apparent that we are living in a culture in which "judge not" is the modus operandi. The problem is that few people who say this understand the context in which Jesus said it. He was speaking against *hypocritical* judging—such as the Pharisees were doing—not against all judging. If no judging were acceptable, then no police officer or judge could do his or her job. Only God knows for sure what people's *motives* are, but we can all see what their *actions* are.

The Bible gives many examples on which we can base our judgment on the actions of other people. If we could not judge others, then there would be no punishment for crimes, including theft, abuse, and even killing. Indeed, the Bible says, "The spiritual person judges all things" (1 Cor. 2:15 ESV). Right judgment is needed for right action. One cannot be a good parent without making good judgments about his or her children. The same is true for any leader.

Paul told the church at Corinth that they should judge unruly and immoral members. He reminded them, "Do you not know that we will judge angels? How much more the things of this life!" (1 Cor. 6:3).

In addition, it's important to point out that those who say not to judge are, in fact, judging others for judging. This is not only contradictory but also hypocritical. Thus, judging people's *actions* is necessary, but judging their *motives* is not.

Application

It's important to remember that God is the Judge, not you. The more you realize this, the less likely you will judge people harshly. Keep focused on the Word of God and seek to apply its truths to your life. In so doing, your judgment will improve and the manner by which you judge others will be done in love.

Bible References

Matthew 7:1–5; Luke 6:37; John 7:24; 1 Corinthians 2:15; 6:3; Galatians 6:1; James 4:12

Books

Ethix: Being Bold in a Whatever World, by Sean McDowell

Christian Ethics: Contemporary Issues and Options, by Norman L. Geisler

Love Your Neighbor: Thinking Wisely about Right and Wrong, by Norman L. Geisler and Ryan Snuffer

Website

Roger E. Olson, "To Judge, or Not to Judge," *Christianity Today* website, http://www.christianitytoday.com/ct/2005/july/22.52.html

DVD

Christian: It's Not What You Think, Andy Stanley

Online Video

Bobby Conway, "Should Christians Judge Others?," The One Minute Apologist, http://www.oneminuteapologist.com/searchpage#judge-others

73 Is Abortion Murder?

Answer

Undoubtedly, abortion in America is our modern holocaust. Since Roe v. Wade, it's been estimated that over fifty million babies have been murdered in the United States. That's an average of three thousand abortions a day and over one million a year!

Despite this atrocity, the debate keeps raging over whether an embryo (from fertilization to start of gestation) or fetus (after the eighth week to birth) is considered a human life. The pro-abortion side argues that neither an embryo or fetus is human; therefore, abortion is not murder. But modern science and strong evidence indicate otherwise. The evidence overwhelmingly shows that a fetus is a tiny, innocent human life.

Murder, by definition, is the intentional taking of an innocent human life. If that's the case (and it is), then abortion, by definition, is murder. The arguments detailed below show that abortion is indeed a murderous act.

First, abortion is not *accidental*; it is an *intentional* act. Both the mother and the doctor knowingly consent to do it.

Second, an embryo is an individual *living* human being. When twenty-three chromosomes from a female ovum unite in conception with twenty-three chromosomes from a male sperm, the result is a forty-six-chromosome human life. This is a scientific fact. At human conception, there is not a *potential human* but a human life with *great potential*.

Furthermore, an embryo or fetus is an individual human life. It is not part of the mother's body, as is evidenced by these facts:

1. The embryo has his or her own sex. If he is a boy, he is definitely different from his mother.
2. The fetus has his or her own individual fingerprints.
3. The fetus has his or her own DNA, which is different from the mother's.
4. If a dark-skinned embryo is transplanted into a light-skinned woman's womb, she will have a dark-skinned baby.
5. Embryos can be conceived in a petri dish, but they are clearly not part of the dish. Likewise, a baby in his or her mother's womb is not part of the mother. He or she is an individual human being who is *nesting* there until birth.

Third, an embryo or fetus is an *innocent* human being. He or she has not committed any crime or even been charged with any crime. He or she has not been given an attorney or been provided with due process under the law. Yet abortion is an intentional act of capital punishment on a living, innocent human being, who, if given the chance, would certainly not consent to being murdered.

Abortion fits all the qualifications of an act of murder because it intentionally ends the life of an innocent human being.

Application

King David captures the words of every single unborn baby: "My frame was not hidden from you when I was made in the secret place, when I was woven together in the depths of the earth. Your eyes saw my unformed body; all the days ordained for me were written in your book before one of them came to be" (Ps. 139:15–16).

Don't just stand idly by and watch as more unborn babies are stripped of their right to live. Ask the Lord how you can get involved in fighting for unborn babies and protecting their right to live.

Bible References

Genesis 2:7; Job 10:8–9; Psalm 139; Jeremiah 1:4–5

Books

The Raging War of Ideas: How to Take Back Our Faith, Family and Country, by Jason Jimenez

Christian Ethics: Contemporary Issues and Options, by Norman L. Geisler

The Case for Life: Equipping Christians to Engage the Culture, by Scott Klusendorf

Why Pro-Life? Caring for the Unborn and Their Mothers, by Randy Alcorn

Stand for Life, by John Ensor and Scott Klusendorf

Website

Life Training Institute, http://www.prolifetraining.com

DVD

Unplanned: The Dramatic True Story of a Former Planned Parenthood Leader's Journey across the Life Line, Tyndale House

Online Videos

Bobby Conway, "Is Abortion Sin?," The One Minute Apologist, http://www.oneminute apologist.com/searchpage#is-abortion-sin

Mark Mittelberg, "What Should Be the Church's Tone on Abortion?," The One Minute Apologist, http://www.oneminuteapologist.com/searchpage#church's-tone-on-abortion

74 Does God Approve of Human Cloning?

Answer

The advancement of science and the increased knowledge of how the body works have clearly opened the door to the possibility of human cloning. The truth is that human cloning frightens people. Most surveys show that the majority of people not only are against human cloning for reproductive purposes but also believe it is morally wrong. Yet it seems as though most politicians, researchers, and academics are fighting for more funding for research on human cloning.

But is this the right thing to do? Does God approve of people tampering with human life?

To answer this question, it's necessary to demonstrate the significant difference between a Judeo-Christian view and a secular humanistic view on life-and-death issues. The following chart compares the two:

Judeo-Christian View	Secular Humanist View
There is a Creator.	There is no Creator.
Humans were created in the image of God.	Humans evolved from animals.
God is sovereign over life.	Humans are sovereign over life.
Sanctity of life is key.	Quality of life is key.
The end does not justify the means.	The end does justify the means.

The next chart compares the two views regarding biomedical issues:

Judeo-Christian View	Secular Humanist View
Serving God	Playing God
Improving human life	Creating human life
Repairing human life	Re-creating human life
Maintenance of life	Engineering of life
Cooperation with nature	Control over nature
Conformity to nature	Power over nature

In light of the radical difference between the two views, it is clear that Christians should be opposed to cloning human beings. We should not *play* God with our knowledge. Rather, we should *serve* God with it. It is our God-given responsibility to *repair* life, not to *duplicate* it.

Some false humanistic principles also need to be exposed: (1) What is being done should be done. (2) What can be done should be done. (3) The end justifies the means. (4) Two wrongs make a right.

These four humanistic principles do not define the standard of the *good*, nor are they able to determine the ultimate outcome of applying the principles. For instance, with principle 4, adding the wrong of fetal experimentation to the wrong of abortion does not equal a right. Both are evil actions and, therefore, result in destroying the greater good, which is life. On the other hand, the *principle of double effect* affirms that when one action has both a good and an evil consequence, we should choose the ultimate good consequence and then not be held responsible for the evil one. A good example of this is amputating a leg to save a life. You may not want to amputate a person's leg, but it's necessary in order to save his or her life. The amputation is the evil consequence, but it resulted in a greater good because it saved a life (good consequence).

Christians, by contrast, make bioethical decisions based on principles like (1) the *sovereignty* of God over life (Deut. 32:39; Job 1:21); (2) the *dignity* of humans made in God's image (Gen. 1:27; 6:9); (3) the *sanctity* of life; and (4) the *mortality* of life. Thus, human cloning is condemned because it attempts to correct human deformities at the expense of destroying life in the process.

Application

It was God who breathed life into the first human (Gen. 2:7), and it is God who has numbered the days of every human. In his misery, Job cried aloud, "A person's days are determined; you have decreed the number of his months and have set limits he cannot exceed" (Job 14:5). Thus, humans are limited in what they can and can't do, but God has unlimited power to give and take life (Rom. 14:7–8).

Bible References

Genesis 1:27; 2:7; 6:9; Deuteronomy 32:39; Job 1:21; 14:5; Romans 14:7–8

Books

Christian Ethics: Contemporary Issues and Options, by Norman L. Geisler

Christianity and Bioethics: Confronting Clinical Issues, by Mark Foreman

How to Be a Christian in a Brave New World, by Joni Eareckson Tada and Nigel M. de S. Cameron

What Does the Lord Require? A Guide for Preaching and Teaching Biblical Ethics, by Walter Kaiser Jr.

Ethics for a Brave New World, by John Feinberg and Paul Feinberg

Website

Ken Ham with Mark Looy, "The Scientific and Scriptural Case against Human Cloning," Creation Ministries International, http://www.creation.com/the-scientific-and-scriptural-case-against-human-cloning

DVD

New Life, Stem Cells, and Cloning: Answers in Genesis, Tommy Mitchell

Online Video

Norman L. Geisler, "Does God Approve of Human Cloning?," The One Minute Apologist, http://www.oneminuteapologist.com/searchpage#human-cloning

75 What Is Wrong with Same-Sex Marriage?

Answer

I (Jason) remember teaching a seminar about how same-sex marriage is not morally good for society. Afterward, a young girl with a distressed look on her face came up. I asked her if she was waiting to ask me something. She nodded and proceeded to ask, "I know you demonstrated that it's morally wrong for homosexuals to marry, but what if their love for one another is genuine? Is it still not okay?"

I remember another time when a troubled student asked me, "I know the Bible condemns homosexuality and all, but . . . what if God really did make people gay and they're just expressing what comes naturally to them?"

Both of these questions reveal the struggle to make sense of what is right. One reason for the moral confusion comes from the explicit exploitation of homosexuality in the media. The gay agenda has been very effective in capturing the young minds of today by using television sitcoms, Hollywood, corporations, politicians, and educators to promote and endorse the gay lifestyle. What was once considered taboo is now on display in every major media outlet in America. The more hearts and minds the gay agenda wins over for homosexuality, the easier it will be for same-sex marriage to be legalized in all fifty states.

But there are several problems with homosexuality and same-sex marriage. First, the Bible declares that God instituted the covenant of marriage to be between one man and one woman only (Gen. 2:24–25; Heb. 13:4). The union between a male and a female in marriage is the most sacred and cherished rite in all of civilization. This union was reaffirmed by Jesus:

> Have you not read that he who created them from the beginning made them male and female, and said, "Therefore a man shall leave his father and his mother and hold fast to his wife, and the two shall become one flesh"? So they are no longer two but one flesh. What therefore God has joined together, let not man separate.
>
> Matthew 19:4–6 ESV

It's evident that Jesus did not support same-sex marriage as an acceptable union. Furthermore, plain common sense tells us that marriage is meant for one man and one woman. That is how we all got here—namely, by a father and a mother.

Second, the natural law, written on the hearts of all people (Rom. 2:2–15), teaches us that homosexuality is wrong. The apostle Paul exhorted against homosexual acts as "contrary to nature" (Rom. 1:26 ESV). Moreover, homosexuals (or anyone for that matter) who claim a person is born gay are wrong. There is absolutely no scientific evidence to support the existence of a gay gene. It's also necessary to point out that the argument for *inherited tendencies* can be used for any type of sin (e.g., alcoholism, pedophilia, incest, or violent behavior); however, such an argument doesn't make any of these other sins or unnatural behaviors right. Thus, to say a person is born gay is unfounded because homosexuality is unnatural.

Third, the practice of homosexuality is self-destructive. Those who practice homosexuality are unable to produce any more of their kind, and the sexual act of homosexuality is unnatural and inflicts damage on the body, both physically and mentally. Homosexuality also carries with it a high degree of promiscuity, sexual diseases, and lower life expectancies. At one time, every state in the United States had laws against homosexual practice called *sodomy laws*. The very name, *sodomy*, is a grim reminder of God's destruction of Sodom and Gomorrah for the depraved behaviors of their people (Gen. 18–19). Indeed, God condemned the Canaanites for their homosexual practice, declaring that the land "vomited out its inhabitants" because of it (Lev. 18:25). God's problem wasn't with homosexual *tendencies*—we all have tendencies to sin in one way or another. The real problem God had with the Canaanites (and still does with people today) was with homosexual *practices*. Thus, it should be neither legally nor morally permissible to redefine marriage for the sole purpose of promoting homosexual predilections.

Fourth, same-sex marriage does not add up anatomically, and it also fails to provide a natural balance of masculinity from the male and femininity from the female. A same-sex couple is unable to meet the God-given requirements of any normal heterosexual relationship because their relationship is a distortion of natural marriage. Once again, this causes more damage than good.

As for the charge that the Bible and those who propagate its message are homophobic, we must remember that God loves everyone, including homosexuals. So while we hate the practice of homosexuality, it is our duty to minister to the homosexual, just as it is our duty to help the alcoholic even though we may detest alcoholism and all its evil results. We were all born, as St. Augustine said, with the propensity to sin and the necessity to die (cf. Rom. 3:23; 5:12; 7:17–20). Therefore, we ought not embrace the sinner (homosexual) and overlook the sin (practice of homosexuality). Real love means confronting the sinful practice in the hope of saving the homosexual from his or her self-destructive behaviors.

Application

Just because it is hard not to sin doesn't make it right to sin. Paul argues strongly that God is faithful and has made a way to overcome temptations in life (1 Cor. 10:13). With the help of God, you will always be able to resist sinning by the grace of God. Hence, look for ways to minister to homosexuals and share with them the gospel of Jesus Christ.

Bible References

Genesis 2:24–25; Leviticus 18:25; Romans 1:26; 2:2–15; 3:23; 5:12; 7:17–20

Books

The Raging War of Ideas: How to Take Back Our Faith, Family, and Country, by Jason Jimenez

Christian Ethics: Contemporary Issues and Options, by Norman L. Geisler

The Truth about Same-Sex Marriage: 6 Things You Need to Know about What's Really at Stake, by Erwin Lutzer

Same-Sex Marriage: A Thoughtful Approach to God's Design for Marriage, by Sean McDowell and John Stonestreet

Website

"Ten Arguments from Social Science against Same-Sex Marriage," Family Research Council, http://www.frc.org/get.cfm?i=if04g01

DVD

Culture Shock: Responding to Today's Most Controversial Topics, Living on the Edge

Online Videos

Frank Turek, "Is Same-Sex 'Marriage' Wrong apart from the Bible?," The One Minute Apologist, http://www.oneminuteapologist.com/searchpage#same-sex-marriage

Michael Brown, "Leviticus Laws and Homosexuality," The One Minute Apologist, http://www.oneminuteapologist.com/searchpage#leviticus-laws

Mark Mittelberg, "Did Jesus Ever Talk about Homosexuality?," The One Minute Apologist, http://www.oneminuteapologist.com/searchpage#did-jesus-ever-talk-about-homosexuality

76 Is Lying Ever Right?

Answer

The Holocaust of the 1940s is one of history's darkest periods. The German Nazis embarked on a campaign to search out every single Jew who lived in their dominion. Many people, however, formed an underground resistance against the Nazis and sought ways to hide and protect Jewish families. In Holland, Corrie ten Boom and her family were part of a group that helped Jews escape. Eventually, Corrie and her family were imprisoned for lying and hiding Jews in their Haarlem home. Was the ten Boom family right in lying to the Nazi soldiers in order to save the lives of a few Jews?

This question is troubling to many because the Bible emphatically points out that God's word is truth (John 17:17), and according to the ninth commandment, "You shall not bear false witness" (Exod. 20:16 ESV).

So can lying ever be justified?

First and foremost, we must distinguish between lying *as such* (which is always wrong) and lying *as an act of mercy* (e.g., to save a life). There are examples in the Bible when lying appears to be the merciful thing to do. Rahab lied to save the spies and all the Israelites (Josh. 2:1–11), and she made it into the faith hall of fame (Heb. 11:31; see James 2:25). Some people reason that she was saved *in spite of* her lie, not because of it. But it is a different case in Exodus 1, when the Hebrew midwives lied and disobeyed the king's command to kill innocent babies. The text reads, "Because the midwives feared God [and therefore lied], he gave them families of their own" (Exod. 1:21).

Furthermore, it's important to distinguish between higher and lower ethical obligations. When the two conflict, we are always obligated to follow the higher one. For example, we should always obey our parents as such. But if they command us to kill the neighbor's child, then we should disobey them in order to keep our higher obligation to the life of an innocent child.

Jesus said there are "more important matters of the law" (Matt. 23:23) and there are "greater sin[s]" (John 19:11). There are even greater virtues (1 Cor. 13:13). Jesus also said that loving God is a greater obligation than loving others, calling it "the first and greatest commandment" (Matt. 22:38).

Given that there are higher and lower ethical duties and that the Bible provides examples of divinely approved obedience to higher commands when they conflict with lower ones (Exod. 1; Dan. 3; 6; Acts 4–5), we can say it is sometimes necessary to break a lower command in order to keep a higher one.

Nonetheless, it is always wrong to lie *as such*. It is only right when it's done because of an unavoidable conflict with *a higher duty*. Just like right-of-way laws for driving are designed to avoid conflicts, so ethical right-of-way laws permit exemption from lower duties in order to fulfill higher ones. As much as one loves his or her parents, if they command that person to deny God or Christ, then he or she must disobey them in order to obey the higher law of God. Similarly, in the case of Rahab, she lied to save the lives of the Israelites (which was the higher duty).

Application

Solomon writes, "The LORD detests lying lips, but he delights in men who are truthful" (Prov. 12:22). Though cases like those of Rahab, the Hebrew midwives, and Corrie ten Boom are rare, it's important to note that their obedience to God's higher law was far superior to obedience to man's conventional law.

Bible References

Exodus 1; Joshua 2:1–11; Proverbs 12:22; 19:9; Matthew 23:23; John 19:11; 1 Corinthians 13:13

Books

Christian Ethics: Contemporary Issues and Options, by Norman L. Geisler

The Abolition of Man, by C. S. Lewis

Love Your Neighbor: Thinking Wisely about Right and Wrong, by Norman L. Geisler and Ryan Snuffer

Website

Greg Koukl, "White Lies and Other Deceptions," Stand to Reason, http://www.str.org/articles /white-lies-and-other-deceptions#.U1_u7PldX74

DVD

Doing the Right Thing: Making Moral Choices in a World Full of Options, Chuck Colson, Robert George, and Brit Hume

Online Video

Norman L. Geisler, "Is Lying Ever Right?," The One Minute Apologist, http://www.one minuteapologist.com/searchpage#is-lying-ever-right

77 How Should Christians View Euthanasia and Physician-Assisted Suicide?

Answer

There is a growing movement across the United States and the world to end the lives of those experiencing extreme pain. It is considered an act of mercy— whether it's done as a suicide or a physician-assisted suicide. Accordingly, if euthanasia and physician-assisted suicide are viewed as acts of mercy, should Christians support them?

213

Christians believe that human life from conception to natural death should be protected and preserved. Since it is wrong to intentionally take the life of an innocent human being, then suicide is as wrong as homicide.

But what do we do about those in extreme pain? We *relieve* them of their pain, not *remove* their life from them. Here are several good reasons not to engage in euthanasia or physician-assisted suicide:

1. It is *unbiblical*. It is prohibited in the Ten Commandments. Exodus 20:13 reads, "You shall not murder." Moreover, it violates God's sovereignty over life: "The LORD gave and the LORD has taken away; may the name of the LORD be praised" (Job 1:21; see Deut. 32:39; 1 Chron. 29:11–12).

2. It is *unethical*. Since ancient times, doctors have pledged the Hippocratic oath, which (essentially) affirms to protect and preserve life, not destroy it. Today the Hippocratic oath is being replaced by the *hypocritical* oath, as people pledge to preserve life while they destroy it. The purpose of a doctor is to save and preserve life, not to end it.

3. It is *unconstitutional*. The Declaration of Independence boldly affirms, "We hold these truths to be self-evident, that all men are created equal, that they have been endowed by their Creator with certain unalienable rights, that among these are Life, Liberty and the pursuit of Happiness." In addition, the Fifth Amendment of the US Constitution states, "No person shall be . . . deprived of life, liberty, or property, without due process of law."

4. It is *uncompassionate*. Euthanasia is not *caring for* the dying; it is *killing* the living. Euthanasia is more along the lines of an act of cowardice than an act of compassion. It replaces bravery with incompetence.

5. It is *easily corruptible*. Legalization of euthanasia has a high risk for overexpansion and corruption, which would result in even more personal and social harm. Providing euthanasia for competent, terminally ill adults could be expanded to include incompetent adults. Eventually, voluntary euthanasia would give way to involuntary euthanasia.

6. It is *detrimental*. Legalized euthanasia would erode patient trust that the health care system will do everything possible to *relieve their suffering* rather than *relieve them of their life*. Knowing that a state has legalized their death, how can patients be sure the health care system will do everything possible to cure them of their sickness? Legalized euthanasia could develop into a policy that if you don't fit the physical standards set forth by the state, then you would be terminated.

7. It is *irreversible*. Euthanasia cuts off the opportunity to correct errors in prognosis and treatment. It also cuts off the discovery of future benefits

in terms of helpful therapy or a possible cure. It ultimately cuts off the spiritual lessons that can be learned in the dying process.

8. It is *unnecessary*. Natural death is going to occur in due time. There is no need for us to hasten it. Proverbs 31:6–7 says, "Give strong drink to the one who is perishing, and wine to those in bitter distress; let them drink and forget their poverty and remember their misery no more" (ESV). Hospice serves this function today. In extreme cases, an induced coma is a relief from pain.

Application

Human life should be respected from conception to natural death. Death is in God's hands, not ours. Therefore, it is the duty of all Christians to preserve life in the womb as well as out of the womb.

Bible References

Exodus 20:13; Deuteronomy 32:39; 1 Chronicles 29:11–12; Job 1:21

Books

Christian Ethics: Contemporary Issues and Options, by Norman L. Geisler

Christianity and Bioethics: Confronting Clinical Issues, by Mark Foreman

How to Be a Christian in a Brave New World, by Joni Eareckson Tada and Nigel M. de S. Cameron

What Does the Lord Require? A Guide for Preaching and Teaching Biblical Ethics, by Walter Kaiser Jr.

Website

Kerby Anderson, "Euthanasia: A Christian Perspective," PROBE Ministries, http://www.probe.org/site/c.fdKEIMNsEoG/b.4218277/k.27C4/Euthanasia.htm

DVD

Turning the Tide: Dignity, Compassion, and Euthanasia, Vision Video

Online Video

John Stonestreet, "How Should Christians View Euthanasia and Physician-Assisted Suicide?," http://www.oneminuteapologist.com/searchpage#euthanasia

78 What Is the Bible's Position on Capital Punishment?

Answer

Since the fall of man, criminals have poured out innocent blood on the earth. The sad truth is that some criminals have gotten away with their crimes, while others have paid for the crimes they committed.

Take, for example, a few notorious murderers who received capital punishment for their crimes. Allen Lee Davis was executed for murdering a mother, her unborn baby, and two children. The question is whether Allen Lee Davis deserved execution by electrocution in Florida.

What about the infamous serial killer Ted Bundy? It's estimated that he raped, tortured, and brutally murdered over thirty women. Did he deserve the electric chair? Or what about Saddam Hussein, an evil dictator who ruled for more than three decades and performed mass genocide on millions of his own people? Would you say the death penalty was a justifiable sentence for him?

These are but a few of the thousands of death penalty cases. No matter how controversial the subject of the death penalty is, it's necessary to know its purpose and, therefore, its justification in extreme cases.

Those who oppose capital punishment argue that if taking a human life is murder (Exod. 20:13), then how can we justify the death penalty? This is a fair question and needs to be further examined.

First, murder is always wrong, but capital punishment is not murder. Murder is the intentional killing of an *innocent* human being. A murderer is not an innocent human being. A murderer is a *guilty* human being who committed a capital crime worthy of capital punishment.

The Bible notes several occasions when taking a guilty human life is justified:

1. It is justified in self-defense (Exod. 22:2).
2. It is justified in a just war, such as a war in defense of the innocent (Gen. 14).
3. It is justified in the case of a capital crime. Genesis 9:6 declares, "Whoever sheds human blood, by humans shall their blood be shed; for in the image of God has God made mankind."

When is capital punishment justified? When someone has committed a capital crime. The biblical principle of "a life for a life" should be applied. Those who steal one hundred dollars owe one hundred dollars, and those who take a life owe their life.

As for whether capital punishment deters crime, two points should be made: (1) It deters all future crimes by that person, for no person given capital punishment has ever committed another crime. (2) The primary purpose of applying the law is not to deter other crimes, though it is hoped that it will do this. The primary purpose is justice, not results; it is penal, not remedial.

But wasn't the practice of capital punishment in the Old Testament instituted under the law of Moses—by which we are no longer bound in the New Testament (Rom. 10:4; 2 Cor. 3:7, 11, 14)? The fact is that capital punishment was instituted in Genesis 9, long before the law of Moses was given (Exod. 21).

Further, capital punishment was reaffirmed in the New Testament when God said he gave the sword to human government to use on the unruly (Rom. 13:1–4). Indeed, Jesus recognized that Pilate had authority from God to take his life (John 19:11). Paul also recognized the capital authority of government in Acts 25:11. As a matter of fact, if capital punishment had not been in effect in New Testament times, then Jesus would not have been able to die for our sins (1 Pet. 2:24).

But didn't Jesus do away with capital punishment when he refused to stone the woman taken in adultery and said, "Go, and from now on sin no more" (John 8:11 ESV)? Not really. Technically, there were no witnesses since they all left (John 8:10–11), and there had to be at least two. Since no man was brought forth, it was probably just a trumped-up charge to trap Jesus. Further, capital punishment was in the hands of the government (Rome) and not in the hands of any citizens (in this case the Jews).

Some object to capital punishment because mistakes are made in administering it. But no one would close down all hospitals because fatal mistakes are sometimes made. The solution is not to do away with hospitals but to correct the problem. The same is true with capital punishment.

Application

Until the new heaven and new earth, sin will continue to have its effect on the world. But justice can be administered to a high degree to punish those who sin and break the law. Psalm 58:10 says, "The righteous will be glad when they are avenged, when they dip their feet in the blood of the wicked." Thus, capital punishment is a just act on those who act unjustly.

Bible References

Genesis 9:6; 14; Exodus 20:13; 22:2; 2 Samuel 12:5; John 19:11; Acts 25:11; Romans 13:1–4; 1 Peter 2:13–14

Books

Christian Ethics: Contemporary Issues and Options, by Norman L. Geisler

The Ethics of Capital Punishment: A Zondervan Digital Short, by Scott Rae

Website

Greg Koukl, "The Bible and Capital Punishment," Stand to Reason, http://www.str.org/articles/the-bible-and-capital-punishment-2#.U1_x5fldX74

DVD

Doing the Right Thing: Making Moral Choices in a World Full of Options, Chuck Colson, Robert George, and Brit Hume

Online Video

Norman L. Geisler, "What's the Bible's Position on Capital Punishment?," The One Minute Apologist, http://www.oneminuteapologist.com/searchpage#capital-punishment

Questions about Culture and Politics

79 What Is the Role of Government?

Answer

History has seen the rise and fall of many empires. After the Assyrian Empire, the Babylonian Empire arose (612–539 BC), which was eventually conquered by the Medo-Persian Empire (539–331 BC). Then came the Greek Empire (331–63 BC), followed by the Roman Empire (63 BC–AD 476). Though each empire of ancient civilization brought with it a certain level of skill, aptitude, and military power, a common trait shared among the empires was the cruel dictators who ruled them.

Consider also the British Empire. At the height of its glory, it stretched over a third of the world—a feat no other empire has achieved. Yet even the power and rule of the former British Empire sometimes carried with it brutal tactics orchestrated by evil kings.

Then throughout the twentieth century, evil dictators emerged such as Adolf Hitler (ruler of the Nazi Party), Josef Stalin (ruler of the Communist Party), and Mao Zedong (ruler of the People's Republic of China). These governments rejected the laws and standards of God and enacted injustice—which led to mass genocide and destruction.

It is obvious that these empires and their rulers were wicked and inhumane. Nonetheless, God has a good purpose in establishing government. According to the Bible, it is God who sets up the kingdoms and rulers of the world:

> No one from the east or the west or from the desert can exalt themselves. It is God who judges: He brings one down, he exalts another.
>
> Psalm 75:6–7

> In the Lord's hand the king's heart is a stream of water that he channels toward all who please him.
>
> Proverbs 21:1

He changes times and seasons; he deposes kings and raises up others. He gives wisdom to the wise and knowledge to the discerning.

Daniel 2:21

The living may know that the Most High is sovereign over the kingdoms of men and gives them to anyone he wishes and sets over them the lowliest of men.

Daniel 4:17

Jesus answered, "You would have no power over me if it were not given to you from above."

John 19:11

God is perfectly just and right in using unrighteous kingdoms to accomplish his sovereign purposes. For example, God used the Assyrians (Isa. 10) and Babylonians (Dan. 4) to punish his people for turning away from him to sin. And yet even the Assyrians and Babylonians were not free from the wrath of God. They too were judged and received harsh punishment for their wickedness and evil deeds toward Israel (Assyria, Isa. 31:8; Babylon, Isa. 13:1–11 and Jer. 50–51). God even used King Cyrus (2 Chron. 36:23; Isa. 45) to end the Babylonian captivity (Dan. 5) and permit the Jews to return to rebuild Jerusalem and the temple (Ezra 1).

Despite the power and influence many of these empires and dictators had at one time or another, it's obvious their forms of government didn't align with the Word of God.

The apostle Paul writes plainly the purpose and role of government:

Everyone must submit himself to the governing authorities, for there is no authority except that which God has established. The authorities that exist have been established by God. Consequently, he who rebels against the authority is rebelling against what God has instituted, and those who do so will bring judgment on themselves. For rulers hold no terror for those who do right, but for those who do wrong. Do you want to be free from fear of the one in authority? Then do what is right and he will commend you. For he is God's servant to do you good. But if you do wrong, be afraid, for he does not bear the sword for nothing. He is God's servant, an agent of wrath to bring punishment on the wrongdoer. Therefore, it is necessary to submit to the authorities, not only because of possible punishment but also because of conscience. This is also why you pay taxes, for the authorities are God's servants, who give their full time to governing. Give everyone what you owe him: If you owe taxes, pay taxes; if revenue, then revenue; if respect, then respect; if honor, then honor.

Romans 13:1–7

In essence, government is an institution (servant) established by God to enact justice and preserve order by punishing wrongdoers and rewarding those who do right (1 Pet. 2:14). It is, therefore, the duty of every citizen to submit to such authorities and obey the common laws of the land (Titus 3:1; 1 Pet. 2:13–17).

But more specifically, what is the role of the federal government of the United States? Listed below are two pieces of our founding documents that erected the structure of both federal and state governments.

We hold these truths to be self-evident, that all men are created equal, that they are endowed by their Creator with certain unalienable Rights, that among these are Life, Liberty and the pursuit of Happiness.—That to secure these rights, Governments are instituted among Men, deriving their just powers from the consent of the governed.—That whenever any Form of Government becomes destructive of these ends, it is the Right of the People to alter or to abolish it, and to institute new Government, laying its foundation on such principles and organizing its powers in such form, as to them shall seem most likely to effect their Safety and Happiness.

Declaration of Independence

We the people of the United States, in order to form a more perfect union, establish justice, insure domestic tranquility, provide for the common defense, promote the general welfare, and secure the blessings of liberty to ourselves and our posterity, do ordain and establish this Constitution for the United States of America.

US Constitution

Thus, the United States government is built on natural law ordained by God. Our nation's founders believed that we are all created equal and have the right to life, liberty, and the pursuit of happiness. To protect and preserve these God-given rights, our founders established a republic with a three-branch system of government: executive, legislative, and judicial. They also established checks and balances to avoid centralized power.

Hence, from our country's founding documents—the Declaration of Independence, United States Constitution, and Bill of Rights—come the purposes of the United States government:

- to preserve the unalienable rights of the people
- to maintain a military to protect its people
- to not overpower the self-government of the people (except in cases of the right of eminent domain)

- to enact justice
- to enforce the laws legislated by elected officials who represent the people
- to regulate commerce among the states and maintain a strong currency
- to secure liberty, not infringe on it

Application

Much has changed from the original purpose of the United States government. What the founders intended to remain limited is now interfering with the privacy and freedoms of Americans. Stay involved in city, state, and national elections, and remain steadfast in studying the Declaration of Independence, United States Constitution, and Bill of Rights. (See question 80, *Why should Christians care about the United States Constitution?*)

Bible References

Romans 13:1–7; Titus 3:1; 1 Peter 2:13–17

Books

God and Government: An Insider's View on the Boundaries between Faith and Politics, by Charles Colson

The Raging War of Ideas: How to Take Back Our Faith, Family, and Country, by Jason Jimenez

The US Constitution, Coughlan Publishing

Website

Doug Bandow, "Biblical Foundations of Limited Government," Acton Institute for the Study of Religion and Liberty, http://www.acton.org/pub/religion-liberty/volume-7-number-1/biblical-foundations-limited-government

DVD

Biblical Foundations of Government, American Family Association

Online Video

Norman L. Geisler, "What's the Role of Government?," The One Minute Apologist, http://www.oneminuteapologist.com/searchpage#role-of-government

80 Why Should Christians Care about the United States Constitution?

Answer

Americans should care a great deal about the US Constitution because it is the basis of our federal republic. Indeed, it is our country's longest-enduring governing document, written in 1788. From the US Constitution comes the structure of the federal government as well as the guiding principles for governing and protecting its citizens. (See question 79, *What is the role of government?*)

The US Constitution is not just for elected officials, attorneys, or judges. It's for every single American. If Americans fail to understand the purpose of the US Constitution, more than likely they will not appreciate the immense value it brings to our livelihood and the future survival of the nation. To put it another way, America's future liberties are dependent on whether Americans choose to preserve and protect the US Constitution.

But Christians, especially, should care about the US Constitution because it is built on natural law and its framework is derived from the Bible:

- The US Constitution is the supreme law of the land, which originates from God (Exod. 18:16; Deut. 17:18–20).
- The US Constitution limits, enumerates, and divides the power of government into a three-branch system (separation of powers with checks and balances) meant to specifically account for the human depravity described in Isaiah 33:22 and Jeremiah 17:9.
- The US Constitution designates civil authorities meant to uphold laws that protect people, not harm them (Exod. 20–22; Deut. 5; 19:11–13; 2 Sam. 5:1–4; 2 Kings 23:1–3).

Application

America is a country specially blessed by God, and it ought to be defended by every American. Its special status isn't simply based on freedoms, military power, or economic strength; it is unique because of its rich Christian heritage. The Judeo-Christian ethic evident throughout the writings of the early

225

settlers, founding fathers, and various colonists in early America has helped shape one the freest and most prosperous nations in history.

Bible References

Exodus 18:16; 20–22; Deuteronomy 5; 17:18–20; 19:11–13; 2 Samuel 5:1–4; 2 Kings 23:1–3; Isaiah 33:22; Jeremiah 17:9

Books

The Raging War of Ideas: How to Take Back Our Faith, Family, and Country, by Jason Jimenez

Indivisible: Restoring Faith, Family, and Freedom before It's Too Late, by James Robison and Jay Richards

Our Constitution Rocks, by Juliette Turner

Website

"The Bible and Government," Faith Facts, http://www.faithfacts.org/christ-and-the-culture/the-bible-and-government

DVD

Drive thru History, American History Series, Dave Stotts

Online Video

Norman L. Geisler, "Why Should Christians Care about the US Constitution?," The One Minute Apologist, http://www.oneminuteapologist.com/searchpage#constitution

81 Should Christians Be Involved in Politics?

Answer

Any time the subject matter turns to politics—look out! Most people will tell you it's never a pleasant thing getting into political debates with relatives or friends. Regrettably, scores of Christians have lost hope in their representatives and have increasingly removed themselves from political matters. If you asked Christians on the street to describe politics in their own words, they would probably say it's nothing more than a bunch of bureaucrats and crooked politicians vying for votes to keep themselves in power—which is often why Christians avoid politics altogether.

But this is a great shame because politics plays an extremely important role in all our lives. *Politics* literally means "relating to citizens." That is, *politics has to do with electing the right officials through a democratic system who will uphold the law and legislate public policies that are good for the citizens they represent.*

Avoiding *partisan politics* can be a good thing, but avoiding *moral issues* in our society and not taking a stand on them is not a good thing. As Christians, we must be salt and light in our world. We cannot afford to stick our pious heads in the sand and allow the world "to go to hell in a hand basket."

There is more to politics than political parties, broken promises, and bad policies. It involves a way of life. So the questions Christians must answer are: What kind of life do we want to live in America? Do we want the government encroaching on our liberties and religious freedoms? Do we want the government to remove our parental rights or force us to pay taxes to fund abortions?

When it comes to politics, there are so many different views being promoted, agendas being pushed, and laws being passed. Without Christian involvement, the issues, policies, and laws will reflect only the values of the world, not of God.

Take, for example, abortion, contraceptives, same-sex marriage, and gambling. These aren't merely political issues—they are moral issues. Whatever morality is legislated becomes the law of the land. That's why Christians should be involved in politics. The more participation and representation Christians have in the governing of our society, the greater chance the moral landscape of American society will improve.

Serving in public office is considered a high honor, but serving with a good conscience is even better. God works through people as conduits to bear his name and uphold his truth. It is God who establishes the governing authorities (Rom. 13:1–2), and it's the moral duty and responsibility of Christians to submit to, pray for, and obey their leaders (1 Tim. 2:1–2).

The bottom line is that our society could use some more salt and light (Matt. 5:13–16).

Application

Who will be an advocate for justice and speak out against evil and corruption if Christians don't? It's not a matter of putting your faith in a politician but rather praying for and supporting leaders who fear God, respect the law, and count it an honor to serve their people.

Just think of the influential men and women in the Bible who made a difference by being involved in the politics of their day:

- Elijah confronted Ahab (1 Kings 17–18).
- Nathan rebuked King David (2 Sam. 12).
- John the Baptist spoke against Herod (Matt. 14:1–4).
- Esther stood against the king's edict (Esther 7:1–10).
- Paul defended his rights as a Roman citizen (Acts 22:24–29; 23:12–33; 25:10–12).

Bible References

2 Samuel 12; 1 Kings 17–18; Esther 7:1–10; Matthew 14:1–2; Acts 22:24–29; 23:12–33; 25:10–12; Romans 13:1–2; 1 Timothy 2:1–2; 1 Peter 2:13–17

Books

God and Government: An Insider's View on the Boundaries between Faith and Politics, by Charles Colson

Wall of Misconception: Does the Separation of Church and State Mean the Separation of God and Government?, by Peter Lillback

The Raging War of Ideas: How to Take Back Our Faith, Family, and Country, by Jason Jimenez

How Would Jesus Vote? A Christian Perspective on the Issues, by D. James Kennedy and Jerry Newcombe

Legislating Morality: Is It Wise? Is It Legal? Is It Possible?, by Norman L. Geisler and Frank Turek

Website

"Why Christians Should and Must Be Involved in Politics," American Family Association, http://action.afa.net/Blogs/BlogPost.aspx?id=2147492044

DVD

Charles Colson on Politics and the Christian Faith, Zondervan

Online Video

Frank Turek, "Why Should Christians Be Involved in Politics?," The One Minute Apologist, http://www.oneminuteapologist.com/searchpage#should-christians-be-involved-in-politics

82 Is There an Agenda behind Public Education?

Answer

Our nation is drifting further and further from God and his eternal truths. The Judeo-Christian ethic that formed our nation and was once considered the standard belief system now faces extinction. One primary reason for this moral downgrade is the subversive nature of the public education system, shown in its promotion of humanism, religious discrimination, sex-education programs, and the gay agenda (to name a few).

Now this is not to say that all school teachers and administrators uphold or support the secular agenda within the public schools. We know many hard-working and God-fearing people who have devoted their lives to caring for and educating young people. And despite the growing problems and the low compensation packages they receive for their selfless work, many teachers continue their work because they feel called to be salt and light in a dark and troubled place. And for that, we commend them and pray God continues to embolden them.

That being said, it's our intent to expose the real agenda behind the Department of Education, not take issue with persons within the school system. So let's now review a few public attacks that reveal the secular agenda behind public education.

For starters, the public schools have banned God from the classroom and replaced him with naturalism. No longer are students taught they were created in the image of an intelligent God (Gen. 1:27). Instead, they learn they are the result of random processes by unintelligible matter.

Public schools have also banned absolute truth and have replaced it with cultural relativism—a belief that denies absolute truth and rejects objective morality. No longer are students taught that objective morality exists; instead, they are encouraged to determine their own truth and set of morals.

The more successful the public education system has been in removing God and redefining truth, the easier it's been to influence students with a humanist way of thinking. The schools say they are advocates for tolerance and acceptance, yet, with the blessing of the Supreme Court, they forbid school prayer (Engel v. Vitale, 1962), banned Bible reading in classrooms (Abington School District v. Schempp, 1963), discriminate against students who want to participate in Bible clubs, and threaten the jobs of Christian teachers and administrators if they speak up about their faith (see recommended resources at the end for testimonials).

It's ironic how, on the one hand, public schools silence Christianity but, on the other, allow the promotion of humanism (which is identified as a religion), and publically endorse openly gay teachers and students. What parents need to realize is that public schools aren't just academic facilities; they have been turned into "churches" to advance the newfound faith of humanism.

Consider this. Schools happen to be the biggest platforms for influencing tens of millions of students each year with these humanistic ideologies:

- transgender equality
- same-sex marriage
- pro-abortion laws
- sex-education programs
- free contraceptives
- environmentalism (green agenda)
- socialism

While more young people are being indoctrinated with naturalism and humanism, student grades are at record lows, and school crime is at an all-time high. Accordingly, schools are producing little results that help improve the nation innovatively or economically.

The bottom line is that things in the public schools aren't getting any better—they are getting worse by the day. Parents may not be able to change what course or curriculum the school chooses to use, but they certainly can speak out against any agenda that runs contrary to their religious convictions. But for this to happen, parents must be better educated on what's really being taught and willing to stand up for biblical truth.

Application

Christians need to count the cost of funding a secular system that is anti-Christian at its core. What is more, parents need to be aware of the dangers of subjecting their children to this secular institution called public education.

The more Christians awaken to the truth and take the time to educate their families according to the Word of God, the better equipped the next generation will be to stand up for biblical truth. Jesus calls each one of us to be the "salt of the earth" (Matt. 5:13) and the "light of the world" (Matt. 5:14). (See question 94, How can I train my children in the ways of the Lord?)

Bible References

Deuteronomy 11:19; Proverbs 1:7; 4:13; 9:10; Ecclesiastes 7:12; 12:12; Ephesians 6:4; 2 Timothy 2:15

Books

The Raging War of Ideas: How to Take Back Our Faith, Family, and Country, by Jason Jimenez

The War against Hope: How Teachers' Unions Hurt Children, Hinder Teachers, and Endanger Public Education, by Rob Paige

Brainwashed: How Universities Indoctrinate America's Youth, by Ben Shapiro

Website

Randy Douglass, "Closing the Back Door: The Need for Christian Education," http://www.normgeisler.com/articles/GuestAuthors/RDouglass-NeedForChristianEducation.htm

DVD

IndoctriNation, Gunn Productions

Online Video

Jason Jimenez, "What's the Real Agenda behind Public Education?," The One Minute Apologist, http://www.oneminuteapologist.com/searchpage#public-education

PART 11

Questions about Worldviews and World Religions

83 What Are Some Worldviews That Oppose Christianity?

Answer

The Christian life isn't only about knowing what you believe; it's also about being aware of the philosophies and worldviews that challenge Christianity. Paul warned the Christians in Colossae, "See to it that *no one takes you captive through hollow and deceptive philosophy, which depends on human tradition and the basic principles of this world* rather than on Christ" (Col. 2:8). Jude, the half brother of Jesus, wrote these words: "Dear friends, although I was very eager to write to you about the salvation we share, I felt I had to write and urge you to *contend for the faith* that was once for all entrusted to the saints" (Jude 3).

As you can see, it is of utmost importance for Christians to be aware not only of false views but also of how to combat them. (See question 2, *Whose truth is true?*; question 3, *Is there a God?*; and question 71, *Who determines what is morally right and morally wrong?*)

There are seven worldviews or ways to view the world. With respect to their view of God, they are listed as follows:

1. *Theism*: There is an infinite, personal God beyond the world who created the world, upholds the world, and can miraculously intervene in the world.
2. *Deism*: An infinite, personal God created the world but does not uphold it since it runs on its own. God does not miraculously intervene in the world.
3. *Finite Godism*: God is not infinite but is limited in his power or perfection or both.
4. *Polytheism*: There are many finite (limited) gods in the world but no one, all-powerful God over the whole world.
5. *Pantheism*: God is the world and the world is God. There is no God beyond the world who created it. There is no real difference between the universe (whether it is material or spiritual) and God.

6. *Panentheism*: It literally means "all in God" or "God in all." God is to the world what a soul is to a body. The world is God's body. Thus, God has two poles: an actual material, temporal, and changing pole, and a potential pole that is not material, temporal, or changing.

7. *Atheism*: There is no God (infinite or finite) either beyond the world or in the world. Agnostics hold the same worldview as atheists but claim they cannot (or do not) know if there is a God.

It's important to note that every nontheistic worldview mentioned in the summary above opposes theism. Hence, if any one of them is true, then theism is false. Correspondingly, if theism is true, then all the nontheistic worldviews are false. (See question 84, *Can all religions be true?*) We have given strong reasons elsewhere for the truth of Christianity (see question 15, *Is the Bible true?*), and those along with other strong arguments prove that the nontheistic worldviews are false (see Norman L. Geisler, *Christian Apologetics*, part 2).

Of course, there are several major religions that are theistic, namely, Judaism, Christianity, and Islam. Which of these is true depends on which one has evidence to support its claim to be unique. (See question 25, *Isn't it intolerant to say Jesus is the only way to God?*) Christianity alone provides evidence that its leader, Jesus Christ, is the Son of God. (See question 19, *Who is Jesus Christ?*) Hence, Christianity is the true religion, as opposed to Judaism and Islam.

Application

Jesus warned, "Watch out for false prophets. They come to you in sheep's clothing, but inwardly they are ferocious wolves" (Matt. 7:15). Stand up for what you believe and be sure to stand against the false worldviews that seek to destroy it (Col. 2:6–8).

Bible References

Matthew 7:15; Colossians 2:6–8; 1 John 4:1–4; Jude 3

Books

Worlds Apart: A Handbook on World Views, by Norman L. Geisler
Christian Apologetics, by Norman L. Geisler
Understanding the Times, by David Noebel
The Universe Next Door: A Basic Worldview Catalog, by James Sire

Website

Worldviews, http://www.allaboutworldview.org

DVD

Worldview Academy Lecture Series: Worldviews, Worldview Press

Online Video

Norman L. Geisler, "How Many Different Worldviews Are There?," The One Minute Apologist, http://www.oneminuteapologist.com/searchpage#worldviews

84 Can All Religions Be True?

Answer

Have you ever come to a stoplight and the car in front of you has the "Coexist" bumper sticker? As peaceful as that bumper sticker may seem, the truth is that it's absolutely false. Not all religions can be true since they hold opposite beliefs, and opposites cannot both be true. (See question 1, *What is truth?*)

For example, there are *atheistic* religions (like secular humanism) that are opposed to *theistic* religions (like Christianity). There are *polytheistic* religions (like Wicca) that are opposed to *monotheistic* religions (like Judaism). There are *pantheistic* religions (like Christian Science) that are opposed to *deistic* religions (like early Unitarianism). (See question 83, *What are some worldviews that oppose Christianity?*)

Let's take two major religions, Christianity and Islam, and see how they cannot both be true because their core doctrines are different:

	Christianity	Islam
God (in one nature)	three persons	one person
Humans	evil by nature	good by nature
Jesus	both God and man	merely man
Death of Christ (for us)	died on the cross for sins	didn't die on the cross for sins
Bible	not corrupted in essentials	corrupted in essentials
Salvation	faith alone without works	faith plus good works

237

Clearly, Islam and Christianity are opposed on every major doctrine compared in the chart above. This means that if Islam's understanding of these doctrines is true, then Christianity's understanding is false on all these essential beliefs. Likewise, if Christianity's essential beliefs are true, then Islam's beliefs are false. Both religions cannot be true. Of course, there are other nonessential things on which both religions agree. But a counterfeit is not identified as genuine by its similarities but by its crucial differences. It is the differences that make all the difference.

This same kind of comparison could be made among all major religions with the same results. Not all of them can be true because some have false beliefs. For example, some believe in only one God (*monotheism*), and others believe in many gods (*polytheism*). Some believe there are many roads to God, but Christianity declares that there is only one way to God—through the work of Christ. Both cannot be true. (See question 2, *Whose truth is true?*)

Therefore, it is contradictory to make the claim that all religions are true—not to mention that adherents of most world religions don't even believe that very statement.

Application

It is false to believe that all religions lead to God. Paul didn't compromise and say that Judaism was true while holding to the teachings of Jesus Christ. He warned against this when he said, "But even if we or an angel from heaven should preach a gospel other than the one we preached to you, let them be under God's curse!" (Gal. 1:8).

Bible References

John 3:16; 6:44; 11:25; 14:6; Acts 4:12; Galatians 1:8; Colossians 2:6–8; 2 Timothy 3:5; Revelation 1:1–20

Books

Worlds Apart: A Handbook on World Views, by Norman L. Geisler

Christian Apologetics, by Norman L. Geisler

The Universe Next Door: A Basic Worldview Catalog, by James Sire

Jesus among Other Gods: The Absolute Claims of the Christian Message, by Ravi Zacharias

Website

"Aren't All Religions Equally Valid?," Ravi Zacharias International Ministries, http://www.rzim.org/a-slice-of-infinity/arent-all-religions-equally-valid/

DVD

The Unshakable Truth, Josh McDowell and Sean McDowell

Online Videos

Bobby Conway, "What Is Religious Pluralism?," The One Minute Apologist, http://www.oneminuteapologist.com/searchpage#pluralism

Craig Hazen, "What Distinguishes Christianity from Other Faiths?," The One Minute Apologist, http://www.oneminuteapologist.com/searchpage#distinguishes-christianity-from-other-faiths

85 What Do Muslims Believe?

Answer

Islam is now the fastest-growing religion in the world. It is second in size only to Christianity among the great world religions. A once distant Middle Eastern faith, Islam is now having a great impact on Western culture, education, and politics.

Background of Muhammad

Muhammad lived from AD 570 to 632 in Saudi Arabia. He believed in one supreme God who created the world and miraculously intervened in it. Muhammad's mission was to turn people from polytheism (false gods) to monotheism—the one true God.

Muhammad received his first revelations when he was forty. He first thought they were demonic, but he was later convinced by his wife, Khadija, that they were from God. Muhammad preached his revelations in Mecca with little results and had to flee from there to Medina in AD 622. This flight is called the *Hijra*, and Muslims divide time into before the Hijra and after the Hijra (i.e., AH). Muhammad later returned to Mecca in 630 with an army and conquered it two years before his death in 632.

After Muhammad

Within a hundred years of his death, Muhammad's followers had spread the Islamic faith (with the use of the sword) all the way from Saudi Arabia to France. Fortunately, in AD 732 Charles Martel was able to defeat the Muslim armies at the Battle of Tours. Today, nearly one out of every five people on earth claims to be Muslim.

The Five Beliefs of Islam

1. *There is one God (Allah)*. God has ninety-nine names, none of which is *Father* since there is only one person in God. To attribute other partners to God or to say that Allah has a son is blasphemy worthy of death.
2. *There are numerous angels, both good and bad*. Angels are spiritual beings created by Allah to serve him. The good angels obey Allah, and the evil ones have disobeyed him. Nonetheless, Allah commands all of them to do his will, and the evil ones will be punished for not doing it.
3. *There are many prophets, and Muhammad is the last*. There have been some 124,000 prophets down through the centuries—one for every people group. Muhammad is the *seal* of the prophets; that is, he is the last one who summed up and sealed all that came before. They all had the same basic message: turn from idolatry to the one true God.
4. *The Quran is the word of God*. Muslims refer to the original Bible as the Law (*Tawrat*), Psalms (*Zabur*), and Gospels (*Injil*). Muhammad urged his followers to read it and trust it (Sura 5:68). Most Muslims, however, believe that the versions of the Bible that exist today have been corrupted (*tahrif*) either in text or in interpretation and, hence, cannot be trusted. So Christians and Jews are urged to accept the Quran, which has not been corrupted and has been copied perfectly down through the ages from the original. Muslims believe Muhammad got the Quran word for word from the angel Gabriel, who dictated it from the golden Quran in heaven, which many Muslims believe is eternal (Sura 85:21–22).
5. *Final day of judgment—heaven and hell*. After death, each person will stand before Allah on the final day of judgment. The angels will recite their good and evil deeds, and Allah will weigh them in the balance. If the good outweighs the bad, they will go to heaven. If the evil outweighs the good, they will be sent to hell. The only exception is for those who died in a jihad (holy war). According to the Quran, they will get a direct ticket to heaven (Sura 8:60; 4:74) and, according to some Muslim

traditions, will receive seventy-two virgins and delicious wine (Sura 37:45–47).

Most Muslims are Sunnis, who believe in separation of religious and political authorities. The minority Shiites, however, believe the religious authorities, Imams, rule over the political leaders.

The Five Pillars of Islam

1. *Shahadah*: To become a Muslim, one must recite the creed, "There is no God but Allah, and Muhammad is his messenger."
2. *Salat*: Muslims should pray five times a day facing toward Mecca.
3. *Sawm*: Muslims have a duty to fast during the daylight hours of Ramadan (which is the ninth lunar month of the year).
4. *Zakat*: Muslims are directed to give one-fortieth of their income to the poor and needy.
5. *Hajj*: All Muslims who are physically and financially able have a duty to make the pilgrimage once in their lifetime to Mecca, in Saudi Arabia.

Muslims also believe in jihad (holy war), which many see as the sixth pillar of Islam. For more *moderate* Muslims, jihad is understood as a spiritual struggle. But the more *militant* Muslims justify jihad as the use of the sword to defend Islam and promote worldwide conquest for Islam. They appeal to these verses from the Quran:

> Fight those who do not believe in Allah . . . until they pay the tax in acknowledgment of superiority and they are in a state of subjection.
>
> Sura 9:29

> Fight with them until there is no more persecution and religion should be only for Allah; but if they desist, then surely Allah sees what they do.
>
> Sura 8:40

> Then, when the sacred months have passed, slay the idolaters wherever ye find them, and take them [captive], and besiege them, and prepare for them each ambush.
>
> Sura 9:5

Listed below is a contrast between Muhammad and Christ (whom Muslims believe to be a prophet but not the Son of God) found in the Quran and Islamic teaching:

Jesus	Muhammad
Virgin born	Not virgin born
Sinless	Not sinless
Called the Messiah	Not called the Messiah
Called the Word of God	Not called the Word of God
Did many miracles to support his claims	Did no miracles to support his claims
His body ascended to heaven	His body is in the grave

Strangely enough, it is clear that, according to the Quran and Islamic teaching, Jesus is superior to Muhammad.

Application

Jesus commands his followers to make disciples of all nations (Matt. 28:19–20). That includes reaching Muslims. And although the Islamic faith is embedded in a history of violence that opposes both Jews and Christians, reaching Muslims with the gospel needs to be a top priority. Use the material below to become more familiar with Islam, and make an effort to share Christ with Muslims.

Bible References

Proverbs 30:5–6; John 8:24; 14:6; Acts 4:12; 1 John 5:12–13

Books

Reasoning from the Scriptures with Muslims, by Ron Rhodes

Answering Islam: The Crescent in Light of the Cross, by Norman L. Geisler and Abdul Saleeb

Brotherhood: America's Next Great Enemy, by Erik Stakelbeck

Website

Answering Islam, http://www.answering-islam.org

DVD

Christianity and Islam, Timothy George

Online Videos

Bobby Conway, "What Are the Main Beliefs of Islam?," The One Minute Apologist, http://www.oneminuteapologist.com/searchpage#beliefs-of-Islam

Richard Howe, "What Do Muslims Believe?," The One Minute Apologist, http://www.one minuteapologist.com/searchpage#muslims-believe

Bobby Conway, "How to Witness to a Muslim," The One Minute Apologist, http://www.one minuteapologist.com/searchpage#witness-to-a-muslim

86 QUESTION What Do Mormons Believe?

Answer

You may have seen them: a pair of young, sharply dressed missionaries riding their bicycles down your street. Chances are they may have knocked on your door. Who are they? They are Mormons.

On the surface, Mormons seem to be Christians. They carry with them the Holy Bible and refer to themselves as *followers of Jesus Christ*. But the truth behind the disguise is that Mormonism is a cult. As we shall see, official Mormon teaching denies many orthodox doctrines of Christianity including the Trinity, the deity of Christ, and salvation by grace alone through faith alone.

Background of Mormonism

Joseph Smith Jr. (1805–44) was born in Sharon, Vermont. According to Joseph Smith, at the age of fourteen, when he was living in Palmyra, New York, he was praying that God would reveal to him what church he needed to join. Smith described how God the Father and Son (two different personages) appeared to him. They told him that all the religions were wrong and not to join any of them. Smith described his encounter in these words: "My object in going to inquire of the Lord was to know which of all the sects was right, that I might know which to join. . . . I was answered that I must join none of them, for they were all wrong; and the personage who addressed me said that all their creeds were an abomination in his sight."[8] Thus, from these revelations, Smith started Mormonism, which later became known as the Church of Jesus Christ of Latter-Day Saints (LDS). The nickname "Mormon" comes from their early American prophet named Mormon, mentioned in the Book of Mormon.[9]

When Smith was killed in Carthage, Illinois, in 1844, Brigham Young became his successor, and the majority of Mormons moved with him to Utah.

The remaining Mormons, however, followed Smith's son, Joseph Smith III, and launched the Reorganized Church of Jesus Christ of Latter-Day Saints (which was renamed the Community of Christ in 2001).

Mormon Beliefs

1. *The doctrine of God*: The Trinity is comprised of three separate and distinct entities, a *plurality of Gods*. They are only one in *purpose*, not in essence. This is known as tritheism or polytheism.

2. *A succession of gods*: A previous god begot each succeeding god, in an endless series of gods. Elohim (God the Father) has a tangible body of flesh and bones. He was once a finite, mortal man who became God the same way Mormons hope to attain godhood someday. (For more details read Bruce McConkie's *Mormon Doctrine*.)

Christian View of God	Mormon View of God
One God (monotheism)	Many gods (polytheism)
Tri-unity in God	Tritheism of three Gods
Immaterial spirit	Material body
Sexless	Generates children
Heavenly Father	Heavenly Father and Mother
Unchanging	Changing
Necessary being	Contingent being
Infinite	Finite
Eternal	Not eternal
Creation out of nothing	Creation out of matter
All-powerful	Not all-powerful

3. *The doctrine of creation*: Mormons believe the universe is eternal. Accordingly, creation was not from nothing (*ex nihilo*) but from preexisting material (*ex materia*).

4. *The Bible*: Mormon doctrine holds that the Bible is not complete and is full of errors. The Bible is true only insofar as it has been translated correctly (but it has not been copied accurately). The Bible is not above the other standard works of the LDS.

Christian View of Scripture	Mormon View of Scripture
Infallible	Fallible
Complete	Incomplete
Uncorrupted	Corrupted
Confirmed by miracles	Not confirmed by miracles
No false prophecy	False prophecy

5. *The Book of Mormon*: According to the LDS, the Book of Mormon is the most correct of any book on earth. Mormons believe the Book of Mormon, not the Bible, contains the fullness of the everlasting Gospel.

6. *Doctrine and Covenants*: This book contains 138 revelations, 133 of which came from Joseph Smith (between 1823 and 1844). The rest came from his successors in the presidency. *Doctrine and Covenants* speaks about baptism for the dead, eternal marriage, polygamy, polytheism, and exaltation to godhood. It was first published in 1833 with the title *Book of Commandments*.

7. *The Pearl of Great Price*: This contains the Book of Moses, the Book of Abraham, the writings of Joseph Smith, and the Articles of Faith. Mormons believe that Joseph Smith translated the Book of Abraham from Egyptian papyri in 1835.

8. *The doctrine of Christ*: In heaven, Jesus was the first spirit child begotten of Father and Mother God through a sexual union. He is the brother of Lucifer, another spirit child begotten by the Father. On earth, Jesus was not begotten of the Holy Spirit, but was conceived when the heavenly Father had sex with Mary. (Strangely, Mormons claim this left Mary a virgin since she didn't have sex with a mortal man.) Jesus is divine in the same sense we are; the difference is only in degree, not in kind.

9. *The doctrine of human beings*: According to Mormonism, humans preexist before birth. Mormons believe that prior to spirit birth, people exist in their individual intelligence.

10. *The living prophets*: The living prophets—from Joseph Smith to the current president of the Mormon church—are inspired by God and are given divine authority to receive and speak new revelations.

11. *Sin and salvation*: Christ provided *general* salvation (namely, the resurrection) for all people by his death and resurrection. According to Mormon doctrine, however, *individual* salvation (called "exaltation") can be attained only by good works. Polygamy in heaven is necessary for exaltation. In addition, it is necessary for the Mormon priesthood to perform baptisms in order to forgive people of their sins.

Christian View of Salvation	Mormon View of Salvation
Fall of humans was bad	Fall of humans was good
Atonement complete	Atonement not complete
Faith alone needed	Works needed
No levels of heaven	Levels of heaven
Living *with* God	Living *as* God
Marriage for life	Marriage forever

12. *Baptism for the dead*: Baptism by proxy is possible for all who have died. It is the gate to the celestial kingdom.

13. *The doctrine of the church*: Joseph Smith was given a revelation that the original, true gospel was lost, and thus, he was given the Book of Mormon and the authority to restore the true gospel to the LDS as the true religion.

14. *The doctrine of last things*: Christ will return to earth and reign for a thousand years with two resurrections, one before and one after the millennium. Following this, there are different levels of eternity: (1) The *celestial kingdom* has three levels, but only faithful Mormons who are married for eternity in a Mormon temple and who will procreate children forever attain this status. (2) The *terrestrial kingdom* is where all good, moral people go, as do those who do not accept Christ until after death. (3) The *telestial kingdom* has less glory and is for those whose sins call for suffering before they enter this lower glory. Hell has two levels: (1) *Temporary suffering* (purgatory) is for those who need to suffer for their sins before entering the telestial kingdom. (2) *Permanent suffering* (hell) is for the *sons of perdition*, who refused even their second chance for heaven.

Application

The next time Mormons come knocking on your door, don't send them away. Be intentional to engage them with the Word of God. Mormons need to hear the gospel of Jesus Christ just like you did. They need to know that salvation isn't attained by doing good works but comes by faith through grace.

Bible References

Proverbs 13:13; 30:5–6; Isaiah 40:8; Matthew 24:35; Romans 4:5; Ephesians 2:8–9; Titus 3:5–6

Books

Understanding the Book of Mormon: A Quick Christian Guide to the Mormon Holy Book, by Ross Anderson

Mormonism 101, by Bill McKeever and Eric Johnson

Reasoning from the Scriptures with the Mormons, by Ron Rhodes

Website

Ryan Turner, "Verses to Know When Witnessing to Mormons," Christian Apologetics & Research Ministry, http://carm.org/verses-witnessing-to-mormons

DVD

Secret World of Mormonism, Jeremiah Films

Online Videos

Richard Howe, "What Do Mormons Believe?," The One Minute Apologist, http://www.one minuteapologist.com/searchpage#what-do-mormons-believe

Norman L. Geisler, "Are Mormons Christian?," The One Minute Apologist, http://www.one minuteapologist.com/searchpage#are-mormons-christians-geisler

Bobby Conway, "Can Mormons Become Gods?," The One Minute Apologist, http://www. oneminuteapologist.com/searchpage#can-mormons-become-gods

87 What Do Jehovah's Witnesses Believe?

Answer

Jehovah's Witnesses are one of the most zealous religious groups. Their door-to-door mission activity and their ability to quote Scripture and explain what they believe are impressive. But Jehovah's Witnesses are a counterfeit of Christianity.

The Beginnings

The Jehovah's Witnesses (JWs) began with Charles Taze Russell's (1852–1916) teachings in 1870. The Zion's Watch Tower Tract Society was incorporated in 1884 by Russell. He wrote a six-volume set called *Studies in the Scriptures*. His successor, Judge Joseph F. Rutherford (1869–1942), became president in 1916. He wrote *Harp of God* and nineteen more books (1921–41). The name Jehovah's Witnesses was chosen to distinguish them from a splinter group of Russellites.

The JWs were incorporated in 1931 as the Watchtower Bible and Tract Society, and their offices were located in Brooklyn, New York. President Nathan Knorr began the Watchtower Bible School of Gilead in 1943 and published the *New World Translation of the Holy Scriptures*. In 1975, the governing body of about twelve men became the supreme authority of JWs.

The JWs publish *The Watchtower* and *Awake* magazines, and their foundational works include *Studies in the Scriptures* (7 vols.); *Deliverance*; *The*

Harp of God; *The New Heavens and New Earth*; *What Has Religion Done for Mankind?*; *Let God Be True*; *Reasoning from the Scriptures*; *Let Your Name Be Sanctified*; *Aid to Bible Understanding*; *Should You Believe in the Trinity?*; and *Make Sure of All Things*.

The Beliefs of JWs

1. *Beliefs about God*: There is only one God, and only one person is God (the Father), who is called Jehovah. Jehovah has a body and is not omnipresent. He uses angels to know what is happening everywhere. The Son is one with God in purpose, not in nature. He is a lesser god. The Holy Spirit is not a person but a force emanating from the Father. Thus, JWs believe the Trinity is a pagan doctrine. Several examples of their anti-trinitarian bias are found in the *New World Translation of the Holy Scriptures* (emphases added):

   • Genesis 1:1–2: "In [the] beginning God created the heavens and the earth. . . . And *God's active force* was moving to and fro over the surface of the waters." The use of "active force" was an action to eliminate the trinitarian understanding of the Spirit of God.

   • John 1:1: "In the beginning was the Word, and the Word was with God, and the Word was *a god*." The JWs removed "the Word was God" in order to fit their belief that Jesus was a created angelic being (a little god).

   • Colossians 1:15–17: "He is the image of the invisible God, the firstborn of all creation; because by means of *him all* [*other*] things were created in the heavens and upon the earth." The word *other* was inserted so that the text reflected that Christ is not eternal but a created being.

2. *Beliefs about the Bible*: The Bible is the inspired Word of God; however, most Bible translations distort the Word of God on crucial doctrines. The only trustworthy translation is the *New World Translation of the Holy Scriptures* (1961). But according to many noted Greek scholars (including the renowned Dr. Bruce Metzger), the *New World Translation* is an erroneous translation of the Greek in many places.

3. *Beliefs about Jesus Christ*: JWs teach that Jesus (only begotten Son) is Michael the Archangel. The JWs render John 1:1 to read that Jesus is "a god." This unfitting interpretation of the text was influenced by a spiritist named Johannes Gerber, who authored *Communication with the Spirit World* in 1932. They believe:

   • *Before Bethlehem*—Jesus was Michael the Archangel, the first created being.

   • *While on earth*—Jesus was a sinless man of flesh (not an angel).

- *After the resurrection*—Jesus became a spirit (Michael) again. Thus, Jesus's resurrection was in a *spirit body*.

4. *Beliefs about human beings*: A human is a soul/body identity (monism). At death, we cease to exist (annihilation). Hell is the grave, not a place of departed spirits; there is no place of conscious torment. At the resurrection, believers are re-created into new persons.

5. *Beliefs about salvation*: JWs believe in works-oriented salvation. They must perform good works in order to ensure their names will be in the Book of Life. The anointed class (the 144,000) gets to enjoy heaven, while the second class (other sheep) experiences earthly paradise. The 144,000 are now finalized, so everyone else is a part of the second class.

6. *Beliefs about the church*: The JWs teach that all Christian churches are apostate and idolatrous instruments of the devil. Their organization claims to be God's prophet on earth, and only the anointed class (the 144,000) is the true theocracy of God.

7. *Beliefs about the future*: Christ began his reign (invisibly) in 1914. JWs believe that the world is headed to the Battle of Armageddon and that the millennium (thousand-year reign of Christ) will follow, during which humans will be resurrected to salvation or to a second-chance trial for life. Anyone who rejects the second chance will be annihilated.

8. *Beliefs about cultural matters*: The JWs have peculiar views regarding the government, holidays, and the cross. According to the JWs, every form of the human government is demonically controlled. That's why JWs don't salute the flag, vote, hold political office, or serve in the military. JWs also don't celebrate birthdays or holidays because they believe them to be evil. And lastly, JWs believe wearing a cross is sinful because Jesus didn't die on a cross but on a stake.

Application

Unlike the god of the JWs, the God of the Bible is omnipotent (Job 42:2), omnipresent (Jer. 23:24), omniscient (Ps. 147:4–5), and omnibenevolent (Jer. 31:3). God is not made up of a body but is an immaterial Spirit who exists eternally as Father, Son, and Holy Spirit (Eph. 1:3–14). Moreover, Jesus is not Michael the archangel; he is God (John 1:1–14; 10:30–33; Col. 1:15; Heb. 1:8).

The next time JWs knock on your door, be friendly and take a few minutes to talk with them. Allow the Holy Spirit to use you to share with them the truth of the gospel. Remember, JWs believe they know the truth, but the truth is that they've been indoctrinated into believing a lie. That's why it's important for Christians to be a light to them.

Bible References

Job 42:2; Psalm 147:4–5; Jeremiah 23:24; 31:3; John 1:1–14; 10:30–33; Colossians 1:15; Hebrews 1:8

Books

Reasoning from the Scriptures with the Jehovah's Witnesses, by Ron Rhodes

The Facts on Jehovah's Witnesses, by John Ankerberg, John Weldon, and Dillon Burroughs

Website

"Jehovah's Witnesses," Christian Apologetics & Research Ministry, http://carm.org/jehovahs-witnesses

DVD

In the Name of Jehovah, North American Mission Board

Online Videos

Richard Howe, "What Do Jehovah's Witnesses Believe?," The One Minute Apologist, http://www.oneminuteapologist.com/searchpage#what-do-jehovah's-witnesses-believe

Bobby Conway, "Who Is Jesus according to Jehovah's Witnesses?," The One Minute Apologist, http://www.oneminuteapologist.com/searchpage#who-is-jesus-according-to-jehovah's-witnesses

Norman L. Geisler, "Are Jehovah's Witnesses a Cult?," The One Minute Apologist, http://www.oneminuteapologist.com/searchpage#jehovah's-witnesses-a-cult

88 What Do Hindus Believe?

Answer

One of the main reasons most Americans have heard of Hinduism is due in large part to the widely successful yoga classes throughout America. Hinduism is an ancient religion (2000–500 BC), whose roots are in India. It is a vibrant world religion filled with bright colors, temples, and the elaborate worship of over three hundred million deities.

It's important to point out that there are many forms of Hinduism, as found in the Upanishads (philosophical writings of the Hindu religion): Shankara, Radhakrishnan, Hare Krishna, and Vedanta (which means "conclusion," because it is found in the last section of the Hindu scriptures, Vedas). Vedanta is the more prominent of the Hindu philosophies and the most widespread. It is this form of Hinduism that is represented in this section. The Vedanta beliefs include the following:

1. *View of God*: Brahman is indescribable. He is not known nor can he be known. The theoretical writings of the Hindu religion state, "He truly knows Brahman who knows him as beyond knowledge; he who thinks that he knows, knows not. The ignorant think that Brahman is known, but the wise know him to be beyond knowledge. He who realizes the existence of Brahman behind every activity of his being—whether sensation, perception, or thought—he alone gains immortality."[10]

2. *View of the world*: There is only one reality (monism). All is God and God is all. It appears there is a universe, but in fact, all is just an illusion, or maya. Meditation is what unites maya with mind and matter, which are aspects of the one reality of Brahman. "Brahman alone is—nothing else is. He who sees the manifold universe, and not the one reality, goes evermore from death to death."[11]

3. *View of human beings*: In essence, a human being is merely a reflection of Brahman. Through meditation, one can draw oneself (Atman) to the purity of Brahman. Once a sage attained Brahman and declared, "I am life. . . . I am established in the purity of Brahman. I have attained the freedom of the Self. I am Brahman, self-luminous, the brightest treasure. I am endowed with wisdom. I am immortal, imperishable."[12]

4. *View of ethics*: To be above good and evil, one must unite with Brahman. No longer will the person be plagued by the impurities that separate him or her from Brahman. Thus, different forms of yoga are used to discover the path of mind control, right knowledge, work, and love and devotion.

5. *View of human destiny*: Hindus believe in karma (the moral law of cause and effect). If a person has good karma, then good will come as a result. If a person has bad karma, then bad things will strike. This is an endless cycle known as samsara (the wheel of birth and rebirth). In order to achieve higher planes of existence or consciousness, one needs to be enlightened on how to break the shackles of samsara. This is determined by the fate of each person's current life.

Application

Thankfully, as a Christian, you don't have to worry about trying to become one with God or being reincarnated again and again until you learn your lessons. Paul gives this hope to all believers in Christ: "I consider that our present sufferings are not worth comparing with the glory that will be revealed in us" (Rom. 8:18). Nor will there be any reincarnations, for "it is appointed for men to die once, and after this the judgment" (Heb. 9:27 NKJV).

Bible References

John 3:15–17; 8:32; 11:25; 14:6; Acts 4:12; 17:24; 1 Corinthians 15:22

Books

New Birth or Rebirth? Jesus Talks with Krishna, by Ravi Zacharias

The Hindu Traditions: A Concise Introduction, by Mark Muesse

The Reincarnation Sensation, by Norman L. Geisler

Website

Ryan Turner, "How to Share the Gospel to Hindus," Christian Apologetics & Research Ministry, http://carm.org/how-to-share-gospel-hindus

DVD

Hinduism: An Examination of the World's Third Largest Religion, Charlie Campbell

Online Videos

Norman L. Geisler, "What Do Hindus Believe?," The One Minute Apologist, http://www.oneminuteapologist.com/searchpage#what-do-hindus-believe

Norman L. Geisler, "What Is Pantheism?," The One Minute Apologist, http://www.oneminuteapologist.com/searchpage#pantheism

89 What Do Buddhists Believe?

Answer

Siddhartha Gautama is the founder of Buddhism (563–483 BC). Most Americans know him as "the Buddha" or the big, round statue posed in a happy, meditative state.

Gautama was born into a royal Hindu family. After many years of living richly, he left his home and family in a search for enlightenment. Legend has it that he found it while meditating under a Bo tree.

There are two main branches of Buddhism: Mahayana ("the greater vehicle") and Hinayana ("the lesser vehicle"), which was later called Theravada ("the teaching of the elders"). The former claims enlightenment is open to all, and the latter claims it is only for a few.

The Four Noble Truths of Buddhism

1. Life consists of suffering (*dukkha*). This entails pain, misery, sorrow, and the lack of fulfillment.
2. Nothing is permanent or unchanging in the world (*anicca*). We suffer because we desire that which is not permanent.
3. The path of liberation is to free oneself of all desire or craving of that which is not permanent.
4. Following the Eightfold Path can eliminate desire.

The Eightfold Path of Buddhism

The Eightfold Path is divided into three areas:

Wisdom: (1) right view and (2) right intention

Ethical conduct: (3) right speech, (4) right action, and (5) right livelihood

Mental discipline: (6) right effort, (7) right awareness, and (8) right meditation

Zen Buddhism is the most well-known form of Buddhism in the West. The nature of Zen Buddhism is pantheistic and can be understood both negatively and positively. In the negative sense, Zen is not a philosophical system built on logic and reason. Zen opposes any form of dualistic thinking and doesn't hold to any sacred writings. In a positive sense, Zen is life—it encompasses everything (i.e., air, sky, mountains, trees, humans, animals, etc.).

In essence, *Zen teaches nothing*. It's what you teach yourself as Zen guides you to self-revelation. There is no god to worship or become or any ceremonial rituals or traditions to follow. In a nutshell, Zen Buddhism is living a self-disciplined life that rejects egocentric notions and desires. A Buddhist's ultimate destiny is to achieve nirvana (the state of nothingness). This blissful enlightenment can come only if the Buddhist can transcend inwardly and become completely detached from ignorance and selfishness.

Application

A Zen Buddhist may think that following the Eightfold Path will bring peace and enlightenment, but the truth is that good works can't save a person from sin (Titus 3:5–6). Paul states, "All have sinned and fall short of the glory of God" (Rom. 3:23). Jeremiah says that the "heart is deceitful" (17:9). Isaiah writes, "All of us have become like one who is unclean, and all our righteous acts are like filthy rags" (64:6). Thus, the notion that one can find inner peace in *self* is false. Humans are sinful beings, not divine beings. It is only through Jesus Christ that a person can be saved from sin and given the peace of eternal life (1 Pet. 2:24–25). Jesus gave this promise: "Because I live, you also will live" (John 14:19).

Bible References

Jeremiah 17:9; Romans 3:23; Ephesians 2:8–9; Titus 3:5–6; 1 Peter 2:24–25

Books

Apologetics in the New Age, by Norman L. Geisler and David Clark
Worlds Apart: A Handbook on World Views, by Norman L. Geisler and William Watkins
Pocket Guide to World Religions, by Winfried Corduan
The Compact Guide to World Religions, Dean Halverson, editor

Website

"Bailey the Buddhist," Dare 2 Share, http://www.dare2share.org/worldviews/buddhists/

Online Videos

Bobby Conway, "Who's Greater: Jesus or Buddha?," The One Minute Apologist, http://www.oneminuteapologist.com/searchpage#jesus-or-buddha

The following six videos can be accessed at The One Minute Apologist, http://www.oneminuteapologist.com/searchpage#buddhism:

Richard Howe, "What Do Buddhists Believe?"
Bobby Conway, "What Is the Origin of Buddhism?"
Norman L. Geisler, "What Are Buddhists' Worldviews?"
Bobby Conway, "How Does Buddhism Differ from Christianity?"
Bobby Conway, "What Are the Four Noble Truths of Buddhism?"
Bobby Conway, "How Do I Share My Faith with a Buddhist?"

90   What Do New Agers Believe?

Answer

The New Age Movement (NAM) is a phenomenon in Western culture. It is a popular metaphysical belief system that has gained much notoriety through film producers (e.g., M. Night Shyamalan), musicians (e.g., the Beatles), movies (e.g., *Star Wars* and *Avatar*), books (e.g., Deepak Chopra), celebrities (e.g., Oprah Winfrey), health and fitness exercises, and educational programs. Today, millions of Americans seek out astrology, card readings, palm readings, and speaking to the dead as ways to bring peace and harmony into their lives. (See question 42, *Who are demons and what do they do?*)

In essence, *New Age* is a term applied to a movement of loosely networked religions that hold a common core of pantheistic (God *is* all) and panentheistic (God *in* all) beliefs such as monism, mysticism, and self-realization. (See question 83, *What are some worldviews that oppose Christianity?*; question 88, *What do Hindus believe?*; and question 89, *What do Buddhists believe?*) Notice the contrast between New Age and two main religious movements.

Christianity	Secular Humanism	New Age
Theists	Atheists	Pantheists
God made all	No God at all	God is all
Mind made matter	All is matter	All is mind

The chart below demonstrates the various beliefs held by New Agers. Though not all New Agers hold to all of these beliefs, it's important to point out the general beliefs of the movement as a whole.

General Beliefs of New Agers

God is all.	Pantheism
God is one.	Monism
Man is God.	Self-deification
God is within.	Immanentism
Godhood is obtainable.	Mysticism
Life is cyclical.	Reincarnation
The world is unreal.	Illusionism
The world is living.	Animism
The world is evolving.	Evolution
The world will awaken.	Self-realization
The world will be one.	Globalism
All religions are one.	Syncretism
Morality and truth are relative.	Relativism

1. *God is impersonal (pantheism).* God is the life force that undergirds all other life. This is a huge difference with Christianity, which teaches that God is personal and immaterial.

2. *God is one (monism).* The NAM teaches that there is only one absolute truth, and everyone is that truth.

3. *Humans are God.* Nature is one with God; therefore, humans are particularizations of God. In essence, they are their own god.

4. *Reincarnation.* The NAM employs some form of reincarnation. Notice the difference between the *resurrection* of Christianity and the *reincarnation* of the NAM.

Resurrection	Reincarnation
Into an immortal body	Into a mortal body
One-time event	Many-time event
Ultimate state	Intermediate state
Perfected	In process

5. *Meditation.* This is a mechanism many New Agers use to revert back to the source of all life. There are different forms and levels of yoga—meditations and concentration techniques that New Agers use to find inner peace and to speak to spirit guides.

Finally, contrast traditional education to that of New Age and see the difference between the two.

Traditional Education	New Age Education
Explore external world	Explore internal world
Knowledge from without	Knowledge from within
Cognitive learning	Affective learning
Educate the mind	Change the feelings
Goal is to inform	Goal is to enlighten
Research outer world	Reflect on inner world
Memorization	Meditation
Teacher is an authority	Teacher is a guru

Application

In the end, the NAM holds that all religions are true (pluralism) and that truth is whatever you believe it to be (relativism). Of course, this is contradictory and therefore a false view (see question 2, *Whose truth is true?* and question 84, *Can all religions be true?*). Unfortunately, millions of devoted followers to the NAM are being led astray on a daily basis.

Are you willing to dig deeper into the NAM, pay closer attention to its influences in society, and take a stand against it? If so, read some of the following resources.

Bible References

Exodus 3:14; Habakkuk 1:13; Romans 5:12; 6:23; Ephesians 2:8–9

Books

Apologetics in the New Age, by Norman L. Geisler
The New Age Movement, by Ron Rhodes
Unmasking the New Age, by Douglas Groothuis

Website

Matt Slick, "Biblical Responses to the New Age Movement," Christian Apologetics & Research Ministry, http://carm.org/new-age-biblical-responses

DVD

The New Age Movement: An Examination of Eight Popular New Age Beliefs, Charlie Campbell

Online Video

Norman L. Geisler, "What Is Pantheism?," The One Minute Apologist, http://www.one minuteapologist.com/searchpage#pantheism

PART 12

Questions
about Family

91 Why Do Many Christian Marriages End in Divorce?

Answer

It is heart wrenching to sit across the table from a Christian couple who wants a divorce. I (Jason) remember meeting with a couple I knew very well and respected highly. So when they started sharing their marital problems with me, I was caught off guard. I thought they wanted to meet to talk about how we could disciple more families in the Word of God—not discuss how to save their marriage!

As my initial shock wore off, I offered my full support and cooperation to see that they received all the care needed to save their marriage. I remember that after I prayed for the couple and we said our good-byes, I remained in my office for a moment thinking to myself, *Why are so many Christian couples getting divorced?*

Like that couple, maybe you've been there or know someone who has. The sad reality is that marriages are falling apart because couples fail to keep God in their marriages. It seems like most marriages start out strong, but in a matter of two to three short years, that once glowing marriage darkens and the couple heads down a path of destruction.

Many divorced couples would say that their marriage ended because they were unwilling to forgive any longer. The husband or wife (or both) came to a point in their marriage where they couldn't keep sweeping the wrongs under the rug anymore.

In every broken marriage there was a breaking point when the husband and wife couldn't keep pretending everything was fine. They were sick and tired of hoping the marriage would improve when all they saw and sensed were irreconcilable differences. Attempting to remain positive in the midst of a marital crisis is next to impossible, as is keeping up appearances that everything is fine.

We can sit around and discuss the various constraints on marriage, the rising statistics of infidelity, or couples who cohabitate before marriage, but when it comes right down to it, many Christian marriages end in divorce because couples do not apply God's standards for the husband and wife.

It's not a lack of understanding the problems in the marriage that leads to divorce but the failure to know and apply God's resolutions for the marriage to thrive. (See question 92, *How can I have a good marriage?*)

Application

Marriage is not about meeting needs; it is about reflecting and representing the love Christ has for his bride. Marriage is a beautiful picture of the sacrificial love and grace of Jesus Christ. Therefore, Christian marriages ought to be a storyboard of God's magnificent mercy and redemption.

Bible References

Genesis 2:20–24; Ecclesiastes 4:12; Ephesians 5:21–33; Colossians 3:18–21; Hebrews 13:4; 1 Peter 3:1–8

Books

The Best Advice I Ever Got on Marriage, by Jim Daly

The Meaning of Marriage: Facing the Complexities of Commitment with the Wisdom of God, by Timothy Keller and Kathy Keller

Things I Wish I'd Known before We Got Married, by Gary Chapman

Website

"Marriage," Focus on the Family, http://www.focusonthefamily.com/marriage.aspx

DVD

The Art of Marriage, FamilyLife

Online Video

Jason Jimenez, "Why Do Many Christian Marriages End in Divorce?," The One Minute Apologist, http://www.oneminuteapologist.com/searchpage#christian-marriages-end-in-divorce

92 How Can I Have a Good Marriage?

Answer

My wife and I (Norm) have been married for nearly sixty years. It all starts with putting God first. On our very first date, I prayed for God's will for our lives. My wife (Barbara) was a little startled at the frankness of that prayer, but I was serious. Here we are over a half century later with six children, fifteen grandchildren, and three great-grandchildren—blessed of God and serving the Lord!

There is so much we can talk about when it comes to the topic of marriage. But in response to this question, allow us to highlight three essentials that make for a good marriage.

The first essential for any good marriage is to make a *covenant* with God. Paul states, "Submit to one another out of reverence for Christ" (Eph. 5:21). The husband and wife are in love with each other, but their shared love for God and reverence for him need to be much greater than their love for each other. It is God who has united the two as one flesh and has made a covenant with them in his presence (Gen. 2:24). With God in the equation, the marriage will not be easily broken (Eccles. 4:12). Thus, as Jesus said unequivocally, "Therefore what God has joined together, let no one separate" (Matt. 19:6).

The second essential is *companionship* shared between the husband and the wife. It is the responsibility of the married couple to cultivate companionship together. Thus, the goal for any couple is to remain best friends. Best friends love to spend time together; it doesn't matter what they do, as long as they are together. When friends spend time together, they impart uplifting words to one another. That's precisely what a marriage needs to have if it's going to last.

Proverbs says, "The words of the reckless pierce like swords, but the tongue of the wise brings healing" (12:18). Think about the damage done every time a husband or a wife chooses to say hurtful things to his or her spouse. A true partner is wise in *what* and *how* to say things; the words are not meant to be hurtful but to bring healing. Paul wrote these encouraging words: "Do not let any unwholesome talk come out of your mouths, but only what is helpful for building others up according to their needs, that it may benefit those who listen" (Eph. 4:29).

Along with healing words, a healthy marriage contains laughter. A great indicator of a good marriage is that it is filled with laughter and joy. Proverbs 17:22 reads, "A cheerful heart is good medicine, but a crushed spirit dries up the bones."

The third essential for a good marriage is a *commitment* to remain faithful and pure. Without question, every marriage will have its ups and downs. But God has called marriage partners to remain committed, and he will give them the strength to overcome any trial or testing (1 Cor. 10:13). The bottom line is that if a marriage is to last, the married couple must surrender everything and be willing to do anything to keep trust and commitment strong.

The key to remaining committed is a willingness to change. The honest truth is that every couple wishes for some sort of change, not only in the marriage but also in their spouse. As a relationship evolves, the couple will learn to let go of or remove certain things that can be detrimental to the marriage. Selfishness, greed, lust, defensiveness, lying, fear, rejection, distrust, and regrets must all be stripped away. Paul commanded, "Put to death, therefore, whatever belongs to your earthly nature: sexual immorality, impurity, lust, evil desires and greed, which is idolatry" (Col. 3:5). Did you catch what all those sinful things are? They are idolatry. Any time there is idolatry in a marriage, the marriage is compromised. Thus, a married couple must work very hard to avoid anything that could compromise a spouse and jeopardize the marriage.

Stay Committed

1. Spend time in daily prayer and meditation in the Word of God.
2. Offer daily intercession for your spouse and family.
3. Deliberately seek the Lord together in prayer.
4. Discuss and agree on a plan for the family.
5. Be open and transparent about your feelings.
6. Be a great listener.
7. Treat your family the way you want to be treated.
8. Serve the other person.
9. Always forgive.
10. Build fun memories.

Application

In a good marriage, spouses don't look to win an argument or get everything they want. In a good marriage, spouses work together and seek to use their marriage as a ministry to others (Phil. 2:4). A particular passage in the Bible sums up marriage and life quite well: "Enjoy life with your wife, whom you love, all the days of this meaningless life that God has given you under the sun—all your meaningless days. For this is your lot in life and in your toilsome labor under the sun" (Eccles. 9:9).

Here is a list of biblical truths that will give you a good understanding of a godly marriage:

1. The man and woman are to be united as one (Gen. 2:22–24).
2. The husband and wife are joined together by God and are not to be separated (Matt. 19:4–6).
3. The marriage is to be honored and not defiled (Heb. 13:4).
4. Both the husband and the wife are to submit to each other in the fear of God (Eph. 5:21) and fulfill their marital duties in Christ's love (1 Cor. 7:1–16; 1 Cor. 13).
5. Wives are to submit to their husbands and respect them in obedience to Christ (Eph. 5:22–24; Col. 3:18).
6. Husbands are to love their wives as Christ loved the church (Eph. 5:25–33; 1 Pet. 3:7).
7. The husband is to rejoice over his wife and be satisfied with her (Prov. 5:18–19).
8. The wife is to be honored and cherished by her husband (Prov. 12:4; 18:22; 31:10–31).
9. The wife is to be wise and of noble character (Prov. 19:14; 31:10–31).
10. A marriage is to be without bitterness, rage, or anger. Spouses should be kind, compassionate, and forgiving (Eph. 4:29–32; see Rom. 12:9–21).

Bible References

Genesis 2:22–24; Proverbs 5:18–19; 12:4; 18:22; Romans 12:9–21; Ephesians 5:25–33; 1 Peter 3:7

Books

The Marriage You Always Wanted Bible Study, by Gary Chapman

The Meaning of Marriage: Facing the Complexities of Commitment with the Wisdom of God, by Timothy and Kathy Keller

Family Life Bible Study for Couples, by Dennis and Barbara Rainey

Love and Respect for a Lifetime, by Emerson Eggerich

Website

Steve Arterburn, "Ten Biblical Rules for a Happy Marriage," Christian Broadcasting Network, http://www.cbn.com/family/Marriage/newlife-happymarriage.aspx

DVD

His Needs, Her Needs: Building an Affair-Proof Marriage, Willard Harley

Online Video

Jason Jimenez, "How Can I Have a Good Marriage?," The One Minute Apologist, http://www.oneminuteapologist.com/searchpage#how-can-i-have-a-good-marriage

93 How Do You Grow a Healthy Blended Family?

Answer

In an age when the connection of devices and the sharing of information are getting better and faster by the day, blended families are rapidly becoming the new normal. There is one major problem, however. Unlike the vast improvements in technological devices, more and more blended families struggle to stay connected and share valuable information.

It's enough of a challenge to deal with all the ins and outs of marriage and the growing pains of raising children. But when you factor in a couple of divorces, shared custody, demanding schedules, split times, and different locations—not to mention the differences of opinion and styles of parenting—it's no wonder blended families have an extremely difficult time getting along.

I (Jason) come from a blended family. My mother, Amy, was killed in a car accident at the age of thirty-six. I was only fifteen years old when she died, leaving my father to raise four boys. But in God's providence, my father remarried.

This, of course, brought its challenges. For instance, my brothers and I had not grown up with sisters. Now all of a sudden we had two stepsisters. Fortunately, most of us were already out of the house, so we didn't have to go through all the challenges of sharing bedrooms or fighting to see who got the bathroom first. But there were plenty of unforgettable holidays when difficult dynamics were in play (which is typical with blended families). Though my family certainly had its misfits and experienced its fair share of unpleasant dinners, birthdays, and holidays, for the most part, we put aside our differences and eventually agreed to get along.

Consequently, my experience in a blended family has been very fruitful in my ministry. Most of the people I've counseled in church have come from blended families. I have heard so many depressing stories from stepdads, stepmoms, and stepsiblings through the years. Yet in the midst of it all, the single question I've been asked most often is, *How can we have a healthy blended family?*

The truth is that most divorced couples and stepparents want peace between families, and, may I add, so do the children. Children who come from divorced homes are very fragile and have lost a sense of security, stability, and trust. So the last thing any family member really wants is more drama.

Due to space limitations and the sensitivity of this issue, we want to encourage you to dig deeper into the resources provided below. For now, here are a few helpful pointers that have helped hundreds of blended families get healthy.

1. Most blended families are the result of divorce. Therefore, couples need to make their marriage a priority and avoid failure repeats.

2. Stepparents need to be sensitive and seek ways to earn the trust of their stepchildren. It is not wise for stepparents to assume a role they have not earned.

3. Tell your stepchild up front, "I am not your father/mother, but I would like to be your friend. If you need me, I am here for you any time."

4. Stepparents need to extend a lot of patience and grace.

5. Stepparents should be respectful of the biological parents and keep their personal opinions to themselves.

6. Both the biological parents and the stepparents need to find common ground and work together to raise the children in the Lord.

7. Stepparents should never come between a biological parent and his or her children, unless, of course, the child is in danger.

8. Stepparents have a tendency to exert authority too early. This can get ugly fast. That's why it's best for biological parents to be unified with their spouses (the stepparent) and help them ease into their parental role. This will be hard, but it will pay off in the long run.

9. Bridge the gap. Avoid the mistake of letting the blended family feel like a *divided* family. This can happen quickly when the remarried couple takes sides and argues over how the children should be raised.

10. Be sure to spend time together as a united family. This will help the blended family members become comfortable with one another and avoid playing favorites.

11. Stepparents should look for fun things to do with their stepchildren. This will help reduce stress and provide a change of environment. Have no agenda other than to have fun.

Bible References

Psalm 127:1; Romans 12; 1 Corinthians 13; Ephesians 4:32; 6:1–4; 1 Timothy 3:4; 5:8; Titus 2:3–5

Books

The Smart Stepfamily, by Ron Deal

Help for Stepfamilies: Avoiding the Pitfalls and Learning to Love, by Winston Smith

The Heart of Remarriage, by Gary and Greg Smalley

Website

Ron Deal, "Remarriage and Blended Families," Focus on the Family, http://www.focusonthe family.com/marriage/marriage_challenges/remarriage_and_blended_families.aspx

DVD

The Smart Stepfamily: Seven Steps to a Healthy Family, Ron Deal

Online Video

Jason Jimenez, "How Do You Grow a Healthy Blended Family?," The One Minute Apologist, http://www.oneminuteapologist.com/searchpage#blended-family

94 How Can I Train My Children in the Ways of the Lord?

Answer

Have you ever been given a job that you had no idea how to do? That's how most parents feel when it comes to raising children.

The Bible gives a simple and straightforward assignment for parents: "Train a child in the way he should go, and when he is old he will not depart from it" (Prov. 22:6 NKJV). Simple enough? Not a chance.

Nevertheless, this is the mandate given by God and instructed in the pages of the Bible. So what are parents to do? Go out and buy all the parenting books they can? No. The first thing to realize is that God has everything under control. Your family is a gift from him, which means that God has entrusted you with one child or several children. God has faith in you, and he has given you all you need to raise your family as he commanded.

Let's take a closer look at what it means to "train a child." First, the word *train* means to "dedicate," "instruct," or "consecrate." The Hebrew word translated *train* in Proverbs 22:6 has a rich meaning that involves initiating instruction, cultivating a desire, and reinforcing good habits and interests. Hence, the role of a parent is to cultivate a desire within the child to live rightly and to instruct the child based on his or her natural desires and distinctive abilities. The goal of a parent should not be to *dominate* the child but to *develop* the child's moral character and natural characteristics, whatever they may be.

Allow us to give you five key biblical insights that will help you train up your children in the Lord.

1. *Teach the Bible to your children from infancy.* "How from infancy you have known the Holy Scriptures, which are able to make you wise for salvation through faith in Christ Jesus" (2 Tim. 3:15). We (Norm and Barb) read a Bible story every night to our little children and later a chapter of the Bible to our older children. It is a blessing to visit them and see them do the same with their children.

2. *Instruct and discipline your children in the Lord.* "Fathers, do not exasperate your children; instead, bring them up in the training and instruction of the Lord" (Eph. 6:4). Overdiscipline can be as bad as no discipline. We (Jason and Celia) make sure that we never discipline our children in anger. The main focus ought to be on the child learning a lesson, not on our disappointment.

3. *Live out God's Word to your children every day.* "Only be careful, and watch yourselves closely so that you do not forget the things your eyes have seen or let them fade from your heart as long as you live. Teach them to your children and to their children after them" (Deut. 4:9). Parents should model their faith to their children in a way that is not hypocritical or prideful (Rom. 12:9–21; Gal. 6:3). It's very important that parents set a good example and live out their faith in all that they do. One of the most encouraging things we (Norm and Barb) have heard from our grown children is, "Mom and Dad, thanks for setting a good example for us."

4. *Seek out opportunities to teach your children God's commandments.* "Impress them on your children. Talk about them when you sit at home and when you walk along the road, when you lie down and when you get up" (Deut. 6:7). Make talking about God a natural part of life as events occur. Everything is a teachable moment with your children; therefore, don't be too busy to talk with them.

5. *Prepare the next generation to trust in God's power.* "Things we have heard and known, what our ancestors have told us. We will not hide them from their descendants; we will tell the next generation the praiseworthy deeds of the Lord, his power, and the wonders he has done" (Ps. 78:6–7).

This is the ultimate fulfillment for any parent: knowing that he or she raised up a new generation in the family that walks in truth (3 John 4).

Application

Raising kids isn't easy. There are no guarantees that each of them will turn out right. Proverbs 22:6 is not a universal promise but a general rule. God is a perfect Father. He created perfect creatures (called angels). They lived in a perfect environment (called heaven). Yet one-third of them rebelled against him and never returned (Rev. 12:3–4). Certainly God was not to blame for their sin. God doesn't expect you to do better. Nonetheless, you are responsible to rear your children in the nurture and admonition of the Lord (Eph. 6:4). Studies show that when this is done faithfully in love, a higher percentage of children grow up as mature followers of Christ.

Bible References

Deuteronomy 6:5–9; Psalm 78:6–7; Proverbs 22:6; Ephesians 6:4

Books

Shepherding a Child's Heart, by Tedd Tripp
Why Family Matters, Focus on the Family
Grace-Based Parenting, by Tim Kimmel
Parenting beyond Your Capacity, by Reggie Joiner and Carey Nieuwhof

Website

"Parenting," Focus on the Family, http://www.focusonthefamily.com/parenting.aspx

DVD

Shepherding a Child's Heart, Tedd Tripp

Online Video

Jason Jimenez, "How Do I Train My Children in the Ways of the Lord?," The One Minute Apologist, http://www.oneminuteapologist.com/searchpage#godly-kids

95 Why Are So Many Young People Abandoning the Faith?

Answer

The teen sat there, hunched over in his chair, staring at the ground. Motionless. Like he was frozen in time. I (Jason) motioned toward him to get some sort of response from him. The only reply I got was a little shrug acknowledging my presence, but nothing more.

The teen was acting this way because he and his parents had gotten in a huge fight. The parents had gotten on him for his bad attitude, and he was upset over how his parents had overreacted and punished him.

As the parents continued to express their disappointment and struggled to figure out what to do, I leaned toward the teen and asked, "Do you believe your parents live Christ at home?"

The teen rose from the chair and shot back, "You kidding me? They're the biggest hypocrites I know!"

Dead silence.

I leaned back in my chair and shifted my focus to the parents. Without saying a word, tears began rolling down their faces. It was at that moment that Mom and Dad realized their son was right. Yeah, they went to church every Sunday, but they certainly weren't living out their faith the rest of the week.

I wish I could say this family got its act together. Last I heard, the teen had abandoned the faith and was having sex and doing drugs.

So what's going on with our young people? Why are so many of them abandoning the faith? There are essentially seven key points that will help answer this question:

1. Many millennials (eighteen- to twenty-nine-year-olds) who claim to be Christians never had a true conversion to begin with. The pat Sunday school prayers that churches and revivals have people recite don't guarantee salvation. Many young people never come to a point where they truly believe in Jesus Christ (Acts 16:31), repent from their sins, and give their lives to God (Acts 3:19; 8:22). (See question 36, *How does one become a Christian?*)

2. The simple fact is that a large majority of Christian parents have done a poor job living out their faith and raising their children in the Bible (Eph. 6:4). Many millennials have been raised to be legalistic rather than to live a biblical life. There's been a greater emphasis on rewarding good behavior than on being obedient to God's Word. As a result, many young people rebel and fail to see the discipline of God's grace in their lives. (See question 94, *How can I train my children in the ways of the Lord?*)

3. Doubts about the Bible and common objections about Christianity often get the best of millennials. You would think that after being raised in a Christian home and attending church for years most millennials would have a strong faith in the Bible. But the fact is that they don't. When asked about this, young people say they never really felt they could express their doubts and concerns regarding Christianity at home or in the church. This caused a level of intellectual skepticism to sprout up and choke any roots of faith that may have been left. (See question 15, *Is the Bible true?*)

4. Millennials fail to see the connection faith has to culture. Their lack of involvement in the church damages their ability to connect faith to day-to-day life. When millennials grow up, they have no idea the role faith should play in their careers, personal interests, or future lives. (See question 48, *How can I get my family involved in church?*)

5. Hypocrisy and compromise in the church play a significant role in many millennials abandoning the faith. They see the church as more concerned about money and membership than about teaching the Bible. (See question 47, *How can I know a good church from a bad one?*)

6. The majority of millennials are biblically illiterate. Most of them have neglected reading and applying the Bible. So, of course, when a competing belief or religion comes their way, millennials are unable to defend the Christian faith. One way Satan has been able to do this is through the false teaching of naturalism—an ideology that teaches there is no God, absolute truth, meaning, or afterlife. (See question 18, *How do I study the Bible?*)

7. Millennials have never actually been taught about the life, work, death, and resurrection of Jesus Christ. The focus has been more on the celebrity pastor than on the Savior, Jesus Christ. More time and resources have been devoted to launching more satellite campuses than to training up the next generation in the Word of God. The result: millennials never encounter Jesus. (See question 19, *Who is Jesus Christ?*)

In summary, a failure to preach the Word of God (2 Tim. 4:1–5) and "defend the faith" (Jude 3) to our families and in our churches has created a population that was once *churched* but now prefers to be *unchurched*.

Application

The best thing for millennials is for them to see and talk with real followers of Jesus Christ. Few have truly seen how the incarnational Christ can impact a community of people. They need authentic Christians to love them and offer them solid answers to their fears and doubts (1 Pet. 3:15). Think about these words that Paul delivered to Timothy and ask yourself if this is the kind of ministry you have to others: "What you heard from me, keep as the pattern of sound teaching, with faith and love in Christ Jesus" (2 Tim. 1:13).

Bible References

Deuteronomy 6:5–9; Psalm 78:6–7; Proverbs 22:6; Ephesians 4:14–16; 6:4; Colossians 2:6–8; 4:5–6; 1 Peter 3:15–16; Jude 3

Books

Almost Christian: What the Faith of Our Teenagers Is Telling the American Church, by Kenda Creasy Dean

Sticky Faith, Youth Worker Edition: Practical Ideas to Nurture Long-Term Faith in Teenagers, by Kara Powell, Brad Griffin, and Cheryl Crawford

You Lost Me: Why Young Christians Are Leaving Church . . . and Rethinking Faith, by David Kinnaman and Aly Hawkins

Preparing for Adolescence, by James Dobson

Already Gone: Why Your Kids Will Quit Church and What You Can Do to Stop It, by Ken Ham, Britt Beemer, and Todd Hillard

Website

"5 Reasons Millennials Stay Connected to Church," Barna Group, http://www.barna.org/barna-update/millennials/635-5-reasons-millennials-stay-connected-to-church

DVD

Sticky Faith Teen Curriculum with DVD: 10 Lessons to Nurture Faith beyond High School, Kara Powell and Brad Griffin

Online Videos

Jason Jimenez, "Why Are So Many Young People Abandoning the Faith?," The One Minute Apologist, http://www.oneminuteapologist.com/searchpage#abandoning-the-faith

Bobby Conway, "What Is New Atheism?," The One Minute Apologist, http://www.oneminuteapologist.com/searchpage#new-atheism

96 How Can I Win Back a Prodigal Child?

Answer

No parent wishes to have a prodigal child. But they exist, and some even come from the most saintly of homes. As a matter of fact, many respected Christian leaders and pastors have had prodigal children. The world's greatest evangelist, Billy Graham, suffered through years of pain as he watched his son, Franklin Graham, rebel and pursue the pleasures of the world. (Franklin Graham now heads the Billy Graham Evangelistic Association and Samaritan's Purse.)

But that's not the only prodigal in the Graham family. Billy Graham's grandson Tullian Tchividjian also had bouts of rebellion. One particular incident got so out of hand that the police were called, landing Tullian in the back seat of a police car. (Tullian now pastors Coral Ridge Presbyterian Church.)

Then there was the time when John Piper, prominent Reformed preacher and author, had to exercise church discipline on his own son, Abraham Piper. (You can read about Abraham's return to Christ in "Let Them Come Home.")[13]

We draw your attention to these two prominent Christian families not to pass judgment but to make a point: no Christian family is immune to having a prodigal child. But there are steps parents can take early on in the hope of preventing a child from rebelling. (See question 94, *How can I train my children in the ways of the Lord?*)

The term *prodigal* comes from the classic parable of a son who took his inheritance, ran away, and eventually squandered all he had (Luke 15:11–32). Hence, *prodigal* depicts a sense of wastefulness, reckless behavior, and carelessness. Some key indicators of a prodigal child are rebellion against God; a lustful desire to commit sinful acts; destructive behavior; a flagrant disrespect of people, rules, and authority; and a tendency to never take full responsibility for anything.

The best advice for parents of a prodigal child is to be devoted to a life of prayer. The Bible says, "Devote yourselves to prayer, being watchful and thankful" (Col. 4:2). The word *devote* carries the idea of giving constant attention and care to something. The constant worry over a prodigal can defeat any good parent, which is why constant prayer is vitally important. It will help take away your burden and help you trust that the Holy Spirit is working on your prodigal child (Hannah's prayer, 1 Sam. 1:9–13; David's prayer, 1 Sam. 17:45; Jairus's prayer, Matt. 9:18). The key is not losing hope but having faith that God is in control. Proverbs 19:21 puts it like this: "Many are the plans in a person's heart, but it is the LORD's purpose that prevails." Your prodigal may think he or she is living it up, but the Lord's purposes will last.

Another key to winning back a prodigal is showing him or her constant love and grace. Many people struggle with this, and for good reason. The amount of pain and emotional damage brought on by prodigals seems unbearable. But the Bible makes it clear that Christians are to forgive:

> Forgive us our debts, as we also have forgiven our debtors.
>
> Matthew 6:12

> For if you forgive other people when they sin against you, your heavenly Father will also forgive you. But if you do not forgive others their sins, your Father will not forgive your sins.
>
> Matthew 6:14–15

> If your brother or sister sins against you, rebuke them; and if they repent, forgive them. Even if they sin against you seven times in a day and seven times come back to you saying "I repent," you must forgive them.
>
> Luke 17:3–4

> Jesus said, "Father, forgive them, for they do not know what they are doing."
>
> Luke 23:34

Jesus said the prodigal's father saw his son in the distance and was "filled with compassion for him; he ran to his son, threw his arms around him and kissed him" (Luke 15:20). That is true forgiveness. Make sure your prodigal knows that their sinful behavior doesn't change the fact that you are still their loving parent. Let your child know that you love them and are waiting if they decide to repent of their sins. Remember that the more a parent extends grace and forgiveness, the softer a wayward child's heart will become.

Furthermore, even as you keep open lines of communication with your prodigal, make sure solid boundaries are in place as well. Because prodigals aren't always to be trusted and are often argumentative, it is wise to have safeguards to protect you and the rest of your family from possible harm or danger. Proverbs 14:7 states, "Stay away from fools, for you won't find knowledge on their lips" (NLT). Another wise proverb says, "Don't answer the foolish arguments of fools, or you will become as foolish as they are" (Prov. 26:4 NLT).

Arguing will cause more separation than healing. The general rule of thumb is to pray more and say less.

Finally, as you seek to pray for and love your prodigal, recruit a few godly people who are willing to talk to him or her. Prodigals often feel uncomfortable talking with their parents because of the many fights, disagreements, emotions, regrets, and disapproval. This way, if your prodigal is open to talk, he or she will have someone who will offer a biblical perspective. This person can be a close friend, relative, or pastor. If you don't have someone in mind, give it to God in prayer. He will bring the right person at the right time.

Application

The story of the prodigal son is really about the father (Luke 15:11–32). It is a beautiful picture of the mercy and grace of God. No matter the sin or how far it seems your prodigal is from God, remember the promise from the Bible that "love covers a multitude of sin" (1 Pet. 4:8).

Bible References

Deuteronomy 31:8; Joshua 1:8; Psalms 27; 55:22; Proverbs 22:6; 23:13; 26:4; Luke 15:11–32; 1 Peter 4:8; 3 John 4

Books

Setting Boundaries with Your Adult Children, by Allison Bottke

Come Home: A Call Back to Faith, by James MacDonald

Bringing Home the Prodigals, by Rob Parsons

Website

"Will a Prodigal Child Always Return?," Dr. James Dobson's Family Talk, http://www.drjamesdobson.org/Solid-Answers/Answers?a=a4651318-9f2a-4a75-87c7-4da7b76e3ede

DVD

Raise Up a Child, Walk thru the Bible

Online Video

Jason Jimenez, "How Do I Win Back a Prodigal Child?," The One Minute Apologist, http://www.oneminuteapologist.com/searchpage#prodigal-child

97 Should a Christian Date an Unbeliever?

Answer

Broken relationships are a leading cause of regrets. At one point or another, everybody has experienced a bad friendship or has been heartbroken over an awful breakup.

Relationships are tough. They bring with them so many variables and emotions, making it seemingly impossible for people to work them all out.

If relationships come with so many difficulties, is it wise for a Christian to date an unbeliever? Does the Bible consider that an acceptable relationship? This is a topic that stirs up people on both sides of the issue. But before we attempt to answer it, allow us to pose this question: If relationships are naturally difficult, and the Bible says to be like-minded, then is it wise for two people with different beliefs to be intimately involved?

When you pose the question like that, it is clear the answer is a resounding no! We are not saying that two people who don't share the same beliefs don't have anything in common. We are merely pointing out the biblical and practical aspects of every dating relationship.

Paul writes:

> Do not be yoked together with unbelievers. For what do righteousness and wickedness have in common? Or what fellowship can light have with darkness? What harmony is there between Christ and Belial? What does a believer have in common with an unbeliever? What agreement is there between the temple of God and idols? For we are the temple of the living God. As God has said: "I will live with them and walk among them, and I will be their God, and they will be my people."
>
> 2 Corinthians 6:14–16

The term *unequally yoked* (2 Cor. 6:14 ESV) comes from the law regarding not mixing cattle of diverse kind (Lev. 19:19; Deut. 22:10). This conveys that opposites cannot fellowship together. Notice the five contrasts Paul lists to make his point: (1) righteousness has *nothing in common* with wickedness; (2) light has *no fellowship* with darkness; (3) Christ has *no harmony* with

Belial; (4) a believer has *nothing in common* with an unbeliever; (5) there is *no agreement* between the temple of God and idols.

Paul stresses that Christians should not be intimately involved with unbelievers. Of course, the Bible isn't suggesting that Christians have nothing to do with the world. If that were the case, then it would be impossible for Christians to "let [their] light shine before others" (Matt. 5:16) and "make disciples of all nations" (Matt. 28:19). The Bible is clear that Christians are to befriend unbelievers in the love and grace of Jesus Christ—while making sure they choose their friends wisely. "The righteous choose their friends carefully, but the way of the wicked leads them astray" (Prov. 12:26).

If Christians aren't careful, the temptations and influences of unbelievers can and will corrupt their character and witness for Christ. Paul warns, "Bad company corrupts good character" (1 Cor. 15:33). That's why a Christian and an unbeliever just don't mix in a dating relationship. Nor should "missionary" dating be something Christians engage in. The Bible nowhere endorses or commands such a practice. And Christians don't need to date unbelievers in order to lead them to Christ. More often than not, Christians who are lonely, heartbroken, or desperate to marry will eventually compromise their beliefs. This doesn't usually end well for either person in the dating relationship.

Of course, there are some cases in which a Christian was able to lead an unbelieving spouse to the Lord. But that isn't license for every unmarried Christian to undertake marriage in order to do the same. A marriage with an unbeliever is strongly opposed by God.

The purpose of dating is to help prepare two Christians who are committed to a pure relationship and desire to get married someday. Sharing a marriage with a like-minded believer will bring more blessing and unity as the couple matures, has children, and serves the Lord together.

Application

The most important thing for any unmarried Christian is to keep his or her relationship with Christ first and foremost. No relationship, object, or marriage should come between a Christian and his or her relationship with Christ. Remember the words of the prophet Amos: "Do two walk together unless they have agreed to do so?" (3:3).

Bible References

1 Kings 11:4; Proverbs 6:20–7:27; 1 Corinthians 6:9–7:19; 11:1–34; 2 Corinthians 6:14–18; Ephesians 5:3; 1 Thessalonians 4:1–8

Books

The Sacred Search, by Gary Thomas

I Kissed Dating Goodbye and *Boy Meets Girl: Say Hello to Courtship*, by Joshua Harris

Is This the One? Insightful Dates for Finding the Love of Your Life, by Stephen Arterburn

Website

Scott Croft, "Biblical Dating: How It's Different from Modern Dating," http://www.bound less.org/relationships/2012/biblical-dating-how-its-different-from-modern-dating

DVD

The New Rules for Love, Sex, and Dating, Andy Stanley

Online Video

Jason Jimenez, "Should a Christian Date an Unbeliever?," The One Minute Apologist, http://www.oneminuteapologist.com/searchpage#can-a-christian-date-a-nonbeliever

98 Am I a Bad Parent for Not Having Family Devotions?

Answer

This question is not often presented this way, but it certainly is implied in indirect ways. Many parents feel a sense of guilt, frustration, or ignorance when it comes to family devotions. Some parents express that they would love to have family devotions but are too busy to get the family together. Others have told us they tried to do family devotions but found it to be too stressful.

Whatever the reason, no one seems to have time for the family. Everyone is off doing his or her own thing. Tragically, the spiritual development of the family tends to suffer.

Rather than answer this question by offering some tips on how to have family devotions (see resources below), allow us to give some biblical advice.

A key thing for parents to realize is that a Bible study is not the only thing that qualifies as family devotions. It is much more than that. Deuteronomy 11:19 reads, "Teach them to your children, talking about them when you sit at home and when you walk along the road, when you lie down and when you get up."

The biblical mandate for parents is to live out their faith in front of their children by teaching the Word of God to them as a way of life. Thus, it shouldn't be called family *devotions* but family *life*.

Parents who are focused on family *life* take advantage of the daily experiences they have with their children. They take these opportunities to share a lesson or talk openly about struggles, regrets, or mishaps. They are alert and sensitive to observe a good time to apply biblical truths to a particular situation or circumstance.

Many godly parents share God's Word with their children daily and make it a point to talk about spiritual matters as much as they do sports, politics, and movies. And many of them will tell you that they don't have a designated time—they just live out their faith and incorporate the reading and teaching of the Bible into their daily activities.

Another key thing is for parents to make dinner around the table with the family a top priority. Before excuses flood your mind, let us say this: dinner is a great way to spend time together and recap the day.

It's amazing what dinnertime can do for children. It's a great time to gather the family after a hard day of work and school and give thanks to God for his many blessings. It's also a time for the family to talk about the day and use a Bible or guitar after dinner to worship God. This is something my wife and I (Jason) do with our four kids practically every night. We spend time together as a family to give thanks, share a good meal, talk about the day, and read Scripture together. I can't help but think of the words spoken by Moses to the Israelites: "Know therefore that the LORD your God is God; he is the faithful God, keeping his covenant of love to a thousand generations of those who love him and keep his commands" (Deut. 7:9).

The final key to family *life* is to pray together. Paul writes, "Devote yourselves to prayer, being watchful and thankful" (Col. 4:2). Similarly, Paul told the Romans to be "faithful in prayer" (Rom. 12:12). Families should carve out a special time to share prayer requests and pray for the needs in the home.

Those are just a few special insights we hope will help guide you into doing not just family *devotions* but family *life*.

As you seek to do family *life*, be advised to follow these tips:

1. Be flexible. Things aren't always going to turn out perfectly.
2. Be open and sensitive to the work of the Holy Spirit.
3. Look for ways to share with your children about God and the Bible.
4. Spend quality time with your kids, together as a family and individually.

5. Make dinnertime with the family a top priority.

6. Always pray for and with your children.

7. Be consistent.

For thirty years we (Norm and Barb) had family time while our family was growing. Our guide was not how long but how consistently we did it. Most of the time it amounted to reading one chapter from the Bible, singing a song, and saying a prayer. But we were consistent in doing it every day, even if only for a few minutes.

Application

Remember that family *devotions* are worth the time, but family *life* matters the most. Don't be harsh on yourself, but trust in the Lord as you seek to cultivate Deuteronomy 6:6 and 11:19 into your home with your family.

Bible References

Deuteronomy 6:4–9; 11:19; Psalms 73; 101:2; Proverbs 11:29; Ephesians 5:21–33; 6:1–4; 1 Timothy 3:4–5

Books

Step into the Bible: 100 Family Devotions to Help Grow Your Child's Faith, by Ruth Graham

The NIV Family Reading Bible: A Joyful Discovery: Explore God's Word Together, Zondervan

Character Stories for Families series, by Barbara Rainey

A Family Guide to the Bible, by Christin Ditchfield

Website

"Family Mealtime Devotions," Focus on the Family, http://www.focusonthefamily.com/par enting/spiritual_growth_for_kids/family_mealtime_devotionals.aspx

DVD

GodQuest, Sean McDowell

Online Video

Jason Jimenez, "Am I a Bad Parent for Not Having Family Devotions?," The One Minute Apologist, http://www.oneminuteapologist.com/searchpage#family-devotions

99 How Can I Deal with Pornography in the Home?

Answer

Pornography is mainstream, and the demand for it grows by the day. Because of the internet, pornography has quickly become the top addiction in the world. It is a multibillion-dollar industry that now dwarfs Hollywood entertainment and the sports industry in America.

Roughly 90 percent of children are exposed to pornographic images by the age of ten. Shocked? Well, you shouldn't be.

The porn industry is a master manipulator that preys on the innocent by seducing them with its toxic product. Yet in the midst of the rise of porn in the home, the church has remained largely silent on the pandemic of this sexual sin.

Marriages are crumbling. Families have been ruined. Young lives are enslaved. All thanks to porn.

The same sort of measures taken by families to protect their homes with alarm systems, weapons, and law enforcement are needed when addressing the threat of pornography in the home. As mentioned above, porn is toxic, and therefore, families need to take every precaution to prevent its toxic waste from killing marriages and enslaving young lives.

But before you jump online and download the best software filter, you first need to make sure porn isn't in your marriage. The truth is that many parents are addicted to porn, and not many spouses are aware of it. If this happens to be you, we beg you to get help immediately. Pornography may be enjoyable in the moment, but it's destroying your witness, your marriage, and the family you love. You need to trust in the Lord for strength and confess this sexual sin to your spouse. It's not about

Signs of Porn Addiction

1. Your child is more secretive and removed from family gatherings.
2. Your child spends a lot of unsupervised time on the internet or in the bathroom.
3. Your child has access to soft or hard porn on television or gaming devices.
4. Your child won't let anyone view his or her smartphone.
5. Your child expresses anger or struggles with guilt.
6. Your child makes sexual comments about the opposite sex.
7. Your child is moody and acts distant when talking about the Bible.
8. Your child has a hard time praying.
9. Your child tends to ask vague questions about sin, forgiveness, sex, and relationships.
10. Your child may feel the urge to speak to or touch others inappropriately.

how you feel, but *what* this is doing to you and your family. If you are unable to speak privately about this addiction with your spouse, we advise you to set up a meeting with a pastor or counselor to act as a mediator.

If your marriage is clean from sexual sin, formulate a plan for discussing sex and pornography with your kids in age-appropriate ways. Always tell them the proper standard of sex and the function it plays in marriages and families, and then talk to them about the improper use of sex for selfish pleasure. They need to know that sex is good and healthy in marriage but that sex outside of marriage is morally wrong.

Having these open conversations with your kids about sex and pornography is a great way to teach them the truth while protecting them from harm.

Next, make sure all smartphones and computers are monitored by parents and contain the latest software filter to block inappropriate activity (see resources below). Technology and websites are continually evolving, so make sure you keep up with what is offered by your cell phone provider and the latest filter apps and blocks offered by the major social networks.

If you do find out that your teen is addicted to porn, don't freak out. The last thing your child needs is for you to go off on him or her. Most teens who are addicted to porn already feel guilty and are experiencing some level of depression as a result. The best thing is for you to act in grace and give your child an opportunity to come clean. If at all possible, let dads talk with sons, and moms talk with daughters. If you are a single parent, try to get an older sibling, uncle or aunt, or pastor to help you discuss this with your child of the opposite sex.

Parents can't afford to be naïve about the dangers of porn in their family. They need to be willing to do anything and everything to remove this threat from the home. Not only should parents install filters on every device in the home, but they should also make sure they routinely monitor their children. Kids may not like being accountable, but parents are ultimately accountable to God.

Application

There are many ways to block pornography, but how do you block it from consuming your soul? Heed the words of King David on how not to sin against God: "How can a young man keep his way pure? By living according to your word. I seek you with all my heart; do not let me stray from your commands. I have hidden your word in my heart that I might not sin against you" (Ps. 119:9–11).

Bible References

Job 31:1; Psalms 51; 101:3; 119:9–11; Matthew 5:28; Romans 8:1–11; 1 Corinthians 6; 2 Corinthians 10:4–5; Galatians 5; 1 John 1:9; 4:4

Books

Every Man's Battle: Winning the War on Sexual Temptation One Victory at a Time, by Stephen Arterburn, Fred Stoeker, and Mike Yorkey

Wired for Intimacy: How Pornography Hijacks the Male Brain, by William Struthers

Straight Talk with Your Kids about Sex, by Josh McDowell and Dottie McDowell

Finally Free: Fighting for Purity with the Power of Grace, by Heath Lambert

Website

Covenant Eyes Internet Accountability and Filtering, http://www.covenanteyes.com

DVD

Trapped: Finding Freedom from Pornography, Day of Discovery

Online Video

Jason Jimenez, "How Do We Deal with Pornography in the Home?," The One Minute Apologist, https://www.youtube.com/watch?v=wyIzv50486U&list=UUXkgIl5W-HXG8-srQdyAbDw

100 Should I Let My Child Join Social Networking?

Answer

Right now, all over the world, hundreds of millions of people are logging onto Facebook, Twitter, Instagram, Vine, and other social networks to connect, post, tweet, and chat.

This is the age of social networking, where most interaction happens online, through FaceTime, or via text. Sharing life instantly on social networking has changed the way the world communicates. This may be a fun and easy way to communicate, but it definitely poses a risk to people's safety.

That being said, each family has to determine what they believe is the right course of action when it comes to social networking. Like any other medium, it can be our servant or our master. If it starts becoming our master, then obviously we should stay away from it.

If parents do decide to allow their child to join any form of social networking, they should follow certain guidelines:

1. Make a covenant with your child to remain pure in what he or she sees, posts, and shares.
2. Establish boundaries and agree to certain consequences if those boundaries are crossed.
3. Install filters that block and monitor your child's online traffic.
4. Initiate frequent checkups on all the devices and apps your child owns.
5. Sign up for your own social networking accounts to track your child.
6. Stay up to date with the current safety tips for online usage.
7. Maintain an open dialogue with your child about social networking.
8. Pay close attention to signs of cyberbullying, cyberstalking, and exposure to sexual content or violent material. If your child is a victim or perpetrator of any one of these things, seek professional help.

Disclaimer: Parents should never allow children total access to social networking without any kind of supervision. Even the most innocent of users are exposed to some level of risk. You can never be too sure of the dangers your child is exposed to. (See question 99, *How can I deal with pornography in the home?*)

Application

People love to express themselves. This is especially true of young people. And social networking makes that really easy to do. Therefore, tread with caution. Be wise in how you deal with social networking in your home, and maintain the knowledge necessary to keep up with it all. Consider this: what you don't know can hurt you!

Bible References

Job 31:1; Psalm 101:3; Matthew 6:22; Luke 11:33–36; 1 Corinthians 6:18; 10:13; 1 Peter 2:24

Books

Who's in Your Social Network? Understanding the Risks Associated with Modern Media and Social Networking and How It Can Impact Your Character and Relationships, by Pam Stenzel and Melissa Nesdahl

Generation iY, by Tim Elmore

Download: Teaching Teenagers to Filter Their Media Choices, by Walt Mueller

Website

Get Safe Online, http://www.getsafeonline.org

DVD

Captivated: Finding Freedom in a Media-Captive Culture, Phillip Telfer

Online Video

Jason Jimenez, "Should Our Kids Use Social Media?," The One Minute Apologist, http://www.oneminuteapologist.com/searchpage#social-media

Notes

1. Throughout the book we provide URLs for video interviews on The One Minute Apologist website, http://www.oneminuteapologist.com. This site is hosted by pastor, author, and speaker Dr. Bobby Conway. It provides quick, credible answers to apologetic questions for people with a hunger to defend their Christian faith.

2. C. S. Lewis, *Miracles* (1960; repr., New York: HarperCollins, 2009), 169.

3. Josephus, *Antiquities* 18.3.3, quoted in Norman L. Geisler, *The Big Book of Christian Apologetics: An A to Z Guide* (Grand Rapids: Baker Books, 2012), 173.

4. Ibid., 76–77.

5. C. S. Lewis, *Mere Christianity* (1952; repr., San Francisco: HarperCollins, 2009).

6. C. S. Lewis, *The Abolition of Man* (1943; repr., San Francisco: HarperCollins, 2009).

7. Julia Pimsleur, "Is the U.S. Education System Bad for Business?," Forbes.com, April 4, 2014, http://www.forbes.com/sites/juliapimsleur/2014/04/04/u-s-education-system-is-bad-for-business/; S. Robers, J. Kemp, and J. Truman, Indicators of School Crime and Safety: 2012, National Center for Education Statistics, U.S. Department of Education, and Bureau of Justice Statistics, Office of Justice Programs, U.S. Department of Justice (Washington, DC, 2013), http://nces.ed.gov/pubs2013/2013036.pdf.

8. *The Pearl of Great Price*, 2:18–19.

9. The Book of Mormon, 3 Nephi, chapter 5.

10. Kena Upanishad, 2.3.

11. Prabhavananda Upanishad, sec. 36.

12. Taittiriya Upanishad, 1.10.1.

13. Abraham Piper and John Piper, "Let Them Come Home," First Boynton Church, http://www.firstboynton.com/2012/04/04/let-them-come-home-john-and-abraham-piper.

Also Available

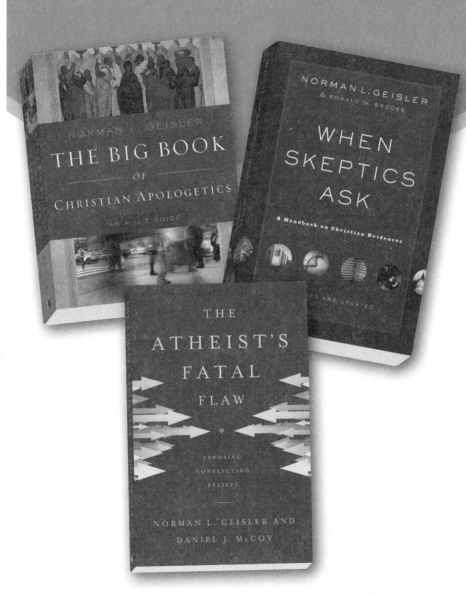